CHRIST

CW00536922

A Study Manual of Professional Competence in Road Transport Management

A Study Manual of Professional Competence in Road Transport Management

NINTH
EDITION

DAVID LOWE

KOGAN
PAGE

YOURS TO HAVE AND TO HOLD

BUT NOT TO COPY

First published in 1978
Reprinted 1979
Second edition 1980 and reprinted with revisions 1981 and 1982
Third edition 1983
Fourth edition 1984
Fifth edition 1986
Sixth edition 1988
Seventh edition 1989
Eighth edition 1991
Ninth edition 1995

Kogan Page Limited
120 Pentonville Road
London N1 9JN

British Library Cataloguing in Publication Data

A CIP record for this book is available from the British Library.

ISBN 0 7494 1814 1

Typeset by Kogan Page Ltd
Printed and bound in Great Britain by Biddles Ltd, Guildford & Kings Lynn

Contents

Preface

The syllabus for the professional competence examinations in road haulage published by the Royal Society of Arts (RSA), effective from 1 January 1991 has been updated by a new edition introduced in October 1993. The 1991 syllabus was extensively revised from the previous version and completely restructured to reflect the modular system applied to the examinations. Readers will find this structure easy to follow and particularly beneficial where an examination candidate needs to study a particular module (eg A or B) in isolation.

This latest edition of the manual has been revised and restructured in line with the 1993 revised syllabus and updated to reflect changes in legislation since publication of the previous (eighth) edition. Its contents follow the new RSA syllabus with the text separated into modules A, B and D and each part number within the modules starting on a new page. To help the reader further, a series of typical examination questions have been included, with the answers, at the end of the manual.

Where the syllabus is either not relevant to, or varies from, the Northern Ireland road haulage national examination, an appropriate note is included in the text.

The manual is written primarily for those studying for the national and international examinations in road haulage but since the module A syllabus is common to both road haulage and road passenger examinations, this part of the manual can be studied with equal benefit by passenger examination candidates. They may also find much of the other material useful and of interest, if not directly relevant in their studies.

As with the previous professional competence examination syllabus, the current syllabus on which this manual is based is largely concerned with legislative matters which change frequently. Consequently, the contents are always being overtaken by new regulations. Experience too results in changes to examination questions.

Every effort has been made to ensure that the text of this manual is correct and sufficiently comprehensive and up-to-date at the time of writing. But since changes, for the various reasons explained, are inevitable, the reader is recommended to check that the information being studied is still current. Readers are invited to contact the author or the publisher if they have any doubts in this connection. Copies of the official syllabus may be obtained from the Royal Society of Arts Examination Board, Westwood Way, Coventry CV4 8HS.

The reader should note that this manual is published for study purposes only and while the legislative content is intended to be accurate, it is not recommended as a legal work of reference for normal operational purposes. Other works by the same author, such as the annual publication *The Transport Manager's and Operator's Handbook* (Kogan Page), give much greater detail on specific points for operational guidance but in the event of conflict with the law, proper legal advice should always be sought from a solicitor.

Terminology
Many regulations are framed in negative terms rather than positive ones, for example: 'It is an offence to ...' or 'No person may ...' etc. For the sake of brevity, frequent use is made in the text of the word 'must' in connection with legal requirements. Readers should, therefore, take the use of this word to mean one or both of the following:

1. that the law specifies certain actions to be taken; or
2. that the law specifies that an offence is committed if certain action is not taken.

To avoid over-complicating the study material, only limited reference, where absolutely essential, is made to the actual statutes themselves. Concentration has been on presenting the *facts* which are likely to comprise the answers needed to achieve an examination 'pass' result.

Masculine pronouns are used throughout this manual to avoid ugly and cumbersome language. No discrimination, prejudice or bias is intended.

Acknowledgements

Much of the success of this manual depends on the information available to the author. In preparing the original text a great deal of research was necessary, and considerable help was provided by contacts and friends in many spheres of business in general and transport in particular. It is not possible to list all those who made valuable contributions to the original and to subsequent editions, but I extend my sincere thanks to them all.

Reference was made to many books and documents in preparing the manual to check and cross-check facts, and while these cannot all be individually acknowledged, the following are worthy of special mention: *Your Lorry Abroad*, The International Road Freight Office, *Croner's Reference Books for Exporters and Employers*, Kogan Page's *Personnel and Training Databook* and a host of statutory instruments, command papers and official publications including *The Highway Code* for which acknowledgement is made to the Controller of Her Majesty's Stationery Office. Acknowledgement is also made to the Royal Society of Arts whose syllabus and example examination papers were the source of valuable information.

Special thanks are due to my publisher whose persuasion and tolerance once again ensured the completion of a revised manuscript.

Since publication of the first edition of this manual in 1978 many readers have notified me of their successes in the examinations as a result of using it. It is particularly gratifying to the author to receive such complimentary comments because they confirm the validity of the manual for the purpose for which it is intended. I also know that it has been widely used for reference by those studying at college courses and by home study means because many of them write with comments and to report their successes in the examination. I would like to thank these readers for taking the trouble to write to me and to others who also wrote in with helpful comments about the contents of earlier editions. These points have been included, where appropriate, in the revised editions.

David Lowe, 1995

Introduction

UK legislation (implementing EC Directive 561/74) specifying new standards of professional competence for those responsible for the operation of goods vehicles was introduced on 1 January 1978 as one of the conditions under which a Standard Operator's licence may be granted for carrying goods for hire or reward.

Provisions in the regulations originally enabled certain people in the road transport industry to claim their 'professional competence' on the grounds of qualifying experience gained by working in transport prior to 1975. This scheme finally ended on 31 December 1979. People who did not qualify under this 'Grandfather Rights' scheme may satisfy the requirements through membership, at specified grades, of certain of the professional transport institutes.

For those who do not qualify by these methods, and for young people and other newcomers to the industry, an examination system provides a qualification to meet the legal requirements for professional competence.

This study manual is aimed principally at those people taking up positions in transport who need or want to become professionally competent by examination. Its purpose is to provide a comprehensive and self-contained course of study based on the official RSA syllabus, which leads the reader to a point where both the national and international examinations in road haulage may be taken successfully.

The manual enables examination candidates to study privately, at home and elsewhere, either when it is convenient to devote long periods to study or when just a few spare moments are available for revision. It is self-contained, providing sufficient knowledge of all the syllabus subjects to meet the examination requirements. To avoid unnecessary length and volume the information has been presented as briefly as possible, dispensing with irrelevant narrative and concentrating on the basic informative facts which the reader needs to learn to pass the examination.

The syllabus covers a broad subject range, from matters directly concerning legal and administrative aspects of road haulage operation to technical matters of goods vehicle construction, use and maintenance, road safety measures, and then on to the much wider issues of management such as business administration, financial controls, marketing, legal knowledge, and the complexities of social legislation.

Overall, the extent of the syllabus is such that the successful examination candidate can justifiably claim to have acquired a sound grounding in the broader aspects of management and the running of a business, in addition to the more specialised knowledge of road haulage operation. It is this aspect of wider education which will undoubtedly induce many other managers in transport, who have qualified for professional 'competence' on the grounds of past experience, to attempt the examination to prove that they too can meet the demanding standards it imposes. Or they may just wish to brush up their knowledge even if they decide against the rigours of sitting the examination. For these people, the manual will make valuable reading and reference material.

While the scope of the study syllabus is broad and the nature of the examination such that the candidate's knowledge is tested in full, it should be recognised that there is much more to managing a road haulage fleet than just passing the professional competence examination. Prospective professional managers will need to broaden their knowledge further with more detailed reading on legal points, financial control and management techniques, marketing and the intricacies of industrial relations. But reading alone will not produce the truly professional manager. Transport is an industry where practical operating experience is a vital ingredient of success and examination candidates who read this manual should also seek ways of widening their practical knowledge.

Requirements for Professional Competence

The European Union under its directives EC 561/74 and EC 438/89 sets out requirements for admission to the occupation of road haulage operations. These provisions are implemented in the UK by means of the Goods Vehicles (Operators' Licences, Qualifications and Fees) Regulations 1984 (SI 176/84) (as amended SI 666/86, 1391/86, 841/87, 2170/87, 2128/88, 1849/90, 2640/90, 2239/91, 2319/92 and 1209/94) which require that transport operators who wish to engage in the carriage of goods for hire or reward and, consequently, hold a standard operator's licence, must satisfy the requirement of professional competence with either the firm's proprietor holding the qualification or by the employment of a person who meets the qualification.

People who were responsible for road transport operations under an Operator's licence before 1 January 1975 could qualify for professional competence by virtue of their experience (known as Grandfather Rights) but the issue of certificates (ie CPCs) under this scheme ended on 31 December 1979.

People who did not qualify under the Grandfather Rights provisions may gain 'exemption' through membership in an appropriate grade of one of the professional transport institutes (see pages 143–4), thereby qualifying for professional competence.

Anyone else who did not qualify under the Grandfather Rights provisions or who is not exempt on the basis mentioned above must sit the official Royal Society of Arts examination in order to qualify for professional competence.

Transfer of professional competence qualification

Holders of the professional competence qualification gained in Great Britain can transfer the qualification to Northern Ireland or to any other member state of the European Union (ie Austria, Belgium, Denmark, Eire, Finland, France, Germany, Greece, Italy, Luxembourg, Netherlands, Portugal, Spain and

Sweden) should they wish to operate in road haulage or obtain a position as a transport manager in any of those states. A Certificate of Qualification for this purpose can be obtained on application (and on payment of the relevant fee) to a Licensing Authority. Similarly any person holding nationality of an EU member state (as well as those from Northern Ireland) may obtain confirmation of their qualification in their own country and apply to use it in the UK.

The Official Examination

Examinations for professional competence in road transport operations are conducted at centres throughout the country on behalf of the official examining body, the Royal Society of Arts.

Normally, examinations will be held four times a year, usually in March, June, October and December, on dates which are published by the Royal Society of Arts.

On the day of the examinations, the module A 'core' examination and the modules B and C national examinations are held in the morning. The module A examination taken by both road haulage and road passenger candidates lasts for 30 minutes and comprises 20 questions. Prior to that, with a 15-minute interval between, the separate freight module B national examination is held. This lasts for one hour and comprises 40 questions. For passenger transport candidates the module C examination is held after the module A examination, again with a 15-minute interval, and also comprises 40 questions to be completed in 65 minutes. The international examination (module D for freight) lasting 45 minutes and comprising 30 questions, is held in the afternoon of the same day so that candidates can sit all modules comprising the national and the international examinations for both freight and passenger on the same day at the same location if they so wish (and provided the examination centre has sufficient entries to run all sections).

Candidates who pass a single module of the national examinations will be granted a 'credit' until they pass the remaining module at which time they will be fully qualified as professionally competent in national road haulage or road passenger operations and can obtain a certificate to this effect from the RSA. Each module of the examination can be taken and paid for separately. A candidate who passes the international examination (ie module D or E) but has not secured a pass in both modules (ie A and B or A and C) of the national examinations cannot utilise this until the national qualification is obtained.

Northern Ireland candidates also follow the modular pattern of examination described above based on the current syllabus as covered in this manual. However, relevant omissions or variations in the text are taken into account.

Examination questions are of the objective testing or multiple-choice type, whereby the candidate has to choose the correct answer to each question from a number of given alternatives, or has to indicate whether statements of fact are true or false. Examples of typical questions of the type used in the examinations are included in this manual with the correct answers shown at the end of the book.

Full details of the examination and copies of the current syllabus, which includes details of the examination regulations, may be obtained from:

The Royal Society of Arts Examinations Board,
Westwood Way,
Coventry CV4 8HS
Tel: 01203 470033
Fax: 01203 468080

Current fees for the examinations, until August 1995, are as follows:

1. Module A (core) £8.00
2. Module B (national freight) and C (national passenger) £14.70 each
3. Module D (international freight) and E (international passenger) £19.90 each.

Additional local administrative fees will be charged by examination centres.

Unsuccessful candidates may apply for details of their performance using an application form obtainable from the RSA.

Special note to readers

This manual has been prepared in accordance with the official Royal Society of Arts syllabus for the professional competence examinations. However, despite the author's efforts to ensure conformity with the syllabus, experience has shown that odd questions are included in the examination which may not appear to be taken from within the published syllabus material. The examination has been criticised for the inclusion of questions which are believed to be outside the stated scope of the syllabus. The author and publisher, therefore, will be pleased to hear from readers who can provide information or advice on any such questions so that they can be included in new editions for the benefit of future readers and examination candidates.

National Syllabus

Module A

Part 1: Law

1. Elements of law

Law is a word which describes a general rule of conduct. In the context of our study it may be defined as 'the body of principles recognised and applied by the State in the administration of justice' (Sir John Salmond, *Jurisprudence*). 'The law as a body has as its aim the attainment of justice in society' (R S Sim and D M M Scott, *'A' Level English Law*).

Relationship of common law, statute law and legal precedent

The laws observed in operating transport are derived from common law or statute law and also legal precedent. Additionally, European Union law and the requirements of international agreements and conventions, to which the UK is signatory, must be observed.

Common law
Common law is established by practice or custom over a long period of time rather than being enacted by the State, but many aspects of common law or 'practice' have become absorbed into our legal system as a result of being adopted by Courts in the past as the basis for judgements. Once customs and practices are adopted by the Courts they become precedents which other Courts either *must* follow (binding precedents) or *may* follow (persuasive precedents).

Before 1873 law existed in the form of common law and equity, which was a system designed to overcome defects in the common law system. The Judicature Acts 1873/75 were responsible for drawing together the processes of common law justice and equity, which had previously been separately administered – common law in the common law Courts and equity in the Chancery Court.

Statute law
Statute law is created by Act of Parliament to which, after the due processes of debate and approval in both the House of Commons and the House of Lords, the Sovereign gives approval with the Royal Assent. Legislation is law enacted by Parliament, in which all legislative power in the UK is vested. Parliament has the power to enact any law and remove or repeal any law (but cannot overrule or fail to implement EU

law). In legislating, Parliament may delegate legislative powers to other bodies and even to individuals. For example, an Act of Parliament may authorise the Privy Council to legislate, it may authorise a Minister of the State to make 'provisional orders' which later require legislative confirmation by Parliament or it may authorise a Minister to make regulations. These are published as Statutory Instruments and have the statutory force of law.

Precedent
A precedent or judicial precedent is a statement or judgement of interpretation of the law by a Court. It is recorded in law records and is followed by other Courts when dealing with future cases in similar circumstances. Precedents may be authoritative pronouncements on the law setting standards for future judgements.

Precedents are usually binding for cases where similar matters are at issue in Courts below that which set the precedent. Therefore, for example, a House of Lords decision on a particular matter will set the pattern to be followed for judgements in identical circumstances in the Court of Appeal, the High Court and the County Courts.

However, not all the pronouncements made in a Court become 'binding'. A judge may make a particular decision in a case but may also make additional comments and observations which are recorded. While these ancillary comments may be studied and considered in future cases, they are not part of the actual judgement and are not 'binding' on other Courts. They are only 'persuasive' (ie they give an indication of the line of thinking which may be followed).

Judicial precedents form what is known as 'case law'. A substantial amount of case law exists in Britain; in effect every case which comes before the Courts is likely to be prejudiced by particular judgements in previous instances. However, Judges exercise discretion in taking into account all the information available, and make reasoned decisions based on the facts of the particular case *and* observing the principles of any precedents which apply.

Parliament and the Courts
It is Parliament's role to establish the law (except where EU law directly applies) and the Court's role to interpret it. In transport terms, this means that if you ring a Government Department (the Executive of Parliament) and ask an official to tell you what a particular regulation means, you will be told it means what it says (an official is not permitted to interpret the law). If a case is brought before a Court, it is for that Court to interpret the law

and say how it should be applied. In particular, the Courts may determine the definition of words used in law. As a transport example, a Court will determine the meaning in particular cases of words like 'danger' and 'nuisance' which occur in the C&U (Construction and Use) regulations.

Formation of statute law
New law is created by the publication of a bill which is placed before Parliament for consideration. Such bills may be put forward by the Government through its respective Government Departments and Secretaries of State or they may be put forward by Members of Parliament as private members' bills.

Bills are debated by the House of Commons either in the House, or in committee first and then in the House. The committees are formed from representatives of the major political parties, and they work their way through each section in detail and agree on the principles and the final wording before re-submitting the matter to the House.

After three readings in the Commons, where the bill is accepted either in its original or in an amended form, it passes to the House of Lords for consideration and here again, debate can result in changes and the bill goes back to the Commons.

When the bill is approved, it gains the Royal Assent and is published as an Act of Parliament. An Act may detail new law which is effective on a specific date, or it may give powers to Secretaries of State or statutory bodies to make regulations by publishing Statutory Instruments. In the latter case, the Act would be generally termed 'enabling legislation'.

When regulations are made under powers conferred by an Act, they are placed before Parliament (ie 'placed on the table of the House') for 21 days, after which time they become law on the date specified. Statutory Instruments specify the date made, the date laid before Parliament and the date of their enforcement.

Some items contained in Acts may remain dormant for many years before they are brought into use by regulations or may never be effected (eg Section 65 and Schedule 9 of the Transport Act 1968 providing for transport managers' licensing).

Redundant legislation is repealed by the inclusion, in subsequent Acts or regulations, of provisions which specifically repeal sections of earlier legislation or complete Acts or regulations (eg the goods vehicle plating and testing requirements were originally specified in the 1967 Road Safety

Act, section 9, were repealed by the 1972 Road Traffic Act, Schedule 9 and replaced by section 45 of that Act and subsequently by section 49 of the Road Traffic Act 1988).

Subordinate legislation
As previously explained, legislation is created by Acts of Parliament which may either state the law or confer powers on the Executive (Secretaries of State or statutory bodies) to make regulations. Regulations and orders made by the Executive are referred to as subordinate legislation. This form of legislation is applied extensively to road transport where we see fewer Acts (the Transport Act 1968 and the Road Traffic Acts 1972, 1974 and 1988 being just a few of the significant ones) but there are a great many regulations which set out the detailed requirements on a broad range of subjects, as follows:

- Operators' licensing
- Driver licensing
- Drivers' hours and records
- Construction and use of vehicles
- Vehicle plating and testing
- Vehicle lighting
- Road traffic controls
- Excise duty.

Regulations are frequently published as Statutory Instruments to amend existing legislation (eg to increase statutory fees for licences or testing) or to introduce sections of Acts not previously implemented where the Secretary of State has been given powers to do so.

EU law
Since the UK is a member of the European Union we are bound to comply with the requirements of EU law. This takes two forms; *directives* which member states must apply in principle by means of their own domestic legislation and *regulations* which have direct impact and must be applied to the letter, needing no domestic legislation to bring them into force (eg the EU drivers' hours and tachograph regulations – Regulations 3820/85 and 3821/85).

International agreements/ conventions

The UK is party to many international agreements or conventions which must be followed and which are usually incorporated into British law. For example, in transport, the ADR agreement covering the carriage of dangerous goods by road, the ATP agreement covering the carriage of perishable foodstuffs by road and the CMR agreement which applies to the carriage of goods for hire or reward on international journeys – these are all dealt with in detail in other parts of this manual.

Interpretation of statutory law

As previously explained, it is the role of the Courts to interpret the law. Prosecutions for criminal acts (offences specified in statute law in general terms) are brought by the police (mainly via the Crown Prosecution Service – CPS), the Director of Public Prosecutions or by other specific authorities, like the Consumer Protection Officer representing the local authority. In presenting their case they cite the specific regulation or regulations which have been breached. It is then for the defendant to plead 'guilty' or 'not guilty'; if he pleads 'not guilty' then the Court has to determine whether the defendant or the prosecution is right. This may be quite a straightforward matter, but complications may arise if, for example, the case depends on differing interpretations by the police and the defendant of a particular regulation. The Court must then decide how the regulation should be interpreted, taking account of appropriate precedents and all the relevant facts of the matter.

If the defendant loses the case, he is either convicted and receives the appropriate penalty (fine, imprisonment, driving licence endorsement or disqualification) or is committed to a higher Court (the Crown Court) for trial by jury.

The Courts

Initially, most transport related offences are dealt with in the lowest level of Court – the Magistrates' Court or the Court of Summary Jurisdiction. More serious offences are dealt with by the Crown Court and appeals against the decisions of these Courts are heard by the Court of Appeal. In complicated cases where satisfaction is not obtained from the Court of Appeal, the matter may be taken to the highest Court in our legal system, the House of Lords or, where appropriate, to the European Court of Justice which supersedes even the House of Lords.

Criminal versus civil action

There are two basic forms of legal action: 'criminal' action, which generally deals with offences committed in breach of statutory legislation, and 'civil' action, when one party feels aggrieved by the actions of another party and wishes to obtain some form of restitution by way of damages or restraint (for example, a haulier may seek an injunction to stop a union or a group of workers 'blacking' his vehicles.) An injunction is usually only granted for a short period until the matter concerned can be properly dealt with by negotiation or in Court.

Civil action includes the recovery of debts and deals with other claims concerning failure to comply with contracts. Where small sums of money are involved these matters may be settled in the County Court and in most instances no legal representation is necessary; the plaintiff can make his own case and produce his evidence personally to the District Judge. Where larger claims are to be settled the matter is dealt with in the High Court where legal representation of the claimant (plaintiff) and defendant is usual but not essential.

Licensing Authorities and the Transport Tribunal

There is a further system of legal control which the transport operator must understand. The controlling authorities for operators' licensing and related professional competence requirements are the Licensing Authorities (one for each traffic area) appointed by the Secretary of State for Transport. The LAs have powers to administer these regulations, call operators to appear before them and impose penalties (such as suspension, revocation or curtailment of a licence).

Any transport operator dissatisfied with a decision of an LA regarding the grant of a licence or the refusal to grant a licence, or with any penalty imposed, can appeal to the Transport Tribunal (see module B part 3/1).

Other tribunals
Tribunals deal with certain areas of transport operation and other business, rather than the Courts. For example, claims for redundancy payments, unfair dismissal and other employment matters (such as claims relating to sexual discrimination and equality, race relations and so on) are dealt with by Industrial Tribunals.

Legally enforceable contracts

An enforceable contract must contain the following essential points:

1. An offer and an acceptance.
2. Details of a consideration (ie a benefit or payment).
3. An intention for the parties to be legally bound by the contract (this is always assumed by the Courts unless there is a written provision to the contrary).

A contract exists when an offer has been made and accepted – there is no requirement for it to be in writing.

Carriers' liability for goods – private/ common carriers

In road haulage operations the operator enters into a contract each time goods are accepted from a customer to be carried to a specified destination. In most cases he accepts these goods in the role of private carrier, whereby his liability is limited to the terms specified in his conditions of carriage which are either printed on the back of his business paper, quotation sheets or are posted in the office. If he has no conditions of carriage and holds himself out to carry for all and sundry without reserving the right to refuse to carry goods tendered, he undertakes the role of common carrier (basically under the terms of the Carriers Act 1830) and his liability for loss of or damage to the goods, irrespective of the degree of negligence, is unlimited.

Conditions of carriage

When goods are carried under a specific contract between the owner of the goods and the haulier (in the role of private carrier as opposed to common carrier), the haulier limits his liability by applying conditions of carriage, which are the terms on which a contract is made with the owner of the goods. By contracting to carry goods in accordance with specified conditions of carriage, the haulier limits his liability under the terms of those conditions.

Road hauliers' power to restrict legal liability

The road haulier may include in his conditions of carriage appropriate and easily understood terms and clauses which define the limits of his liability. If this is done, the haulier then remains liable only for his own negligence and that of his servants.

The haulier is also liable for loss or damage which the consignor suffers as a result of unreasonable delay of the goods in transit (in transitu) where such loss was reasonably foreseeable (eg if fruit was consigned to a market it would be known beforehand that delay might result in the market being missed and the fruit becoming worthless). The haulier is not liable if delay is caused by the consignor stopping delivery of the goods while in transit because he does not wish the buyer to receive them due to the buyer's possible inability to pay (for example, because of his insolvency).

Similarly, the haulier is liable for wrongful delivery of goods if this is due to wilful misconduct by his servants, but not if it is merely a negligent misdelivery. The haulier is not liable in respect of dangerous goods where he did not know that the goods were dangerous; had he known, he could have either refused to carry them or imposed special conditions or charges.

In making an offer to consign goods via the haulier, the owner implies acceptance of the conditions where they have been drawn to his attention, directly or otherwise (they may be printed on the back of the quotation or they may be referred to on the haulier's letter heading, literature or consignment notes) prior to the movement taking place.

The conditions of carriage limit the haulier's responsibility for loss or damage to the goods as a result of his own or his servants' negligence, up to a maximum limit of value (usually £800/£1000 or more per tonne). He is not liable for loss or damage to the goods in excess of this value unless he has

27

been informed of their value and undertakes to carry them and become the insurer of the excess amount over the standard conditions. If the haulier is advised that goods to be carried exceed this value, extra cover should be arranged with the Goods in Transit insurers.

Operator liability Torts – negligence

A road transport operator, when under contract with a third party, is, in the execution of that contract, liable for his own negligence and, in many instances, the negligence of his employees. Negligence means that proper care was not exercised in dealing with other people's goods or property or in maintaining vehicles on which goods are carried or premises in which goods may be held or stored.

The operator's liability for torts (a legal term for 'breach of duty', in other words negligence, redressible by a claim for damages by the person who suffers as a result of that breach) in many particular aspects is important.

The operator must exercise proper care in carrying and storing the goods belonging to his customers to ensure that they are not lost or damaged because of his negligence. Negligence could be attributed to such acts as failing to secure the load adequately on the vehicle, failing to sheet the load to protect it from the weather or failing to maintain the vehicle so that as a result of mechanical failure the goods are damaged. Other instances concern delay so that if loss or damage occurs through unreasonable delay the operator is liable. Similarly he is liable for negligence if the load is transhipped in his yard and damage is caused through failure to use suitable lifting equipment or if the goods are left outside and are damaged by the weather.

Legal proceedings for negligence
The customer (the plaintiff) can institute legal proceedings against the carrier (the defendant) for negligence if he has suffered damage or loss through the defendant's negligent actions or omissions. Without evidence of damage or loss there can be no case. Where there is a case and the Court accepts this, it will award 'damages' (ie monetary recompense).

Breach of contract

While the haulier can limit his liability as described previously, he cannot include in the contract a clause which exempts him from liability for a fundamental breach of contract . In other words he cannot fail to do what he has contracted to do and then avoid liability for this failure (eg by failure to deliver goods which he has contracted to deliver although he could avoid liability for failure to deliver at, say, a specific time).

Rights to lien and bailment

The road haulier has a right to lien (ie possession) over goods entrusted to him for carriage until the carriage charges are paid.

Lien falls into two categories: particular lien means that a specific consignment of goods may be held until the carriage charges in respect of that particular consignment are paid, and general lien means that any goods may be held until charges for previous consignments have been paid.

Particular lien is a standing right in law but the right to general lien is only applicable if specified in the haulier's conditions of carriage. The rights to lien only confer a right to detain goods, not to charge for their storage to enforce the lien and not to dispose of them in order to recover lost carriage charges unless such actions are specifically forewarned in the conditions of carriage.

A haulier may detain goods which are consigned for carriage but which cannot be delivered for some reason – known as 'bailment'. He then becomes a 'bailer' of the goods and as such, has a duty to avoid them becoming lost or damaged through negligence. The goods may be held until the carriage charges are paid, either on his vehicle or in his yard, and if his conditions of carriage include the necessary provision, demurrage (ie delay) charges may be raised.

Principals' liability for the actions of their agents

An agent's role is to act on behalf of and represent the business interests of his principal. For example, a firm (the principal) may wish to have another firm (the agent) act as a selling agent in a location where it does not have its own employed sales representatives.

In legal terms an agent is a firm or person who has agreed, on behalf of the principal, to conclude a contract between the principal and a third party. Once the authority to act is given to the agent by the principal, the principal becomes responsible for the agent's actions or omissions.

Any contract established by an agent is a contract between the principal and the third party (ie the customer). The agent is only a link between one and the other and is not a party to the contract.

A principal's responsibility or liability for the actions of his agent cannot be terminated merely by telling the agent not to act. Therefore if the agent continues to act for the principal in an unauthorised capacity (ie by still selling goods to third parties after having his employment as the agent terminated – this *does not* relate to employment as a pure employee), those people contracting with the agent have the right to assume that the agent is still authorised to act until they are informed otherwise.

If the employer or principal wishes to terminate the responsibility of an agent, he should take steps to inform all potential customers that the agent is no longer authorised to act on his behalf. This can be a long-term, extensive and very costly operation involving newspaper and trade paper advertisements, direct mail letters to existing and potential customers and so on.

Secret profits

It is illegal under the terms of a principal/agent relationship for the agent to make secret profits in his dealings with the principal's customers. In the event that such profits are made they must be returned to the principal or alternatively the principal can sue the agent for their return – they do not have to be returned to the customer.

Employers' liability for the actions of their employees

An employer is liable for the wrongful or negligent acts of his employees when such acts are committed within the scope of the employee's terms or position of employment. For example, if an employee is a salesman and commits any wrongful or negligent act in his selling capacity, this would be the responsibility of the employer.

However, if the employee committed a wrongful act in some other respect which could be termed 'deviation or departure' from duty, the employer would not be held liable. Consider the case of a television or a washing machine salesman who, on visiting a customer, strips down or attempts to repair the customer's old machine, having assured the customer that he 'knows about these things'. In the event of a claim, the employer could say that the employee was working outside the terms of his employment as a salesman so the employer could therefore not be held liable for any claim resulting from such action. Such action is generally referred to as the employee engaging in a 'frolic of his own'.

The employer is not completely free of liability if he merely prohibits an employee from doing certain things, or from doing certain things for specified third parties if this is part of the employee's general terms of employment. For example, if a mechanic who services cars was expressly forbidden by his employer to service the car of Mr X but the employee disregards this instruction and a claim results, the employer cannot escape liability by virtue of the instruction to the employee not to commit that act.

Where an employee fails to meet specific legal requirements (for example, relating to his job as an LGV driver), the employer is also held to be responsible for the employee's failure should any claim result and he can also be prosecuted for offences relating to his employee's failure to comply with statutory requirements.

Contractors and sub-contractors

In haulage terms, a sub-contractor is a vehicle operator who accepts instructions to deliver goods which a principal contractor has agreed to deliver. Usually the principal contractor sub-contracts work when his own fleet is fully utilised, when the delivery is outside his normal working territory or when the price is poor but he still feels obliged to accept instructions for delivery. The responsibilities on both sides are as follows:

Main/principal contractor

1. The customer expects him to ensure that the goods are properly carried on a suitable vehicle with a reliable driver, are properly protected against loss or damage and adequately insured.
2. The customer will expect the goods to be delivered to the right place on time and will require proof of delivery.
3. The contractor should vet the haulier who is carrying the goods (ie the sub-contractor) to ensure he is reliable, has proper vehicles, is licensed to do the work, has a properly licensed driver and, most important, is adequately insured.

The main contractor is fully liable to the consignor (ie the customer) for loss or damage to the goods even if this occurred when they were in the possession of a sub-contractor whose fault the loss or damage may have been. In turn, he must seek redress from the sub-contractor.

Sub-contractor

1. Has responsibility to ensure that instructions given regarding collection and delivery and other matters are followed.
2. Must ensure that the load is carried without risk of loss or damage and is adequately covered by insurance.
3. Should provide proof of delivery by producing a signed receipt note for the principal contractor when sending the invoice.

If the shipper (ie the customer or the consignor of the goods) has to make a claim for loss or damage this claim will be made to the principal contractor who in turn will seek redress from the sub-contractor. In acting as an intermediary only the principal contractor does not (in fact legally cannot) escape responsibility for the safe-keeping and proper delivery of the goods.

Nuisance

Public nuisance
It is a crime to cause a public nuisance: a person affected by a public nuisance to the point where he has suffered a loss

31

beyond the discomfort or inconvenience suffered by the public at large may take action in tort against the person causing the public nuisance. A public nuisance may result, for example, from causing obstruction on a highway or public right of way, causing excessive noise at unsociable hours or creating exceptional noise or smell.

For an action to be called a public nuisance it must affect the reasonable comfort and convenience of the life of a 'class' of people. Therefore an action is not normally a public nuisance if it affects only one or two people although the number which constitutes a class is not defined.

In the case of transport, for example, if all the people in a row of houses were subject to excessive noise at night from a vehicle workshop, this could be classed as a public nuisance and the people have recourse to law as well as having the opportunity to make an environmental representation against the operator's 'O' licence.

Private nuisance
If one person only is affected by an unlawful act concerning land, this can be termed 'private nuisance'. This might arise, for example, when the offender interferes with a person's enjoyment of land occupied by him by obstructing access to the land, by blocking light from the land or by allowing that person's land to be affected by noise, smells, water, germs or physical objects, eg rubbish.

Trespass Trespass may be defined as interference with the possession of another person's land without lawful justification. To constitute trespass, the interference must be forcible and direct and therefore to walk on another person's land constitutes trespass and so too does remaining on the land after permission to stay has ended.

NB: This definition is peculiar to English law. In Scotland different circumstances can apply although the same general principle may be effective in similar circumstances.

The transport operator's legal responsibility to trespassers on land which he occupies prevents him from setting traps or other discouraging devices (see also below). The operator has a duty under common humanity to give warning of the dangers on his land to trespassers or to warn them to take reasonable steps to avoid the dangers.

If activities on a transport operator's land are likely to cause danger, even to unauthorised trespassers, the land should be fenced. The operator can be held liable for negligence if a trespasser suffers injuries while on his land.

Occupiers' liability

Occupiers of premises encounter two types of person on their land: visitors and employees, who are there with explicit or implied permission, and trespassers, who have no authority to be there.

The occupier owes a common duty of care towards visitors and employees (under the Occupiers' Liability Acts of 1957 and 1984), to ensure that they are reasonably safe in using the premises for the purpose for which they are invited or permitted to be there. This can be achieved by giving adequate warning of any dangers attached to being on the premises.

It is particularly important to assess the role of children in relationship to this point. The occupier must be prepared for children to be less careful than adults and he becomes liable if child visitors are not protected from being attracted to dangerous objects or areas on the premises, although in the case of very young children the occupier may only need to give sufficient warning to the adult or a competent person accompanying the child.

It is also illegal (under the Guard Dogs Act 1975) to allow guard dogs to roam loose on premises or indeed to have such a dog on premises at all unless a notice clearly warns of the danger.

Obstruction of the police

It is an offence to obstruct the police in the execution of their duties. Obstruction in this instance could include failure or refusal to provide information in response to police enquiries about alleged offences and crimes, in connection with the use of vehicles for example, or with any other police investigation. Almost any refusal to follow the direction of a police officer could result in prosecution for obstruction. For example, failure to move a vehicle to or from a particular place, refusal to produce a driving licence or other documents, or even making facetious replies to questions or sarcastic comments when apprehended by an officer could be considered obstruction of the police and could lead to prosecution.

2. Business and company law

Forms of business organisation

Business is conducted in many forms, the simplest organisational structure being the person working on his own account as a sole trader or sole proprietor. Larger organisations are usually formed into partnerships or into limited liability companies and many of the largest national and international firms are formed into public limited companies.

33

Each of these various forms of commercial organisation differs in the nature of the legal obligations to be met and each has relative advantages and disadvantages depending on size, the nature of the trade or commercial activity in which they are engaged, their financial needs and the wishes of the owners. The main legal differences and requirements and the relative advantages and disadvantages of each are briefly described here.

Sole traders   The simplest form of business is the sole trader. Any person can start a business in this way very cheaply and with the minimum of fuss. Setting up costs are negligible, legal requirements are minimal and the owner is mainly only responsible to himself and his customers.

The advantage of operating as a sole trader is the freedom from the need to comply with Companies Act legislation which requires legal registration and other complex formalities to be followed, including the need for accounts to be kept in a proper form and audited annually and completed returns of directors and shareholders to be sent to Companies House.

The disadvantage is that the proprietor has no protection against his personal liabilities for meeting creditors' demands for payment if the business should fail. In this event the proprietor's belongings and even his house may be sold to help pay off what is due to creditors.

If the business succeeds it will need capital for expansion and consequently assistance from the bank, for which security has to be provided. Usually the bank will want to take a second charge on the proprietor's home (if he owns it or is buying it on mortgage). Thus if repayments cannot be made, the bank holds the house which it could sell to recover any outstanding balance on the loan.

All profits made by the business become the proprietor's income (ie rewards for the business risks taken and the effort put into the business), from which he both derives his livelihood and builds up capital resources for future asset replacement or expansion. He must, of course declare these profits for taxation purposes and pay any tax due.

Partnerships   This form of business is an expansion of the sole trader structure. Instead of one person owning the business, two or more people own it, sharing the ownership, the work and the profits either equally or in unequal proportions.

Usually the partners in such a business have a legal agreement setting out their responsibilities and liabilities in proportion to their share of the ownership of the business, and any profits made which are not retained for future use in the business are shared proportionately in accordance with the terms of the agreement. In the absence of such an agreement the law (and the Inland Revenue) looks upon the partners as all having equal shares but with each person 'jointly and severally' liable for any debts of the partnership – in other words, if the other partners have no personal assets one partner with assets could be left to meet the tax liabilities and all the other debts of the partnership should the business fail.

Many professional firms such as accountants, solicitors, surveyors, estate agents and consulting engineers operate as legally constituted partnerships (solicitors and accountants, for example, cannot by law limit their liabilities so they have no choice but to operate as partnerships). In contrast, the road haulage industry comprises many partnerships based on little more than friendship, mutual trust or family relationships (eg father and son, husband and wife, etc).

The advantages of a partnership are that there are more people to contribute initial finance and more people to share the work, the decision-making and the worries. The burden of providing security is also shared.

The disadvantages of partnerships are that people do not always agree, and argument and distrust can lead eventually to the failure of a business. Another major aspect of contention is that profits have to be shared in proportion to ownership rather than in proportion to the work and effort put into making the business a success.

Limited companies (private)

If a person (or persons) forming a business wishes to remove the risk of loss of personal property and possessions in the event of the business failure, he can form a private limited liability company.

This is a legally constituted corporate body (ie a 'company') formally registered with the Registrar of Companies in which the parties to the business hold shares in equal or unequal proportions. The owners of the business are therefore the shareholders (or members) of the company. The company has a registered name which must be approved by the Registrar of Companies and not be a name which may be confused with that of any other registered company or not one which is either sensitive (eg implying royal connections or suggesting that the company is a national body or authority), or offensive. The word limited must be added as the last word of the name.

The legal requirement is for a minimum of two shareholders. One person must be appointed a director of the company (who may or may not be a shareholder) and one person must be the company secretary (who also need not be a shareholder but that person must not be the only director). Invariably, in small companies the secretary is both a shareholder and director. The company secretary is known as the legal officer of the company upon whom all legal notices are served. If the company is prosecuted for offences committed by the company itself, its directors as individuals or its employees, this is done through the company secretary who may not be personally liable but he is the officer of the company who is ultimately answerable to the Court on behalf of the company (the company may, of course, be legally represented in such cases). This person also has responsibility under the Companies Act for ensuring that all statutory requirements are met, for recording the minutes of board meetings, ensuring that annual accounts and a balance sheet are produced, and making the necessary annual returns to Companies House.

In forming the business or in raising capital for expansion, friends or relatives may be asked to invest funds in return for shares in the company *but it is not permitted to advertise for the public to invest in or buy the shares of a private limited company*. Some or all of the shareholders may be elected to be directors of the company (ie the people who control the business and make the important decisions). The directors can choose a chairman from among themselves for the purpose of conducting meetings of the board of directors. The chairman usually has a casting vote, which is intended to resolve any 'stalemate' situations in voting decisions.

When a company is formed, the subscribers (the founders) decide on the amount of shares which will form the legally constituted 'share capital' of the business. This may be, for example, 100 shares at £1 each to make it a £100 share-capital company. These shares are divided among the subscribers according to their contribution and according to the decision on who is to have the controlling interest. One shareholder may have 51 shares and the second one 49 shares, or they may have 50 each which means neither has a controlling interest.

Once the share capital and the holdings of each of the subscribers are determined, this becomes the maximum limit of their personal liability if the business goes into liquidation. So if their shares are fully paid up, the shareholders do not have to make any other contribution towards the debts of the company.

Often the share capital of a company is not fully paid up. For example, two people could form a £100 company of which only two £1 shares are 'issued' or 'paid up' (one each). In the event of liquidation they become liable to pay the balance of their allocation of shares (say, another £49 each if they have equal shares).

Company directors carry considerable legal responsibilities and can be held liable for a whole range of Company Law related offences (some 200 in all). They have a fiduciary duty to the company (ie duty of trust to safeguard the property and assets of the company). They must act in good faith and must not allow their personal interests to conflict with those of the company. Besides this duty to the company (not necessarily to the shareholders of the company) they also have a duty to the employees. If they fail in their duties the directors can be held personally liable for any loss which is attributable to their negligence, or to any act outside their authority or in breach of duty or trust – in other words they could be forced to pay compensation out of their own pockets.

Limited companies (public)

When a company becomes very large and needs to raise more capital for expansion by investment rather than by borrowing, it seeks to become quoted on the stock market so that its shares can be sold on the market to all and sundry and it can become 'public'. In this instance, companies are required to put the letters 'PLC' (public limited company) after the company name.

The money that the new shareholders pay for their shares provides the required capital for the business and the new shareholders become part owners of the business along with the original shareholders. The shares which are sold may be new issue shares if the share capital is increased or they may have belonged to the founders of the business (perhaps a family) who decided to sell all or a proportion of their shares (but in this case the money goes to them rather than into the company).

Shares may be divided into a number of classes (particularly into voting and non-voting shares). Normally shares carry the right to vote and usually the right is for one vote per share. The chairman of the board of directors, as mentioned above, frequently is granted an additional casting vote to avoid stalemate situations.

A limited company needs an authorised share capital of at least £50,000* before it goes 'public'. It must have at least two shareholders and must show a satisfactory history of performance and stability and good future prospects with sound management in order to satisfy the stock market.

NB : A second category of PLC is the unlisted securities market (USM). A minimum share capital of £12,500 is needed for trading.

Once a company has become 'public' its shares are quoted on the Stock Exchange and fluctuations in value are recorded daily and are usually published in the financial columns of the daily press.

Insider dealing in shares, which is the use of knowledge or confidential information of companies' plans etc to make financial gains on the stock market, is an illegal act for which severe penalties can be imposed.

Apart from its size and the more rigorous inspection of its activities, accounts, financial dealings and management, which result from a much larger body of shareholders (they could number thousands), a public limited company is very similar in structure to a private limited company.

Legal procedures relating to companies
Formation and registration

Limited companies may be formed specially to suit the requirements of a particular business, or 'ready-made' companies may be purchased 'off the shelf'. In both cases the formation procedure is the same, but the latter method provides quicker protection from liability and saves some money as such companies are formed by firms specialising in this business. Many of these have offices near Companies House and they can easily make the necessary searches to ensure that the name required has not already been used.

These off-the-shelf companies already have their share capital established, their name registered and their Articles and Memorandum of Association printed plus all the other legal formalities completed for immediate operation and are then sold to anybody wishing to obtain limited liability for a business operation very quickly.

Against the advantages of speed and cheapness, ready-made companies are restrictive because the company name may not be suitable and the Articles may not cover exactly what is required. For this reason a new company may be formed. Usually an accountant or solicitor is employed to deal with a company formation and often his office is quoted as the registered office of the company. In forming a company, the following factors have to be established:

1. A name (which must be acceptable to the registrar of companies – see above) followed by the word 'Limited'.

2. The share capital (eg 100 £1 shares, 1000 10p shares, etc).
3. The names of the original subscribers (at least two persons).
4. The names of the first directors and Secretary.
5. The registered office for the company.
6. The Articles of Association and Memorandum.

The Articles and Memorandum of Association jointly form the 'rule book' for the company because they define the company exactly, its name and the objects for which it was formed. Specifically this document (it is usually combined) contains the following information:

Memorandum of Association
1. Name of company followed by the word 'Limited'.
2. Where the registered office is situated (eg in England and Wales or Scotland).
3. The objects for which the company was formed (ie what it can and cannot do by way of trade).
4. A statement that the liability of the members (ie shareholders) is limited.
5. The amount of the share capital divided into a number of shares of a certain value each.
6. The names of the original subscribers and their respective shareholdings.

Articles of Association
1. A statement that the provisions of the Companies Act apply (currently of 1985 as amended 1989).
2. Details of the capital structure of the company, the types of shares of which it is comprised and how they may be transferred.
3. The voting rights of shareholders.
4. Matters relating to the appointment and duties of directors.
5. The borrowing powers of the company.
6. The appointment of a Company Secretary.
7. The requirements for notifying Company meetings (how, when and to whom details must be circulated).
8. The names of the first directors (not less than one and not more than seven for a private limited company).
9. The names and addresses of the original subscribers (ie shareholders or members).

When the company is registered with the Registrar of Companies it is given a number, and it must have an official seal which is used on legal documents and share certificates.

A Certificate of Incorporation is provided showing the company name, registration number and the date of first registration. This must be displayed at the company's registered office.

When the formation is complete, printed sets of the Articles and Memorandum are lodged with the Registrar of Companies along with other formation documents. It is usual also for a company's bank to require copies of the Articles and Memorandum when it is providing finance by way of overdrafts and loans so it too can see what the company's borrowing powers are and any legal restrictions on its operations.

Legal operation of companies

A limited liability company must be operated within the requirements of the Companies Acts. Among these requirements are the following:

1. The Certificate of Incorporation must be displayed at the Registered Office.
2. The company name must be shown on the outside of all its business premises and on all its documentation including cheques.
3. All business paper must show the following information:
   (a) the registered office address if different from the trading address
   (b) the registration number
   (c) whether registered in England and Wales or Scotland (or Northern Ireland)
   (d) the names of the directors *may* be shown provided the list includes *every* individual director of the company together with their Christian names or initials
   (e) the VAT number if VAT registered (not a requirement under the Companies Act but a legal requirement of HM Customs and Excise).
4. The annual accounts for the company must be audited by a professional auditor (ie by a chartered accountant or by a member of the Association of Certified Accountants – but not if he is an employee of the company) who must also prepare a trading account and balance sheet.
5. An annual meeting (ie the AGM) must be held at which the directors and shareholders approve the annual accounts.
6. An annual return of directors, a copy of the minutes of the annual meeting and the accounts must be lodged with the Registrar of Companies. Small and medium-sized companies (turnover not exceeding £90,000 and £350,000 respectively) may produce

simplified accounts in the form of a 'compilation report' for this purpose.

7. The Registrar of Companies must be notified of any changes of secretary, shareholders, directors or of the registered address.
8. Details of any charge or mortgage against the company or against property it owns or other assets must also be recorded at Companies House.

Records relating to limited companies, including their accounts and balance sheets and details of any charges and mortgages etc, can be examined at Companies House by any interested body or person on payment of a small fee. Alternatively, company search specialists based at Companies House will undertake this task and send copies of all documents for a fee.

Liquidation of a business
If financial difficulties reach a point where a business cannot meet the demands of its creditors, it must cease trading – in other words, when it is insolvent. It is illegal to continue trading whether as a sole trader, a partnership or a limited liability company once this position is reached (viz under The Insolvency Act 1986).

When a business has to cease trading, various courses of action are open to the owners. The first stage may be an agreement with creditors whereby they accept reduction of the debt or deferred payment. The next stage may be imposition of an administration order which preserves the firm intact and prevents creditors making it bankrupt while the appointed administrator tries to rescue the business or sell it off as a going concern. If these alternatives are not relevant a Receiver can be appointed voluntarily to take charge of the affairs of the business (ie voluntary liquidation) and pay off the creditors so far as realisation of the assets permits, followed by winding up of the business (in the case of a limited liability company when its name would be struck off the Companies Register). Alternatively, one or more of the creditors (or all of them collectively) may appoint a Receiver. The former is a much more acceptable means of bringing a business to an end. In many instances creditors take action to make a firm bankrupt without prior notice.

Following the collapse of the business, charges may be brought against the proprietor, partners or directors (who may also be disqualified from taking part in the management of any company under the Company Directors Disqualification Act 1986) for misappropriation of funds, for example, or for trading when insolvent, and they could be adjudged personally bankrupt.

Once the Receiver is appointed he becomes legally responsible for collecting debts due to the business, for selling the company's assets and for paying off creditors (and the employees' wages) so far as possible. The amount paid to creditors depends on the resources available and on their status. Preferential creditors such as banks who have loaned money against security, the Inland Revenue and HM Customs and Excise (for VAT and any duties), the DSS for National Insurance contributions owing and debenture holders are among those who have a first share of any money paid out. The Receiver is permitted to charge his fees first.

When all the assets have been realised and distributed and the shareholders of a limited company have met any outstanding commitment on their shares, that is the end of the matter for them. In the case of non-limited firms the Receiver becomes responsible for securing the personal assets of the proprietor or the partners including, where necessary to meet liabilities, forcing them to sell their home, their car and any luxury items such as TV sets, hi-fi systems, works of art and so on, until all claims are met. In the latter case, the individual may be left with nothing more than the barest amount of essential furniture (a bed, chair, table, etc). A similar misfortune may befall a director of a limited liability company who has given personal guarantees or secured his personal assets (ie home, insurances, other savings/investments, etc) against business loans.

3. Social legislation

Present-day transport managers need to be concerned with many aspects of business operation and administration beyond those relating solely to owning and running haulage vehicles.

The employment of staff for driving, and to work in workshops, warehouses and offices, brings the manager into contact with a very broad and complex body of social legislation which has been built up over many years. .

The legislation can be divided into four principal categories which cover industrial relations and employment protection, social security, health and safety at work and discrimination. Also, there are Codes of Practice covering industrial relations and safety* which, while not having statutory authority in themselves, do have a significant bearing on the way in which the relevant statutes are observed and applied.

*ACAS has published three Codes of Practice as follows:

1. *Disciplinary practice and procedures in employment.*
2. *Disclosure of information to trade unions for collective bargaining purposes.*
3. *Time off for trade union duties and activities.*

Two further Codes of Practice are available from the Department of Education and Employment as follows:

1. *Industrial Relations.*
2. *Picketing.*

The main objectives of each of these pieces of legislation and Codes of Practice are dealt with in this section.

Industrial relations
Trade Union and Labour Relations (Consolidation) Act 1992 as amended by the Trade Union Reform and Employment Rights Act 1993

These Acts consolidate employees' rights in industrial relations terms, which were previously contained in other statutes. The main provisions of these Acts are outlined in this section under the following broad headings:

1. Trade union membership
2. Trade disputes and picketing
3. Contracts and written statement of terms and conditions of employment
4. Itemised pay statements
5. Guarantee payments
6. Suspension on medical grounds under health and safety regulations
7. Time off for union duties and activities and for public duties
8. Maternity rights for the expectant mother
9. Rights on termination of employment
10. Dismissal and unfair dismissal
11. Redundancy – time off for job hunting or to arrange training.

Trade union membership

Recognised trade unions

For the purposes of the legislation described here, a 'recognised' trade union is one which is recognised by an employer or a group of employers for the purposes of collective bargaining on wages and other employment terms and conditions. It is also one which is recognised by the parties to a union agreement within the firm, or one which the Advisory, Conciliation and Arbitration Service (ACAS) recommends as being one which should be recognised. Under the Act, in order to establish an approved union membership agreement (ie 'a closed shop') there must be a positive (yes) vote by at least 80 per cent of those *entitled* to vote in a secret ballot.

Right to belong or not to belong to a trade union
Employees have the right not to be victimised or discriminated against as individuals (short of dismissal) for the purpose of:

1. preventing or deterring them from becoming members of a trade union
2. preventing or deterring them from taking part in trade union activities at any appropriate time (ie outside working hours at a time when the employer gives permission for the employee to take part in those activities)
3. compelling them to be or become a member of a trade union. Employees who genuinely object on religious grounds have the right not to have action taken against them (short of dismissal) for the purposes of compelling them to belong to a trade union

An employee can complain to an Industrial Tribunal if any such action is taken against him. The complaint must be made within three months of the action complained of. The Tribunal can award compensation which is just and equitable in relation to any loss suffered by the employee.

Trade disputes and picketing
A trade dispute is a dispute between an employer and his employees relating to, or in the main relating to:

1. the terms and conditions of employment or the actual physical conditions in which employees are required to work
2. the engagement or non-engagement of one or more workers, the termination or suspension of their employment or the duties of their employment
3. the allocation of work or the duties of employment between employees or groups of employees
4. matters of discipline among employees
5. membership or non-membership of a trade union
6. the provision of facilities for trade union officials
7. the machinery for negotiation or consultation and other procedures relating to any of the above matters, including recognition by employers or employers' associations of the right of a trade union to represent workers in any such negotiation or consultation or in carrying out such procedures.

Trade disputes involving industrial action may take place between employers and employees or between groups of employees. Such disputes will be the subject of legal steps only if they have not been agreed in secret ballot requiring workers to make a straight 'Yes' or 'No' vote to the action.

Without a properly conducted ballot the trade union and its officers have no legal immunity if they take or incite industrial action.

Secondary industrial action where a person is induced to take industrial action against an employer who is not party to a trade dispute in most cases can result in legal action for damages.

Picketing staged in furtherance of a trade dispute is legal if its purpose is to peacefully communicate information or peacefully persuade a person to refrain from working (or conversely to work) and provided it is carried out at or near the place of work. It is not illegal to picket elsewhere but this may result in a claim for damages by those who suffer loss as a result (eg by a firm which cannot get goods or employees into or out of its premises). In the cases described above, those who suffer loss may seek an injunction to put a stop to the action complained of and may also seek damages for the torts (wrongful actions) committed against them to compensate for their losses.

Terms and conditions of employment

Contracts and written particulars of employment
A contract of employment exists as soon as a job offer has been made and accepted by the prospective employee. Acceptance of the terms described verbally at the interview or contained in a letter of confirmation will be assumed if the employee reports at the due time to start the job. The contract does not have to be in writing.

Within two months of starting employment an employee must be given a written statement detailing:

1. the parties to the contract
2. the date when employment began (and if for a fixed term, when it will end)
3. the date when continuous employment began (eg after any probationary period)
4. rates of pay
5. when payment is to be made (eg weekly or monthly)
6. hours of work (normal and otherwise)
7. holiday entitlements and pay
8. sick pay and provisions
9. pensions and pension schemes
10. notice of termination required
11. job title
12. if the job contract is only temporary, how long it may be expected to last
13. if the job is a fixed-term contract, the date of termination

14. where the job is outside the UK for more than one month, details of the length of the posting, the currency in which payment will be made, details of any additional benefits which accrue due to the posting and terms and conditions relating to return to the UK
15. disciplinary rules (unless less than 20 persons employed when continuous employment began)
16. the name of the person to whom appeals on disciplinary matters can be referred
17. the name of the person to whom the employee can apply to seek redress of grievances
18. how such applications must be made.

If the terms of employment set out in the written statement are changed the employer must give the employee details of these in writing within one month.

Itemised pay statements
When wages are paid the employee is entitled (on or before the pay day) to an itemised pay statement in writing showing:

1. the gross amount of pay
2. amounts of any deductions and the reasons for deductions (except if fixed deductions are regularly made and a standing statement has been given plus a cumulative statement of the deductions)
3. the net amount payable
4. where the net amount is paid by different means (eg part cheque/part cash), the method of payment of each different part of the total pay.

Guarantee payments
If the employer cannot find work on any day for an employee who has been employed continuously for at least one month, the employee is entitled to be paid a guaranteed payment for that workless day (ie 24 hours from midnight to midnight). This does not apply if the workless day occurs as a result of a trade dispute. Also payment need not be made if:

1. the employee was offered alternative work which he unreasonably refused,
2. the employee does not comply with reasonable requirements to ensure that his services are available.

Limits are placed on the amount of guarantee pay due and the number of days for which it is due (eg five days in any three-month period for a five-day week worker). Further, payment of guarantee pay does not affect the right of the employee to receive any other pay under his contract of employment.

An employee can complain to an Industrial Tribunal if the employer fails to pay all or part of the guarantee pay due. If the Tribunal upholds the complaint the employer will have to pay the amount due.

Suspension on medical grounds
If an employee is suspended from work by his employer on medical grounds as a result of legal requirements or recommendations based on Health and Safety at Work Codes of Practice, he must be paid for up to 26 weeks.

The employee is not entitled to such payment for any time when he is unable to work if:

1. he had not been continuously employed for at least one month prior to commencement of the suspension
2. the employment is under a fixed-term contract not exceeding three months
3. he is suffering disease or bodily or mental disablement
4. the employer has offered suitable alternative work
5. he does not comply with reasonable requirements to make his services available.

The amount of remuneration payable is one week's pay for every week's suspension, and proportionate payment for part-weeks.

An employee can complain to an Industrial Tribunal if the employer fails to make any such payment. If the Tribunal upholds the complaint it will order the employer to pay the amount due.

Time off   In certain circumstances as described below, employees must be given time off from work either with or without pay.

Trade union duties
An employee must be given (paid) time off work if he is an official of a recognised trade union for the purpose of:

1. carrying out the duties of such an official concerned with industrial relations between the employer and the employees
2. undergoing training in industrial relations which is:
   (a) relevant to the duties mentioned
   (b) approved by the union or the Trades Union Congress (TUC).

The amount of time which may be taken off for trade union duties is that which is 'reasonable in all the circumstances'. When an employer permits an employee to have time off for these purposes he must be paid for that time on the basis of normal pay for the time (where pay does not vary), or average pay for the time (where pay does vary).

Trade union activities
Employees (other than union officials) must be given (unpaid) time off to take part in the activities of a union which is recognised and of which the employee is a member, *excluding* activities which consist of industrial action in relation to contemplation or furtherance of a trade union dispute. The amount of time which may be taken off is that which is 'reasonable in all the circumstances'.

Any employee can complain to an Industrial Tribunal if the employer fails to permit the employee to have such time off. If the Tribunal upholds the complaint it will award just and equitable compensation to the employee.

Public duties
Employees who fulfil certain public duties as listed below must be given a reasonable amount of (unpaid) time off to attend to such duties:

1. A Justice of the Peace (JP – ie a magistrate).
2. A member of a local authority (but not elected councillors).
3. A member of a statutory tribunal.
4. A member of a Regional or Area Health Authority (in Scotland, a Health Board) or of a Family Practitioner Committee.
5. A member of the managing or governing body of an educational establishment maintained by a local education authority (in Scotland, a school or college council or central institution of education).
6. A member of the National Rivers Authority.

For these purposes duties include attending meetings and discharging other functions. The amount of time off to be given is that which is 'reasonable in all the circumstances', having regard to how much time is required to fulfil the duties; the amount of time off already taken in this respect; and the effect on the employer's business of the employee's absence.

A complaint can be made to an Industrial Tribunal (within three months) if the employer fails to allow such time off to be taken.

NB: Although not part of this legislation, employees listed for Jury Service must be allowed appropriate time off for such purposes – without pay.

Looking for work or arranging for training

An employee who has been given notice of dismissal by reason of redundancy (ie after two years' continuous employment) must be given, before the expiry of the notice, reasonable time off during working hours to look for new employment or to make arrangements for training for future employment. An employee who is allowed time off for these purposes must be paid at the appropriate rate. If the employer unreasonably refuses time off the employee is entitled to an amount equal to the pay he would have been entitled to, had he taken time off.

A complaint can be made to an Industrial Tribunal (within three months) if the employer refuses time off for such purposes and compensation of up to two-fifths of a week's pay can be awarded.

Maternity rights for the expectant mother

An employee who is absent from work due wholly or partly to pregnancy or confinement is entitled to:

1. 14 weeks continuous leave before and/or after childbirth
2. paid time off for antenatal examinations
3. no risk of dismissal during the period of pregnancy and maternity leave except in exceptional circumstances wholly unconnected with the pregnancy
4. preservation of her contractual rights during the maternity leave
5. pay at the sick-pay rate during the period of maternity.

The employee is entitled to return to work after her confinement (up to a maximum of 29 weeks from the week of the birth – see below), provided that:

1. she continues working until the eleventh week before the expected week of confinement
2. she has been continuously employed prior to this for not less than two years
3. She informs her employer in writing 21 days in advance of her absence (or as soon as is reasonably practicable) that:
   (a) she will be (or is) absent wholly or partly due to pregnancy and confinement (and the week in which it is due), and
   (b) that she intends to return to work.

These entitlements do not apply unless a medical certificate is produced stating the expected week of her confinement, if the employer requests it.

Maternity pay
Statutory maternity pay (SMP) must be given for a maximum period (ie the maternity pay period – MPP) of 18 weeks continuously or in aggregate while the employee is absent from work wholly or partly due to pregnancy or confinement.

The 18-week pay period commences with the first week of absence beginning in the eleventh week – maternity pay is not paid for absence prior to the eleventh week.

The amount of maternity pay due depends on circumstances; there are two rates, a higher and a lower rate. The higher rate equates to nine-tenths of the employee's average weekly earnings. The lower rate is a fixed weekly rate.

The right of the employee to receive maternity pay does not affect that employee's right to any other remuneration owing under any contract of employment.

If an employer fails to pay the whole or part of any maternity pay due, the employee can complain to an Industrial Tribunal.

Payment of maternity benefits
Maternity payments to employees (with appropriate deductions of tax and National Insurance) are made directly by the employer who may then deduct an equal amount from payments due to the Inland Revenue for both the employer's and the employee's share of National Insurance contributions.

Employee's right to return to work
An employee's right to return to work after pregnancy or confinement is subject to the specified conditions of her return. It must be:

1. to the original employer or his successor
2. up to the end of 29 weeks from the week of the confinement
3. in the job in which she was previously employed
4. under the original contract of employment
5. on terms and conditions no less favourable than those applicable had she not been absent.

If, because of changed circumstances (eg redundancies), the employer cannot permit her to return to the original job, she must be offered any suitable alternative vacancy which exists with the original employer or his successor under a new contract of employment which provides suitable work and is not substantially less favourable than the original contract.

The employee wishing to exercise her right of return must notify the employer in writing at least 21 days before she proposes to return. An employer can write to the employee up to 49 days after the notified date of confinement asking for written confirmation that she intends to return to work. If he does not receive a reply in 14 days the right to return to work is lost. The employer can postpone the return date for not more than 4 weeks providing he notifies the employee that the date is being postponed.

The employee, after giving notice of return, can postpone the return date for not more than 4 weeks – even if this goes beyond the 29 weeks. She must produce a medical certificate showing why she cannot return before the notified day of return or before the end of the 29 weeks.

Termination of employment
Employment may be terminated either by the employee giving notice or by the employer giving the employee notice. In either case specified minimum periods of notice must be given.

Termination by the employer
If a person has been employed continuously for 4 weeks or more he must be given the following periods of notice of termination of employment:

Employment	Notice
Less than 2 years	1 week
More than 2 years but less than 12 years	1 week for each continuous year
More than 12 years	at least 12 weeks

Termination by the employee
An employee terminating his employment after 4 weeks or more of employment must give at least one week's notice irrespective of the length of employment service.

If a contract of employment stipulates shorter notice the above (legal minima) still applies but either party may waive the right to notice or accept payment in lieu of notice.

Dismissal
Where the employer finds it necessary to dismiss an employee, certain conditions must be observed depending on the circumstances of the case. Dismissal includes:

1. termination of employment with or without notice
2. the term of a contract expiring without renewal
3. termination by the employee with or without notice due to the employer's conduct
4. failure by an employer to let an employee return to work after pregnancy or confinement.

51

Statement of reasons for dismissal

An employee is entitled to be provided on request, and within 14 days, with a written statement giving reasons for dismissal if:

1. he is given notice of termination (unless the employment was for less than 26 weeks)
2. he is dismissed without notice
3. a fixed term contract expires without being renewed.

Where the employer fails to give such a written statement (or the reason given in writing is not adequate or known to be incorrect) the employee can complain to an Industrial Tribunal (within three months of the date of dismissal) which will, if the case is well founded:

1. declare the reason for dismissal
2. make an award that the employer pays an amount equal to two weeks' pay.

Fair and unfair dismissal

An employee has a right not to be unfairly dismissed. For an employee to be fairly dismissed the employer must show:

1. the reason for dismissal
2. that the reason was within one of the following areas:
    (a) the capability or qualification of the employee for the work involved including his fitness to perform the work
    (b) the conduct of the employee
    (c) redundancy of the employee
    (d) contravention of legal restrictions by the employee in connection with his work.

In showing that the reason for dismissal was within items 2(a) to (d) above, the employer must show that he acted reasonably in treating it as a sufficient reason for dismissing the employee.

Dismissal relating to trade union membership

It is unfair to dismiss an employee because that employee:

1. was, or proposed to become, a trade union member
2. had taken part, or proposed to take part, in trade union activities
3. refused to become a trade union member.

Dismissal on redundancy

It is unfair to dismiss an employee on the grounds of redundancy if the employee:

1. was selected for dismissal for an inadmissible reason
2. was selected in contravention of customary arrangements or agreed procedures.

Dismissal on pregnancy
It is unfair to dismiss an employee who is pregnant or for any reason connected with pregnancy except if the employee:

1. is incapable of doing her job because of the pregnancy
2. cannot do her job due to her pregnancy without contravention of legal restrictions.

Dismissal on replacement
If an employee is engaged to replace a pregnant employee it is not unfair to dismiss that employee on the return to work of the former employee if the replacement employee was told that dismissal would then occur.

Dismissal on industrial action
It is unfair to dismiss an employee where at the date of dismissal:

1. the employer was conducting or instituting a lock-out, or
2. the employee was taking part in a strike or other industrial action.

Qualifying period and age limit for dismissal
Claims for unfair dismissal can be made to an Industrial Tribunal within three months of the date of dismissal. Unfair dismissal cannot be claimed if the employment was in a firm with more than 20 employees and if:

1. the employee was employed for less than two years – one year if the employment began before 1 June 1985 (if he worked for 16 or more hours per week), or
2. the employee was employed for less than five years (if he worked for between 8 and 16 hours per week), or
3. the employee was at the normal retiring age for an employee or if:
    (a) a man, had attained the age of 65 years
    (b) a woman, had attained the age of 60 years.

In the case of a firm with less than 20 employees, unfair dismissal cannot be claimed if the employment was for less than two years.

Remedy for unfair dismissal
An employee can make a complaint of unfair dismissal against an employer to an Industrial Tribunal (within three months of

the date on which the dismissal took effect) which, if the case is well founded:

1. will order reinstatement or re-engagement (subject to the employee's wishes), or
2. award compensation.

Redundancy   The need to make employees redundant arises either when a particular job ceases to exist, when the demand for a particular product or service falls or ceases, or when a business closes down altogether. In these circumstances the employee or employees are redundant. They are not redundant if they are replaced by new or other employees.

For an employee to claim a redundancy payment under the Act, he must have been continuously employed by that employer for at least two years since reaching the age of 18 years, and must not have unreasonably refused any alternative offer of suitable employment made by the employer.

The redundancy payment received by the employee depends on a number of factors; age, the length of service with the employer and the present weekly rate of pay. The scale of pay rates is as follows:

1. Half a week's pay for each year continuously employed between ages 18-21 years
2. One week's pay for each year continuously employed between ages 22-40 years
3. One-and-a-half week's pay for each year continuously employed between ages 41-64 years.

Payment of the sum due under a redundancy arrangement is made by the employer unless he is insolvent, in which case it is paid by the Secretary of State for Education and Employment. Redundancy payments made by employers are not recoverable from the Government. Redundancy payments and payments in lieu of notice are not normally subject to income tax deductions.

The following employees are *not* entitled to redundancy payments:

1. Self-employed people
2. People who have been employed for less than two years continuously with their employers since reaching the age of 18
3. People aged over 65 years (ie both men and women over normal retirement age)
4. People normally employed for less than 16 hours per week

5. The husband or wife of an employer
6. People who are engaged on a fixed-term contract made before 1965 for two years or more and who have agreed to forfeit any right to redundancy
7. People outside Britain at the time of being made redundant unless they normally work in Britain
8. Share fishermen
9. Merchant seamen (a master or seaman on a British seagoing ship with a gross registered tonnage of 80 tons or more)
10. Registered dock workers.

Consultation/disclosure

When an employer wishes to make an employee redundant he must consult that person's trade union representative about the proposed dismissal. It is important to note that the requirement is to consult, not to inform. Consultation should begin 30 days before dismissal when ten or more employees are to be made redundant in a period of 30 days, and 90 days before dismissal when 100 or more employees are to be made redundant in a period of 90 days.

An employer is required to disclose to trade union representatives:

1. the reason why the employees have become redundant
2. the number and description of employees whom it is proposed to dismiss as redundant
3. the total number of comparable employees at the establishment
4. the proposed method of selecting the employees to be dismissed
5. the proposed methods of dismissal, including the period over which they will take effect.

If trade union representatives ask for this information in writing employers should comply with the request, as there is a provision within the Act which can require the information to be posted to an address provided by the trade union. The employer is obliged to consider any representations made by the trade union representative during consultation, to reply to those representations and, if he rejects them, to state his reasons.

Failure to comply with these regulations enables the trade union to complain to an Industrial Tribunal, which will make a protective award to the employee(s) if it finds the complaint well founded.

An employer is also required to notify the Secretary of State for Education and Employment of proposed redundancies at an establishment. This notification must be 30 days in advance when proposing to dismiss ten or more employees and 90 days in advance when dismissing 100 or more employees.

Training

Industrial Training Act 1982

The aims of the original Act were to improve the quality and standard of industrial training, to ensure an adequate supply of properly trained manpower and to spread the cost of training. It was responsible for the establishment of the Industrial Training Boards covering most major industries. The 1982 Act combines all the earlier provisions concerning Industrial Training Boards under the Training Commission, which in turn became the Training Agency and is now the Training, Enterprise and Education Directorate (TEED) – part of the Department of Education and Employment. Its role is to develop policies for industrial training and to ensure these are implemented through Training and Enterprise Councils (TECs); established to be responsible for assisting people in selection and training for employment and for assisting employers in obtaining suitable personnel.

A number of special employment schemes exist under the auspices of the regional Traning and Enterprise Councils (TECs). These schemes vary from TEC region to region depending upon local requirements, but broadly the TECs provide the following:

1. Training to provide relevant skills to the levels of National Vocational Qualifications (NVQs).
2. Business 'Start-Up' schemes to help those wishing to start in business (but there is no longer any financial help).
3. Business Enterprise Training which provides relevant training for those about to start in business, and subsequent training once a business is established.

Social security
Social Security Pensions Act 1975 and the Social Security Act 1986

The Social Security Pensions Act 1975 (amended by the 1986 Act) which came into operation in April 1978, introduced a two-part scheme for retirement, widows' and invalidity pensions: a basic pension and an additional pension. Both parts are paid for by National Insurance contributions, but employees who are covered by an occupational pension scheme may be contracted out of the additional part of the retirement and widows' pension. In this case, National Insurance contributions are reduced for both employers and employees.

Pensions

Retirement pensions are earnings-related (ie the State earnings-related pension scheme – SERPS) and are in two parts. There is a basic pension corresponding to the previous flat-rate National Insurance retirement pension. As from 6 April 1978, an additional pension builds up at the rate of 1¼ per cent a year of the employee's earnings between the lower and the upper earnings limits until after 20 years, a maximum of 25 per cent of these earnings is reached. The lower earnings limit approximately equals the single person's rate of basic pension and the upper limit is about seven times that amount.

Pensions are protected against inflation. Each year's earnings on which the employee's pension is calculated is revalued in line with the growth in earnings generally up to (but not including) the tax year before retirement. After retirement, the basic pension is kept in line with increased earnings (or prices, if more advantageous) and the additional pension is protected against price increases.

Contributions

National Insurance contributions (see below) are payable by both employee and employer when earnings are at or above the lower earnings limit and by self-employed persons. They are then payable on all earnings up to the upper earnings limit.

Occupational pension schemes and contracting out

Employees who are members of occupational pension schemes that meet certain conditions may be contracted out of part of the State scheme by their employer. Alternatively, individual employees may contract out of the scheme if they have made their own acceptable personal pension arrangements. Under these arrangements the basic retirement pension is paid by the State and the occupational scheme takes broad responsibility for providing the additional pension.

National Insurance Contributions and the Social Security Acts 1975, 1981 and 1986

These Acts consolidate the 1973 Act of the same title together with the National Insurance (Industrial Injuries) Acts 1965 and 1974. The 1973 Act established a basic scheme of social security contributions and benefits replacing those established by the National Insurance Acts. These Acts make provisions for various classes of contributions (ie National Insurance contributions – NICs) which employers deduct from employees' pay, or which self-employed persons pay direct or which employees may voluntarily pay direct. In addition to the contribution paid by employees, employers also pay contributions in respect of their employees. Following deduction of the employees' contribution, the employer adds his contribution and makes the total payment to the Inland Revenue along with any tax deductions from employees' wages or salaries.

The four main classes of contributions made by employees and self-employed persons are as follows:

Class 1: Full or reduced rates for employed people working under a contract of employment based on a percentage of weekly earnings (ie paid under the PAYE scheme). Only Class 1 contributions count for unemployment benefit and a certain minimum of contributions must be paid for benefit to be payable.

Class 2: Fixed rate contributions paid by self-employed people. Additionally, people who pay Class 2 contributions also pay a supplementary contribution annually based on earnings (see Class 4 contributions). Payment of Class 2 contributions by a self-employed person entitles that person to sickness and other benefits but it does not count for unemployment benefit.

Class 3: Contributors who wish to maintain benefits while not employed may make voluntary Class 3 contributions.

Class 4: Contributions paid in respect of annual profits or gains derived from carrying on trades, professions or vocations. The amount of the contribution is based on a percentage of earnings between a lower figure and a higher figure.

In all cases, the level of contribution at any time is determined by the Chancellor of the Exchequer and incorporated in the current Finance Act.

Statutory sick pay (SSP)

The Social Security Contributions and Benefits Act 1992 legislates for the statutory sick pay (SSP) scheme under which employers are required to make sickness payments to employees. The employee must satisfy rules on periods of incapacity, entitlement periods and qualifying days. Certain small employers may reclaim the full payments made to employees (including National Insurance contributions) by deductions from his payments of National Insurance contributions to the Inland Revenue – Small Employers' Relief (SER). State sickness benefit still applies for certain special cases – such as those who have to be regularly off work for long term medical treatment and those who do not qualify for or who have exhausted their SSP entitlements.

Employees qualify for SSP after a specified period of incapacity for work (PIW) – four consecutive days – due to physical or mental illness or disablement. A number of periods can be linked if each is of a minimum of four days. The first three days of each PIW are waiting days – sickness payment is only made in respect of qualifying days which count from the fourth day onwards. The maximum entitlement to SSP in any period of incapacity for work is 28 weeks after which a new PIW will start.

Notification of sickness can be by use of the DSS self-certification form, by submitting a doctor's medical certificate or the employer can institute his own scheme of self-certification of sickness.

The amount of SSP which must be paid is based on the employee's average gross weekly pay and is set at a specified limit by the Government.

Discrimination A range of legislation is applied to prevent discrimination against workers on account of sex, colour, race or creed in relation to their recruitment or training for employment, selection for promotion, their pay and terms of employment or other working conditions.

Equal Pay Act 1970 Any employer who employs women, in whatever capacity, is affected by the Equal Pay Act 1970 (as amended by the Equal Pay (Amendment) Regulations 1983) which was introduced to prevent discrimination between men and women with regard to terms and conditions of employment.

The Act requires employers to ensure that the terms and conditions of employment for men and women who are employed on 'like work' or 'work rated as equivalent' are 'not in any respect less favourable than those of the other'. A term of the contract under which a woman is employed at an establishment in Great Britain must be that she shall be given equal treatment to men in the same employment.

The employer's problem lies in establishing what is 'like work', or 'work rated as equivalent'. In the Act, 'like work' is defined as work of the same or broadly similar nature and the difference, if any, between the work a woman does and the work a man does is not of practical importance in relation to the terms and conditions of employment. Also, in comparing a woman's work with a man's, regard must be given to the frequency with which any differences occur in practice as well as to the nature and extent of the differences.

'Work rated as equivalent' is intended to mean that the woman's job has been given equal value to the man's job in terms of effort, skill and decision.

Employers are required to define clearly 'female' jobs and, where necessary, mixed staff arrangements in offices should have been changed if the jobs of the men and women in these offices were to remain unequal after the Act took effect. For example, in a large accounts/invoices/costs/ wages office both male and female clerks may be employed on work which could easily be defined as 'broadly similar' by the staff or their union.

The employer must consider the requirements of the Act when negotiating any pay deals, because the Act states that discrimination between men and women must be eliminated from any collective agreement, pay structure or wage regulation order made before commencement of the Equal Pay Act. This means that separate rates of pay for men and women employed on similar jobs should have ceased by the end of 1975 and should have been replaced by one rate for the job, applicable to both men and women.

A person who is aggrieved under the terms of this Act and who wishes to make a claim, must take their case to an Industrial Tribunal within six months of termination of their employment or at any time while still employed by the employer. If their case is successful they can be awarded up to two years' arrears of pay.

Sex Discrimination Acts 1975 and 1986

Under these Acts (which apply only to firms with more than five employees) it is an offence for anyone to discriminate between people on the grounds of their sex or marital status in relation to employment, selection for training and promotion and other employment benefits as well as for dismissal.

The sexes must be given equal opportunities in terms of work, training and promotion and for many employers the most significant factor arises when advertising vacancies. The advertisement placed must not be worded in a way which suggests that applicants of only one sex should apply. There are instances when it is clearly necessary to show discrimination in advertising and these are generally exempt from the provisions of the Act. The most obvious is recruitment of females for the women's branches of the armed forces or attendants for toilets (male or female), but the transport operator must exercise care against wording advertisements such as 'tea lady required', 'attractive young lady required as receptionist' or 'female invoice clerk required', all of which will provoke complaints under the Act. Even when seeking driving, maintenance, warehouse or traffic office staff, careful wording is essential to avoid the direct suggestion, for example, that only males will be employed. It is permissible to state that the duties are arduous or include heavy lifting which by implication means that mainly men should apply but would not exclude a strong woman who wished to apply.

In general, the media will not accept advertisement copy which infringes the Act but the employer should consider too the dangers of ambiguous framing of employment requests or opportunities which might be posted internally on notice boards or in staff newsletters for example.

Disabled Persons (Employment) Acts 1944 and 1958

The first of these two Acts was designed to make further and better provisions for enabling persons handicapped by disablement to secure employment or work on their own account.

A disabled person, for the purposes of the Act, is a person who because of injury, disease or congenital deformity, is substantially handicapped in obtaining or keeping employment of a kind which apart from that injury, disease or deformity, would be suited to his age, experience and qualifications, or in undertaking work on his own account.

A register of disabled persons is established and the Act made provision for the establishment of vocational training and industrial rehabilitation courses and for payments to people attending courses. It also established an obligation for employers of a substantial number of employees (ie over 20) to give employment to a certain number of *registered* disabled persons (currently three per cent for a period of 30 hours per week or more) providing the trade carried on is suitable for the employment of such persons.

The 1958 Act amended the 1944 Act in respect of the minimum age for attendance at certain courses (instead of having to be 'over 16 years' the Act uses the term 'over compulsory school leaving age'), registration with the Training Commission under the Act (previously a disabled person was not to be registered unless the disability was likely to continue for six months; it is now 12 months), and the provision by local authorities of employment or other work under special conditions (previously reference to provision of employment was in terms of specially formed companies for the purpose; now local authorities have powers to make the necessary arrangements to provide suitable facilities for the employment of disabled persons).

Race Relations Act 1976

This Act (following on from earlier Acts of the same name) effectively prohibits discrimination in employment on racial grounds between people of different racial groups.

Specifically, the aims of the Act are to make it illegal for a person to:

1. treat another person less favourably on racial grounds
2. apply requirements or conditions to a person or proportion of people of different racial groups which are not shown to be justifiable irrespective of the colour, race, nationality or ethnic or national origins of the person or people to whom they are applied.

It is illegal to discriminate against a person on racial grounds in respect of offering employment, the terms on which employment is offered or refusal of employment. Further, it is also illegal to discriminate against employees by offering or refusing to offer opportunities for promotion, training, benefits or services on racial grounds and to dismiss a person or subject him to other detriment on the same grounds.

Fair Employment (Northern Ireland) Act 1989

This Act (replacing a 1976 Act of the same name), which applies solely to the province of Northern Ireland and which came into effect on 1 January 1990, is intended to ensure that Catholic and Protestant workers in Northern Ireland have equal job opportunities. It established a new Fair Employment Commission and a Fair Employment Tribunal and requires compulsory registration of employers with the Commission. Employers are required to review their recruitment, training and promotion practices and monitor their workforces and job applicants to ensure the aims of the Act are upheld. Failure to comply with the Act can result in both criminal penalties and economic sanctions (eg loss of government grants and contracts) and victims of religious discrimination can be awarded compensation by the new Tribunal (currently up to £30,000). The Commission is to draw up a Code of Practice for use by employers in establishing and reviewing their employment policies.

Safety
The Health and Safety at Work, etc Act 1974

The Health and Safety at Work, etc Act 1974 applies to all persons at work including employers and self-employed persons but with the exception of domestic servants. It replaces certain parts of both the Factories Act 1961 and the Offices, Shops and Railway Premises Act 1963 (which still remain in force), but adds other provisions.

The main aims of the Act are:

1. to maintain and improve standards of health, safety and welfare for people at work

2. to protect people other than those at work against risks to their health or safety arising from the work activities of others
3. to control the storage and use of explosives, highly flammable or dangerous substances, and to prevent their unlawful acquisition, possession or use.
4. to control the emission into the atmosphere of noxious or offensive fumes or substances from work premises
5. to set up the Health and Safety Commission and the Health and Safety Executive.

Approved Codes of Practice set up under the Act (particularly those that cover working with lead and other hazardous products, and working with excessive noise) have special status in providing a simple and flexible extension of the law. Consequently, while a person is not rendered liable to proceedings if a Code is not observed, it could have a bearing on the matter in legal proceedings if advice given in a Code has been ignored.

Duties of employers under the Act

The Act prescribes the general duties of all employers (with five or more employees) towards their employees by obliging them to ensure their health, safety and welfare while at work. This duty requires that all plant and methods of work provided must be reasonably safe and without risks to health. A similar injunction relates to the use, handling, storage and transport of any articles or substances used in connection with the employer's work.

It is the duty of the employer to provide all necessary information and instruction, supported by proper training and supervision.

Workplaces generally, if under the employer's control, must be maintained so that they are safe and without risks to health, have adequate means of entrance and exit and provide a working environment that has satisfactory facilities and arrangements for the welfare of the people employed in that workplace.

Additionally, employers and self-employed persons must ensure that their activities do not create any hazard to members of the general public. In certain circumstances, information must be made publicly available regarding the existence of possible hazards to health and safety.

Written policy statement

The employer must (unless he has fewer than five employees) draw up and bring to the notice of all the workforce a written statement of the company policy regarding health and safety at work, together with all current arrangements for implementation of that policy. The statement must be updated as the need arises and all alterations must be communicated to employees.

Safety representatives and committees

Safety representatives should be appointed in firms by the union (not by the management) from among the workforce and joint safety committees must be established as required by the safety representatives (at the request of two or more) in situations where employees are organised in recognised trade unions. Safety representatives should be persons who have been employed by the firm for at least two years or who have had two years' experience in similar employment 'so far as is reasonably practicable'. In other cases the employer should voluntarily set up a safety committee comprising employees and management.

Duties of employees under the Act

The Act states in general terms that the duty of an employee is to take reasonable care for the safety of himself and others and to co-operate with others in order to ensure compliance with statutory duties relating to health and safety at work. In particular, no person must interfere with or misuse anything provided in the interests of health, safety or welfare, either intentionally or recklessly.

Enforcement of the Act

The Health and Safety Commission (HSC) was established to take appropriate action in furthering the general purposes of the Act while the Health and Safety Executive (HSE) has as its primary duty the exercise of delegated functions and the implementation of directions given by the HSC. In turn, the Inspectorate is appointed by enforcing authorities, ie the Executive or local authority with the purpose of actually enforcing the provisions of the Act. Inspectors with suitable qualifications have powers to enter premises and impose restrictions on work activities by the issue of appropriate notices.

An Improvement Notice may be served on a person by an inspector in cases where he believes that the person is contravening or has contravened, and is likely to do so again, any of the relevant statutory provisions. Such a Notice must give details of the inspector's reason for this belief and requires the person concerned to remedy the contravention within a stated period.

A Prohibition Notice may be served by an inspector on a person in charge of activities which come within the scope of the Act if the inspector believes that these activities do or could involve a risk of serious personal injury . A Prohibition Notice must specify those matters giving rise to such a risk, the reason why the inspector believes the statutory provisions are, or are likely to be, contravened and must direct that the activities in question shall not be carried on (ie work must immediately cease) unless and until those matters giving rise to the risk of serious personal injury, and any contravention of the regulations, are rectified.

Factories Act 1961

The Factories Act 1961 (which although partially replaced by the HSW Act still remains in existence) is concerned with the health, safety and welfare of people employed to carry out manual labour in any premises (including open-air premises). It is also concerned with regulating and controlling the employment of women and young people in such premises.

A factory, for the purposes of the Act, is defined as any premises in which people are employed in any process in manual labour. It includes docks, wharves, quays, warehouses with mechanical power and building and civil engineering premises.

The Act contains the following important provisions:

Cleaning/painting
Premises should be cleaned daily, floors must be cleaned at least once a week and walls and ceilings should be washed with hot water and soap or by other approved methods every 14 months; or whitewashed or colour washed if they are not painted or varnished; if these surfaces are painted or varnished, they should be repainted or re-varnished at intervals of not more than seven years.

Overcrowding
Each workroom must provide a minimum of 11 cubic metres of space for every person employed measured within a height of 4.2 metres from the floor (ie any space above 4.2 metres is discounted).

Temperature
Where workers are required to sit down to do work which does not involve serious physical effort, the temperature must be maintained at at least 16°C (60°F) after the first hour. A

thermometer must be placed in a suitable position in every workroom. The maximum temperature permitted (other than in domestic premises or where industrial processes require more heat) is 19°C (66.2°F).

Ventilation
Workrooms must be provided with an adequate supply of air, sufficient to render harmless any injurious fumes or dust generated in the course of work carried on in that room.

Injurious fumes or dust
Where processes are carried out which result in injurious dust or fumes being generated, measures must be taken to protect workers against inhalation of the dust or fumes by the use of exhaust appliances.

Lighting
Sufficient natural or artificial light must be provided and windows and skylights should be kept clean on both sides and free from obstruction, although these may be whitewashed or shaded.

Drainage of floors
Provision must be made for draining floors.

Toilets
Suitable separate toilets for both sexes must be provided and kept clean. There should be at least one toilet for every 25 female employees and one for every 25 male employees, with four toilets for the first 100 male employees and, provided there is sufficient urinal accommodation, toilets need only be provided on the basis of one for every further 40 male employees in excess of 100. (For example, there should be five toilets for 140 male employees and a minimum of eight toilets for 260 male employees.)

Meals in dangerous trades
Food or drink must not be taken into workrooms in which poisonous substances such as lead or arsenic are involved, or in processes where the work carried out produces siliceous or asbestos dust.

Lifting excessive weights
Workpeople must not be employed to lift, carry or move any load which is heavy enough to cause them injury.

Lead processes
Young people and females must not be employed in
workrooms where processes connected with lead manufacture
are carried out or where any other process involving the use of
lead compounds is carried out which results in dust or fumes
being produced.

Notification of industrial diseases
Where any worker is affected by poisoning or disease as a
result of working in dangerous trades such cases must be
reported to the Factories (ie Health and Safety) Inspector.

Notification of accidents
Accidents causing loss of life or disabling a worker from
earning full wages for more than three days must be reported
immediately to the Factories Inspector and entered in a
General Register (ie Accident Book) kept in the workroom. The
General Register should contain details of people employed in
the workroom and information regarding the cleaning and
painting of the workroom in addition to space for describing
every accident and case of industrial disease which occurs
(see also page 70 regarding RIDDOR).

A certificate from the Fire Authority relating to the means of
escape in the case of fire should also be attached to the
General Register.

Fencing
The moving and working parts of all machinery and other
dangerous mechanical parts in the workshop must be securely
guarded and such guards must be kept in position while the
machinery is in motion or in use.

Power cut-offs
Means must be provided to enable the power for transmission
machinery to be cut off promptly.

Training of young people
Young people must be fully instructed about the danger and
the precautions to be observed when working on dangerous
machines, and they must have had adequate training by an
experienced person before working on such machines or must
be supervised while working. Young persons under 18 years
must not clean, lubricate or adjust dangerous machinery if this
exposes them to risk of injury from the machine being worked
on or from nearby machinery.

Hoists and lifts

All hoists and lifts must be in good mechanical condition and of adequate strength, and must be properly maintained. They must be thoroughly examined once every six months by a competent person and his report must be kept with the General Register. They must be suitably protected by enclosures and gates with efficient locking devices and the safe working load must be marked conspicuously on them.

Air receivers

Air receivers (ie air compressors) and their fittings must be cleaned and examined every 26 months. The safe working pressure must be shown clearly and a safety valve and pressure gauge must be fitted.

Chains, ropes and lifting tackle

Chains, ropes and lifting tackle must be of good construction, of adequate strength and free of patent defect. Such equipment must be examined by a competent person once every *six* months and must be tested and certified before being used for the first time. Chains must be annealed at least once every *14* months. Tables of safe working loads must be displayed except in the case of equipment which has the safe working load clearly displayed on it. A register of all chains, ropes and lifting tackle except fibre rope slings must be kept and so too must certificates of their tests.

Cranes

Cranes and other lifting machines and all their parts and working gear, including anchoring appliances, must be of good construction, sound material, adequate strength and free from patent defect, and must be properly maintained. All such equipment must be thoroughly examined by a competent person once every *14* months. The safe working load must be shown on every lifting machine and in the case of cranes with a jib, an automatic indicator or a table of safe working loads must be attached to the crane.

Construction of floors

All floors, steps, stairs, gangways and passageways must be soundly constructed and kept free from obstruction and any substance likely to cause people to slip. Ladders must be soundly constructed and properly maintained, openings in floors must be fenced and stairs must have handrails.

Safe access

A safe means of access to every place in which a person works must be provided.

Fire
All premises in which more than 20 persons are employed or which have been constructed or converted for factory use and in which more than ten persons are employed on any floor other than the ground floor or in which explosive or inflammable materials are stored or used, must have an adequate means of escape in the case of fire. The means of escape must have been approved by the Fire Authority and a certificate to this effect issued. It must be properly maintained and kept free from obstruction. Effective fire alarms must be provided and should be tested or examined every *three* months and a report on this attached to the General Register.

Protection of eyes
If any process is carried out which involves risk of injury to the eye from particles or fragments (eg from grindstones), suitable goggles or effective screens must be provided.

Drinking water
An adequate supply of fresh drinking water and suitable drinking containers must be provided.

Washing facilities
Clean hot and cold water, soap and towels and other means of cleaning and drying must be provided.

Accommodation for clothing
Adequate facilities must be available for hanging clothing not worn during working hours together with reasonably practicable arrangements for drying clothing.

Facilities for sitting
Where workers have an opportunity to sit down during working time they must be provided with suitable facilities.

First aid
Employers must advise their employees about first aid arrangements and provide training as necessary. A first aid box or cupboard containing only first aid requisites must be provided in every factory and workshop. In low hazard operations there must be one trained first-aider for every 150 employees. In high hazard operations there must be one trained first-aider for 50–150 employees and an additional first-aider for every further 150 employees. In small establishments a responsible person must be able to take charge in the event of accident or injury.

A first aid room should be provided in high hazard operations where more than 400 persons are employed.

Offices, Shops and Railway Premises Act 1963

This Act is concerned with provisions for the health, safety and welfare of people employed in offices, shops and certain railway premises.

The main provisions of the Act are similar in detail to the conditions required under the Factories Act (see page 65).

Reporting of accidents (RIDDOR)

Employers are required to report accidents or dangerous occurrences to the Health and Safety Executive under legislation commonly referred to as RIDDOR (ie the Reporting of Injuries, Diseases and Dangerous Occurrences Regulations 1985) – see also page 67 (Notification of accidents). Reports must be made of the following occurrences:

1. Fatal accidents
2. Major injury accidents/conditions
3. Dangerous occurrences
4. Accidents causing more than three days' incapacity for work
5. Work-related diseases
6. Matters concerning the safe supply of gas.

Full records of all such accidents and occurrences must be maintained by the employer and kept for at least *three* years.

COSHH Regulations

The Control of Substances Hazardous to Health Regulations 1986 which came into effect on 1 October 1990 are intended to control the exposure of employees to hazardous substances at their places of work. In particular, the regulations require employers to make assessments of the use of such substances in their work places and to implement suitable control and monitoring procedures for each substance which falls under this heading (largely all toxic, corrosive, irritant and other harmful substances). The employer has a duty to inform his employees (and specifically provide training where appropriate) about the dangers which exist in handling such substances and the precautions to be taken to ensure safe handling.

Other legislation

A number of other items of legislation have been made under the provisions of the HSW etc Act 1974, most notably concerning manual handling (intended to avoid risk to the health of employees when manually handling loads); display screen equipment (setting minimum standards for the use of VDU screens and providing for employees to be able to request eyesight tests); management of health and safety (making more implicit some of the existing HSW provisions); and waste control (setting duty of care requirements).

Part 2: Business and Financial Management

1. Financial management techniques

Purpose of accounts and balance sheets

Maintaining strict control over the financial affairs of a business is vital for its success. For this reason there should be an organised system of calculating and regularly monitoring direct costs, overheads, revenue and profit. In any event, it is usual at least once each year, for a business to balance its books of account in order to prepare proper financial statements of these items as a reflection of its activities during the past year.

This enables the owners and shareholders of the business and other interested parties to see its performance during that time, what expenditure has been incurred, what revenue received, the value of assets owned, the liabilities of the business in terms of money owed and other commitments and money owing to it by its debtors. Most important, the accounts also show the profit or loss made from the year's trading and the current value of the business (ie the so-called 'bottom line' figure).

These documents together provide a complete picture of the financial affairs of a business at a particular moment in time (ie at the end of the financial year). It is from these documents that shareholders are able to obtain a knowledge of how 'their' company has been managed, the company's bank manager can learn of the true financial state of the bank's client and potential investors can obtain information which may encourage them to invest in the company (ie in the case of public limited companies). The accounts are also of interest to other institutions and firms to whom the company may have applied for loans or other financial facilities or with whom it hopes to do business.

For limited liability companies it is a legal requirement that annual accounts are prepared and independently audited and, of course, a return of income or profit must be made to the Inland Revenue (but advising expenditure is not compulsory!) for tax assessment purposes by all businesses ranging in size – and income – from the sole trader to public limited companies.

Annual accounts comprise many separate documents in the case of a large organisation but for simplicity of explanation we are concentrating here on just two documents – the profit and loss (sometimes called the trading) account and the balance sheet – which are found in all accounts whether for a very large company or the smallest.

Profit and loss account

The profit and loss (or trading) account identifies the trading activity of the business for the year, showing on one side of the account payments received for work done or goods supplied (ie termed 'sales' or 'sales turnover', just 'turnover' or 'revenue' – and invariably shown as a single figure) and on the other side a record of all expenditure incurred by the business in its trading activities including purchase of materials, administrative and operating costs, salaries, etc (usually broken down into many individual headings).

When both sides of this account are balanced it will show whether revenue exceeded costs or vice versa. If it is the former then the figure indicates a *trading profit*, otherwise there is a *trading loss*. These are not true profits/losses of the business because other factors such as depreciation and other allowances may need to be taken into account later which can alter the situation but, nevertheless, the (gross) trading profit or loss figure gives a good indication of performance

Two particular points should be borne in mind about the profit and loss account. First, any increase or decrease in business expenditure items (ie such as local authority rates or rents on premises, fuel prices, or wages) will appear and have a direct effect on this account – not elsewhere. Second, debtors and creditors *cannot* be established from the profit and loss or trading account, nor can business asset values, bank overdrafts, the value of shareholder funds or other liabilities. These items will be deduced from the balance sheet – see below.

Balance sheet

A balance sheet is a statement of the cumulative 'worth' of a business over its whole life, shown at a certain time (ie at the end of the financial year – and only then). The values of the fixed and current assets of the business are shown, including buildings, land, equipment, money in the bank and money owed to it by debtors, the value of stock on hand (eg in a haulage firm, diesel in a bulk tank, spares and tyres in the workshop stores as well as stationery in the cupboard) and liabilities of the business including tax owed to the Inland

Revenue, amounts due to creditors, outstanding loans and other debts.

The balance sheet entries are in two columns, those on one side being all the assets plus any trading profits (carried forward from the trading and profit and loss account -see above) and those on the other being its liabilities and any trading losses (see also above). Both sides of the balance sheet are totalled at the bottom and one figure is deducted from the other to show a plus or minus balance which represents the value of the business, the so-called 'bottom-line figure'. From the balance sheet it is possible to determine the current assets and current liabilities of the business.

A simple balance sheet may appear as follows:

Fixed assets:	Current liabilities:
Freehold premises	Mortgage
Motor vehicles	Accounts payable (ie creditors)
Plant & equipment	Hire purchase repayments
Fixtures and fittings	Bank loan repayable
	Bank overdraft
	Tax liability

Current assets:	
Accounts receivable (ie debtors)	
Stocks	
Cash at bank	
Petty cash in hand	
Trading profit brought forward	Trading loss brought forward

Total assets:	Total liabilities:

It should be noted that not all of these items would necessarily appear on a particular balance sheet. For example, there would not be both a trading profit and a loss figure brought forward, similarly there may not be hire purchase repayments, a bank loan and an overdraft and a firm may not have cash at bank and an overdraft – usually (but not always) the credit cash balance would eliminate the overdraft. Premises may be rented rather than owned so while the value would not be shown on the assets side no mortgage liability would be shown on the other side (rents for rented property would appear as expenditure on the profit and loss account only).

Debtors and creditors

Here it is important to point out the difference between debtors and creditors. The examination candidate should ensure he clearly understands which is which – it can have a significant bearing on answers to questions in this section.

Debtors are people, firms or organisations owing money to a company. They show on the balance sheet as current assets. Creditors are people, firms or organisations including banks and financial institutions to which a company owes money. They show on the balance sheet as current liabilities. Ideally, a company's balance sheet should show the value of debtors to be greater than that of creditors so that if all moneys owing were received and all debts paid there would be a surplus of funds rather than a deficit.

Legal responsibilities

As mentioned earlier in this section, limited liability companies are required to have their annual accounts audited by professional (ie chartered) accountants and to show copies of the profit and loss account and balance sheet to shareholders each year. They must also submit copies to the Registrar of Companies (at Companies House) where they are retained on file and are available for inspection by *any* person wishing to see them, on payment of a small statutory fee.

There is no legal requirement for non-limited, sole proprietorships and partnership businesses to have their business accounts audited annually but they must prepare satisfactory annual financial records and submit a statement of their income to the Inland Revenue for tax assessment purposes (see previous note about notifying expenditure – page 71).

Ratios for assessing financial performance

In financial management, a number of basic and very simple calculations are used (such as by an accountant or bank manager) to quickly assess business performance. The important ones are as follows:

Working capital ratio
This is otherwise known as liquidity ratio or acid test, and indicates how readily a business could settle its liabilities. It is calculated thus:

$$\frac{\text{liquid working capital (ie current assets)}}{\text{current liabilities}} = \frac{\text{liquidity / working}}{\text{capital ratio}}$$

Current ratio

This is basically the same as the working capital ratio as shown above and is a measure of a company's current assets in relationship to its current liabilities, and is calculated in the same way as shown above, namely:

$$\frac{\text{current assets}}{\text{current liabilities}} = \text{current ratio}$$

The result of this calculation should ideally be at least 2:1 so that the assets are double the liabilities, but in practice the results may vary from 1:1 (acceptable but not good) or less (which spells problems because basically the firm cannot meet its liabilities), to a much higher figure, particularly in seasonal trading conditions, which indicates a surfeit of funds which should be placed on deposit to earn interest or used for other investment purposes.

Return on capital
This is a means of measuring whether sufficient profit is being made in relationship to the capital invested in the business, and is calculated thus:

$$\frac{\text{net profit}}{\text{capital employed}} \times 100 = \text{x\%}$$

Example: $\dfrac{£30,000}{£300,000} \times 100 = 10\%$

Capital

Businesses need funds – capital – initially when they are established, later for expansion and at all other times to meet day-to-day commitments. These funds fall into a number of different categories – some long term, some short term – which come from different sources and are used for different purposes.

Sources and uses of funds

Finance for establishing and running business activities is available from a number of sources, each of which has particular advantages depending on the purpose for which the finance is used.

Proprietor's and shareholder funds
When businesses are originally founded it is usual for the founder proprietor to introduce some, at least, of his own capital although this may be topped up by business loans and funds from other sources. In the case of limited liability companies the initial capital will come from the shareholders although again this may be increased by funds from other sources. It is quite common for banks and other institutions to invest in new concerns where the ideas are good and the

prospects are sound. These original funds are looked upon as being long-term investments.

Retained Profits
The usual, principal source of funds for the operation and expansion of an established business is the use of retained profits (ie those made in previous years through successful trading which have been retained in the business, not having been distributed to shareholders). This is the ideal method of funding development of a business but in times of recession and during the business's formative years profits may not be sufficient to meet all of its financial needs, so recourse to other sources becomes necessary.

Bank loans
Bank loans are generally provided, against security, for the establishment of a new business or for financing expansion of existing businesses. Banks invariably require security in the form of deposits, personal guarantees given by individuals employed in or with an interest in the business, charges over freehold property or the lodgement of insurance policies with a guaranteed surrender value, or debentures. Repayment of bank loans is invariably by regular amounts over a fixed period of time. Such loans are usually for middle to long-term periods and are not subject to recall at short notice like overdrafts, provided repayments are made in accordance with the terms of the agreement.

Overdrafts
Overdrafts are provided by banks for short-term use in day-to-day business operations to overcome the problems of fluctuating cash flows. They are not intended for long-term capital requirements because they are subject to recall at short notice if, among other things, the Government or the Bank of England places restrictions on credit. Besides the intention, the use of overdraft facilities for capital purchases is not recommended because it reduces credit (ie the availability of ready cash) for more immediate needs such as weekly wages, meeting fuel bills on delivery of new supplies etc. Security in some form is normally required to cover overdraft facilities or at least the surety of a substantial inflow of funds in a short time.

Debentures
These are long-term loans (sometimes called loan stock) secured against the assets of the business (eg by individuals or investment firms) and are repayable with agreed rates of

fixed interest added, usually after a specified period of time. Frequently, the issue of a debenture or loan stock is tied in with a charge on the firm's fixed assets or part of them (its freehold premises for example). In the event of collapse of the company, debenture holders have priority over normal creditors and shareholders (but not over statutory claimants such as the Inland Revenue, the DSS or HM Customs and Excise – for VAT) when that particular asset is disposed of and in any shareout of remaining funds but invariably they lose their investment.

Investment funds

When a business is short of capital to meet development or expansion plans, to obtain more extensive premises, to purchase additional equipment or to meet equipment replacement programmes, assistance may be obtained from a number of sources including merchant banks, investment groups, the ICFC (Industrial and Commercial Finance Corporation) and the 3i's company as well as individual investors sometimes (possibly under the former Business Expansion Scheme – now the Enterprise Investment Scheme (EIS) – whereby if all the qualifying conditions are met they receive taxation benefits). In return for the provision of long-term capital (often termed 'venture capital') the investor will usually want to take a share in the equity of the business, which means that the original owners have to surrender part of their holding and thus some of the control of the business.

Hire purchase and leasing

These two long-term financing facilities provide capital for the acquisition of specific assets: motor vehicles, workshop equipment, office machines, etc. In the case of hire purchase, the finance house loans the money required, the borrower makes the purchase and then repays the loan plus interest over an agreed period of time. At the end of the payment period the asset belongs to the borrower but even while payments are being made he still has title to the goods. In the case of leasing, the lessor provides the money and retains ownership title to the goods while the lessee has their full use during a given period but never actually becomes the owner. The advantage of leasing is that the use of essential items of equipment is obtained with a minimum of capital outlay; a regular predetermined amount is repaid over a period and the item used not to appear on the balance sheet as an asset on the one hand nor as an outstanding debt on the other (hence the term 'off-balance sheet financing') – however, under new accounting rules this situation is being changed so that such items do appear on balance sheets and trading accounts to give a more accurate reflection of a firm's activities in regard to leased assets and leasing commitments.

Factoring

When poor cash flow causes a business financial problems, one source of short-term finance to alleviate this difficulty is the factoring of sales invoices. Factoring companies will pay cash against invoices they consider acceptable, with the deduction of a percentage of the face value for their charges. By this means, prompt payment of invoices is obtained, which improves cash flow and saves the extended periods of delay in waiting for payment, but the amount received is reduced, often substantially. This scheme is not usually acceptable where the firm is working on small profit margins, as in haulage operations, because the commission payable to the factors virtually (or completely) eliminates the profit margin on each invoice. It does not help either with doubtful payers; the factoring house will not accept such invoices.

Use of funds In assessing the various merits of financial sources as described in outline above, it is necessary to consider the uses to which the money is to be put. There is no point in raising fresh capital from shareholders and surrendering part of the equity of the business just to meet short-term demands. These can normally be covered by short-term borrowing and overdrafts with no loss of equity or without tying up valuable securities such as legal charges on freehold property. On the other hand, facilities for short-term borrowing should not be used for expenditure on major capital projects or long-term development as this reduces the availability of ready funds to meet urgent or unexpected short-term needs. Careful financial planning in these matters is essential and this is where the management skill lies in running a successful business whether large or small.

Working capital

A business needs money to operate on a day-to-day basis, paying its suppliers, staff wages, office rent, heating, lighting and telephone bills and so on. The money used for this purpose is called working capital (ie the money which enables a business to function). This includes money in the bank, cash in hand and the value of debtors' invoices which are a quickly realisable asset less any moneys owing to creditors. In other words it is the excess of current assets over current liabilities.

Total capital employed

This is the total of all the money (ie assets) employed in a business. It includes the proprietors'/partners'/shareholders' initial investment which may have been spent on fixed assets such as land and buildings, on plant, equipment and vehicles, on other assets such as office furniture and company cars. It also includes current assets such as cash in the bank and other (perhaps invested) reserves. It is against this yardstick of total fixed and current assets employed in the business that the owners or managers can assess trading or financial performance in the form of return on capital invested.

Budgets

A budget is quite simply a plan for the future. Housewives budget for their expenditure, deciding what has to be spent on essential services (ie gas, water, electricity, rent and rates, etc) and supplies (eg food and clothing). So too must a business budget for its expenditure. Mainly budgets are of a financial nature but an operational plan needs to be made in order to establish what work is to be done to earn a certain level of revenue at a calculated cost (eg a haulier may have work for a vehicle which requires it to work for x days in the year covering x miles consuming x litres of fuel and involving the driver in x hours of work at given rates of pay, etc). From this operating plan the haulier can budget for his likely earnings (ie a revenue budget) and the likely costs of running the vehicle plus his other related costs (ie an expenditure budget). If a project requires a new vehicle or other new plant this would involve making a capital or capital expenditure budget (ie how much capital expenditure – investment – will the potential earnings from the project stand). With the revenue and expenditure budgets calculated a cash flow budget can also be established (see above).

Purchasing and stock control

Control over expenditure is important in any business organisation, particularly in transport where it is possible for staff to purchase indiscriminately spare parts for vehicles and accumulate excessive stocks of incorrect and redundant components, and thus have excessive amounts of capital tied up in slow-moving parts when it could be put to more immediate use meeting day-to-day commitments. Over stocking reduces available cash resources and can create liquidity problems if the stocks could not be sold off quickly enough (or at an acceptable market price) to meet urgent demands (eg to reduce an overdraft quickly). For this reason the establishment of proper systems of purchasing and stock control are necessary, involving (particularly so far as transport operations are concerned) the following:

1. Placing limits on the value or volume of parts which individuals may purchase.

2. Establishing budgets for expenditure which must not be exceeded without authority.
3. Determining the best time to buy in relation to the firm's cash flow position and market forces (ie when prices are likely to be lower or discounts higher).
4. Establishing record systems on which purchases and issues are recorded.
5. Keeping regular checks on stock levels to ensure that stock holdings agree with the records (ie reconciliation).
6. Making stock analyses and examining requisition notes to ensure that correct stock levels of individual items are held according to demand (ie slow-moving and fast-moving items).
7. Checking on suppliers' prices and discount structures to ensure that purchasing is channelled to the most economic supply sources and that maximum discounts are being obtained.
8. Ensuring that obsolete and redundant stocks plus surplus items are returned for credit as soon as possible.
9. Checking supply invoices to ensure that correct prices are being paid and that credits, as appropriate (see item 8 above), are being obtained.

It is important to be able to assess current stock levels from records (such as in the case of bulk diesel fuel storage facility) and this is done as follows:

Opening stock or Balance	+	Deliveries or Purchases	−	Issues or Sales	=	Current stock

Cash flow

Today, control of cash flow is one of the most vital elements of business management. Many firms, especially large ones, have progressively to reduce the speed at which they pay their outstanding debts causing other (usually small) firms to suffer the severe problems arising from a lack of available funds to meet their immediate needs, such as payment for essential supplies and wages. These problems can quickly result in closure (ie liquidation) of a business (see page 41) despite the fact that it is giving its customers good service and may even be showing annual profits.

Planning finances, or budgeting, to ensure a regular cash flow is therefore important. It is done by assessing the levels of revenue to be invoiced and the frequency at which payment is likely to be received, then assessing expenditure which has to be made over the same period. If the latter is greater than the former, plans have to be made to cover the shortfall. These could include measures to ensure faster payment by debtors, to obtain longer periods of credit with suppliers or to obtain bank overdraft facilities to bridge the gap. Net cash flow which the bank may ask about is the difference between cash received in and cash paid out by the business on a day-to-day or week-to-week basis or over longer periods.

Cash-flow forecasting is necessary to ensure the availability of cash to meet future needs. Particularly, a bank manager being asked to provide overdraft facilities to meet short-term cash deficiencies may want to see a cash-flow forecast to indicate the levels of overdraft needed, when it is needed and over what period of time. The forecast would also show him what funds were expected in, and when, to balance the planned overdrawing on the account. Some banks provide blank forms specially designed for completion of cash-flow projections. The time and effort required to produce such a document is well worth while because it provides the business proprietor with a guide as to when and what revenues he has to come and when he can and should – and should not – incur expenditure. It would also indicate to him the months of the year when his cash flow looked deficient, giving him the opportunity to consider possible ways of rearranging work to overcome any financial shortcomings.

2. Commercial business conduct

Terms and documents

Business is largely concerned with administration, which involves many common terms and much documentation designed to keep records, to convey information, to advise customers and so on. Knowing the terminology and the correct document to use for any given purpose is essential otherwise confusion can arise, and worse, costly mistakes could be made. Documents are prepared either manually, mechanically or, mainly these days, by computer. The following documents are commonly found in commercial practice:

Estimate

An estimate is an approximate price for a job usually given without precise details of the work being available. The operator cannot be held to this price should he need to charge more if it turns out that the job was different to that envisaged, took longer, was more complex and, in the case of haulage for example, involved more mileage.

Quotation

A quotation is the notification to a potential customer of a firm price for carrying out a specific job. It details the job or the supply of goods and the price and should indicate the period for which the price will remain valid (eg 30 or 60 days). It also specifies the conditions under which the price is offered (eg 'in accordance with our standard conditions of trade' (for a haulier, for example, it would be 'goods carried in accordance with our standard conditions of carriage'); 'ex-works'; 'delivered to site'; 'to one delivery point only'; etc). Quotations are looked upon as being a fixed price (so long as the job is as originally assessed) unless clauses are incorporated specifying otherwise or unless extreme, unforeseen circumstances arise and then the price can only be altered by mutual agreement with the customer.

Order
: An order is a notification from a customer instructing the supplier to supply goods or services as specified. Full details of the customer's requirements should be specified on an order including the date or period of supply, the quantity of goods, the quality, method of supply, labelling and packing instructions and other special instructions (eg 'loads must be sheeted', 'delivery only accepted between 8am and 4pm', 'notification required before delivery', etc).

Invoice
: This is a notification from the supplier to his customer of the job done and/or the amount owing for the work. It should identify the job clearly and have supporting evidence of supply or delivery, it should show the date of supply, the quantity of goods, the price per unit (eg per tonne) and the total price less any discount offered and plus any VAT due. It is in effect a demand for payment of monies due for goods or services supplied or to be supplied (ie where the agreement or practice is for payment in advance). Usually terms for payment are shown (eg terms 30 days net). A note of discounts offered for prompt payment can be added (eg 2½ per cent discount for payment in 14 days). Often invoices carry the letters 'E & OE'. This means errors and omissions excepted; in other words it gives the issuer the opportunity to go back to his customer for increased payment if he finds later that an inadvertent undercharge was made when preparing the invoice.

Unless clearly stated in the original contract for the job or on the original invoice (or in the case of a haulier, in his conditions of carriage), *it is illegal to subsequently add interest charges to unpaid or late-paid accounts.*

Credit note
: If goods are returned or accepted in a damaged state or are 'short' delivered or an overcharge is made, rather than refund money a supplier can make amends by giving the customer a credit note indicating a refund of part or all of any charge paid or due. This effectively says 'I owe you some money', without actually paying it at that time. The recipient of a credit note may deduct the value of the credit from any amount he may owe the supplier or use it against payment for future supplies

or if there is an account between the two firms the credit will be shown as a reduction of the total amount owing from one to the other.

Debit note

A debit note is effectively the opposite of a credit note or the same as an invoice. It advises the recipient that he owes some money to the issuer. If the issuer owes the recipient money the debit note says 'I will reduce what I owe you by £x (the amount of the debit)'.

Statement

In full, 'statement of account'. A statement is sent out after invoices have been issued and acts as a reminder to the recipient of how the account stands with the supplier. In business transactions, a statement will progressively show outstanding amounts owing, less any payments received since the last statement was issued plus the amount of invoices issued since the last statement (ie the balance of the account). A total of debit or credit is shown and usually a statement will indicate amounts owing as follows: 'this month', 'owing over 30 days', 'owing over 60 days', 'outside our normal credit terms', 'immediate payment required' etc.

Consignment notes

Consignment notes are used in multiple sets which give details of consignor and consignee, the address for collection and delivery, details of the goods (description, weight, size, number of packages, markings), information regarding delivery, details of the vehicle and driver (registration number and driver's name), and a space for the recipient to sign acknowledging safe receipt (ie referred to as a clear signature) or receipt in a damaged condition or short delivery. Frequently, consignment notes are printed on the back with the firm's conditions of carriage. In international haulage operations, consignment notes are particularly significant and must conform to the CMR convention requirements (see pages 262–5).

To help the reader, it is useful to emphasise here the distinct difference between: *consignor* – the sender of the goods, *consignee* – the recipient of the goods. Also: *carriage paid* – where carriage charges are paid by the consignor or in advance by the consignee, and *carriage forward* – where charges are to be paid by the consignee, either on an account basis on invoice or COD (ie 'Cash on Delivery' – in other words, payment must be made before the goods are handed over).

Services offered by financial institutions

Business makes use of the services of a variety of financial institutions as the needs arise and in accordance with its particular needs. The high street banks (the big ones are Lloyds, National Westminster, Barclays and Midland – then

83

there is the Co-op bank, the banks of Scotland and Ireland and the savings banks such as the National Giro Bank) are commonly used for day-to-day financial transactions and in connection with investments.

Where substantial loans are required or investment in business projects then the more specialised merchant banks and other investment organisations are used. In some cases deposits of surplus funds can be made in building societies and loans can be obtained by way of mortgages on property. Normally these organisations are in business to serve the private borrower and investor rather than the business community but increasingly they are seen to offer services in competition with the traditional banking organisations including current accounts. Other finance houses provide hire purchase and leasing facilities for the acquisition of vehicles, plant, office equipment (eg computers) and such like – even furniture. The main services provided by these organisations are outlined here:

Current accounts
: Money is held in current accounts for short-term use and is paid by means of the issue of cheques to creditors. This is the account a business would use on a day-to-day basis for paying in funds received and drawing out money by means of cheques.

Deposit/savings accounts
: Reserve funds are placed in deposit accounts with the high street banks or at the national savings bank (ie via local post offices), or at building societies where interest at the current (variable) rate is earned. Deposit accounts are usually built up by lump-sum transfers while savings accounts are normally built up by regular transfers from a current account.

Overdrafts
: An overdraft is a bank facility (offered normally only by the high street banks and the giro bank) whereby a business can borrow money on a temporary basis, drawing up to an agreed maximum on the current account without an interim need to seek the bank's approval. Interest is charged only on the outstanding balance at any time. The overdraft is reduced by credits paid into the current account. Overdrafts can be recalled at short notice during times of national stringency or for other reasons.

Loans
: These are the provision of finance for capital projects (vehicle purchase, expansion of business, etc) over an agreed and fixed period of time with regular repayments (usually monthly) of agreed amounts, usually by Standing Order payment from the current account. Loans are not subject to short-notice recall as are overdrafts unless the borrower defaults on his repayments.

Credit transfer
: This is an arrangement whereby money can be transferred within the banking system without the need for cheques. Many

firms these days pay their employees by means of credit transfer – in other words pay the money direct to the employees' bank account. This saves the firm the problems of handling cash and cheque writing and ensures more rapid payment for the recipient.

Direct debit

This is a service whereby the bank is authorised to pay amounts direct from a client's accounts, usually on a regular basis (eg monthly, quarterly or annually), on application by the client's debtors (eg for mortgage payments, hire purchase or leasing repayments). This service helps the bank client by saving him the job of writing out cheques every time a payment is due and avoids the problems, firstly, of remembering to make the payment and, secondly, to ensure it is paid on time.

NB: Readers should note the difference between credit transfer and direct debit – the former puts money automatically into an account, the latter automatically takes it out.

Investment advice

Banks will provide advice on the investment of surplus or reserve funds to the best advantage and can act as stockbrokers, buying and selling shares on instruction.

Foreign exchange

Most banks will assist firms in foreign exchange dealings with overseas customers, in exchanging letters of credit, verifying credit-worthiness and helping with exchange of currency, etc. Foreign currency can also be obtained from other organisations such as American Express and from Thomas Cook travel shops as well as at exchange counters at international airports for example.

Financial advice

Bank managers are generally available to give guidance to clients on a wide range of financial matters such as cash flow, capital expenditure, expansion plans, economic trends, etc. Managers of most small bank branches can obtain more extensive advice for their customers from specialists in particular fields within the bank if necessary.

Insurance

Most banks have contacts in the insurance field (or their own subsidiaries) and can assist their client firms with advice on insurance matters and handle all the insurance matters for a business and its proprietors.

Wills and trusts

Banks can act as trustees in relevant matters and can be nominated as executors for administering wills. These services are provided at a charge.

Deposit or security boxes

Most banks can provide security boxes in which clients can place deeds for property, leases and other important documents and valuables for safe-keeping.

Receipts and
withdrawals

When money in the form of cash, bank notes, cheques, postal orders or other negotiable instruments is received, these can be paid into the recipient's current bank account or deposit account by completing a credit slip or a page in a 'paying-in' book and handing this in to the bank with the money. If the payment is made at the firm's own bank the transaction is simple but the payment can be made at any branch of any bank (except 'cash shops') and the amount will be credited to the firm's account at its own branch in a matter of a few days (usually three days must be allowed for the transfer).

Withdrawals are made by writing a cheque which specifies the date, the name of the payee, the amount to be paid in words and figures and bears the authorised signature of the issuer. A cheque can be presented to the recipient's bank for the money to be transferred to his account (again, allow at least three days). If the cheque is 'open' (ie not crossed or the crossing has been cancelled) it may be exchanged over the counter in a bank for cash. This applies also to cheques made out to 'BEARER'.

Although illegal, cheques may have been issued when there are not sufficient funds to cover the amount. The cheque will be returned marked 'Represent' or 'Refer to Drawer'. The former means it is likely to be paid shortly (ie when represented) because the bank expects the issuer to have money coming in. The latter is less promising (ie the cheque 'bounced') and means the recipient must get back to the issuer for a new cheque or payment by other means (see below).

One way of overcoming the risk of non-clearance of a cheque (or if a cheque has been returned 'refer to drawer') is for the payee to request a 'Banker's Draft' which means the bank pays with money it has already obtained from the issuer. So, in effect, it is guaranteed for payment; otherwise the bank would not have issued it.

3. General insurance

Businesses are dependent on many specialised and professional services; insurance, for example, which is overlooked in many firms but is particularly important to protect the risks which occur in business activities. Insurance can cover buildings and property, vehicles and equipment, personal sickness and accident, and life. There is also ancillary cover such as insurance against loss of money, goods in transit and other special risks such as public liability, employers' liability and so on. The cover provided in return for premiums paid (so the insurance company shoulders the risk) reduces the risk of ruination of a business in the event of a serious fire, for example, or the death of a partner or major shareholder, or a substantial claim for damages resulting from the negligence of an employee (eg a driver causing death in an accident for which he was to blame).

It is important for the insured (ie the person or firm who has taken out the insurance) to be aware of any policy exclusions in any of the following policies which may prevent him from obtaining compensation when it may have been expected. In particular, on vehicle insurance the insured should note any actions which can invalidate the cover, such as operating the vehicle outside the requirements of the law (ie in a defective state or with unlicensed drivers). The main types of insurance (both compulsory and voluntary) are described in the following text.

Motor vehicles (compulsory)

Basic motor vehicle insurance covers the insured against claims by injured parties for personal injury (ie death or bodily injury) and medical expenses. This, together with mandatory cover for passengers – except those in the employ of the vehicle owner/operator – and for damage to roadside property, is the minimum legal requirement (often referred to as Road Traffic Act cover). Beyond this a policy may cover other third-party risks including damage to other property, loss of the vehicle by fire or theft or it may be extended to become fully comprehensive cover to provide full protection against third-party claims and to provide compensation for damage to the vehicle (see also pages 124–5 – Module B part 2 dealing with compulsory vehicle insurance).

Excess clauses
In many areas of insurance, and especially vehicle insurance, the insurers require the insured to bear the first portion of any claim. This may be the first £25, £100, £250 or more, depending on the particular circumstances. This amount is referred to as the 'excess' (ie the excess on the policy). Thus if a vehicle is damaged in an accident and requires £500 worth of repairs and the insured has a £100 excess on his policy, the insurance company will reimburse him only £400 leaving him to find the other £100 himself or reclaim this from whoever was responsible for the damage.

Fire (non-compulsory)

Insurance against fire provides cover in the event of loss of buildings, equipment, vehicles and other possessions in the event of fire. The fire brigade would generally need to be called to effect a claim for fire damage. If neighbouring premises catch fire and damage the insured's property for example, the insured must claim on his own insurance. His insurance company will in turn seek reimbursement from the neighbour's insurers.

Storm and flood (non-compulsory)

This is cover to provide compensation in the event of damage or loss sustained as a result of severe weather and flooding.

Theft (non-compulsory)

This type of insurance policy provides cover against loss of possessions by theft but often to substantiate such a claim there needs to be evidence of forcible entry. Policy conditions vary but insurers may not accept claims unless there is sound evidence of a criminal act and the matter has been reported to the police.

Fidelity guarantee (non-compulsory)

When employees are put in responsible positions, particularly if they may be required to handle money or valuables, a firm can take out a fidelity guarantee insurance policy. The insurers investigate the employee's background and if acceptable they will then provide cover (ie by bond or guarantee) against the risk of the employee disappearing with money or valuables belonging to the employer.

Consequential loss (non-compulsory)

It is important to have insurance cover for any consequential loss resulting from an accident or fire. For example, if a warehouse was burnt down the buildings and stock may be covered, but not the resultant loss of trade and business profits. Consequential loss insurance would cover this. The same applies where a haulage vehicle was off the road for an extended period for repair following an accident, the repairs may be covered under the vehicle policy but not the resulting loss of business.

Employers' liability (compulsory)

Employers have a statutory duty to take out insurance cover against the risk of injury to their employees while on the firm's premises or elsewhere (eg on the road in a company-owned vehicle – hence the reason why compulsory passenger cover on motor vehicle policies does not extend to employee passengers – see p 87). Usually such policies provide unlimited cover for any eventuality. A current Certificate of Insurance against employers' liability risks must be displayed on the employer's premises.

Public liability (non-compulsory)

In addition to cover against the risk of injury to employees, a firm should protect itself against claims for loss or injury from the general public. Public liability policies provide such cover. If a member of the public is injured or suffers loss while on a firm's premises or as a result of the action or negligence of its employees (eg a van driver letting a rear door swing open and hit and injure a passing pedestrian or a heating-oil delivery driver leaving a pipe across a pavement so that an elderly person trips over it and is injured), that person has a right of claim for compensation. Such claims can be substantial these days so it is important to have adequate cover against such risks.

Life/sickness and accident/ pension (non-compulsory)

The proprietor of a business is wise to take out personal insurance to cover in the event of his premature death or against extended periods of incapacity due to sickness or accident. This protects (to an extent) his dependents and his business in the event of such a calamity by providing a cash sum (in the event of his death) or an income over a period (in the case of his incapacity) which may be sufficient to keep the business going until it can be sold or until he is fit to work again. Similarly he would be wise to provide for his eventual retirement by paying into a personal pension fund which can be provided via an insurance policy.

Part 3: Road Safety

1. Traffic legislation

Road Traffic Acts

Road traffic in this country is controlled by many separate pieces of legislation – Acts of Parliament, regulations and statutory orders. Mainly the legal provisions are to be found in successive Road Traffic Acts, in particular those of 1972, 1974, 1988 and 1991. These, together with the Road Traffic Offenders Act 1988, the Road Traffic Regulation Act of 1984, the Transport Act 1981 and the Highways Act 1980 (plus others), deal with such matters as traffic offences and penalties, vehicle construction and use, plating and testing, licensing of drivers, vehicle insurance requirements, seat belt fitment and use, speed limits, parking and waiting, motorway driving, powers of police and other enforcement staff and so on.

Speed limits

Speed limits in Great Britain are applied to various types of vehicle on various types of road.

Lower limit

Where speed limits for different classes of vehicle and road vary, *the lower limit always applies.*

Speed limits on roads

The current UK (ie national) maximum speed limits on different classes of road (those for vehicles are to be found in section B5/3) are as follows:

Type of road	Maximum speed any vehicle
Motorways	70mph
Dual carriageway roads	70mph
Single carriageway roads	60mph
Restricted roads	30mph

A 'restricted' road is one which has street lights placed not more than 200 yards apart and with the 30mph (or other indicated speed) limit shown on a circular sign at the beginning of the restricted section of road. On other roads where lower limits are indicated these must be observed (eg 30mph, 40mph and 50mph areas).

Exemptions from speed limits

Fire, police or ambulance service vehicles when necessary in the performance of their duty may exceed maximum speed limits if they can do so in safety.

Advisory/mandatory speed limits on motorways

Advisory speed limits on motorways should be observed. These are shown by illuminated signs and indicate hazardous situations and road works ahead. The amber flashing warning lights located on the nearside of motorways indicate danger ahead – you should slow down until the road is clear. Failure to observe these signs can lead to prosecution for offences such as 'driving without due care' etc.

Mandatory limits may also be found on motorways at roadworks sites (indicated by a white sign with black letters and red border). Failure to comply with these particular signs can result in speeding prosecutions.

Driving in fog and limited visibility
Fog code

When using motorways in fog or adverse conditions the Highway Code recommends the following action:

1. Slow down, keep a safe distance, ensure that you can pull up within your range of vision.
2. Do not keep close to the tail lights of the vehicle in front. This gives a false sense of security.
3. Check your speed; you may be travelling faster than you think.
4. Remember that if you are driving a heavy vehicle you need a greater distance in which to stop.
5. Warning signals are there to help and protect. Do observe them.
6. See and be seen – use headlights or fog lamps.
7. Check and clean your windscreen, lights, reflectors and windows whenever you can.
8. If you must drive in fog, allow more time for your journey.

Segregation

1. Drivers of cars, light goods vehicles and coaches should move out of the left-hand lane when it is safe to do so, unless they will soon be turning off the motorway. When they want to leave the motorway, they should start their move to the left well before the exit. They should be prepared to miss the exit if they cannot reach it safely.
2. Drivers of heavy lorries should keep to the left-hand lane but should be ready to let other drivers into the lane at entry points and well before exit points.

Use of lights in poor visibility

Front and rear position lamps and headlamps must be used during the daytime in poor visibility caused by heavy rain, mist, spray, fog or snow. Rear fog lights, where fitted, should also be used in these conditions. It is an offence to drive in poor visibility without using lights. See also page 171 for section on vehicle lighting.

Parking, waiting, loading and unloading
Clearways

The road sign indicating a clearway is circular, with a red diagonal cross on a blue background surrounded by a red circle. Vehicles must not stop (other than in an emergency) on the carriageway of a clearway or on the carriageway or verge of an urban clearway during the times shown on the sign which indicates the urban clearway, other than for as long as is necessary to let passengers board or alight from the vehicle.

Parking and overtaking

Vehicles must not park or overtake other vehicles in areas where danger or obstruction may be caused, as follows:

1. In a 'no parking' area
2. On a clearway
3. Alongside yellow lines
4. Where there are double white lines
5. Near a road junction
6. Near a bend
7. Near the brow of a hill
8. Near a humpback bridge
9. Near a level crossing
10. Near a bus stop
11. Near a school entrance
12. Near a pedestrian crossing
13. On the right-hand side of the road at night
14. Where the vehicle would obscure a traffic sign
15. On a narrow road
16. On fast main roads and motorways
17. Near entrances and exits used by emergency service vehicles (or near fire hydrants)
18. Near road works
19. Alongside or opposite another parked vehicle
20. In a parking disc zone unless the vehicle displays a parking disc; in a meter zone unless the meter fee has been paid; at bus stops; on a pavement or cycle track; on flyovers, in tunnels or in underpasses.

The police can request a driver to remove a vehicle causing danger or an obstruction or can forcibly remove it themselves and can prosecute the driver/registered owner.

Parking on pedestrian crossings
A vehicle must not be parked within the area marked by zig-zag lines on either side of a zebra crossing or in the zone

indicated by metal studs on the approach to a pedestrian crossing. Overtaking is also prohibited in these areas.

Night parking
Vehicles parked on roads overnight must stand on the nearside except when parked in a one-way street or in a recognised parking place.

Goods vehicles *over* 1525kg unladen must always display lights when parked on roads at night.

Goods vehicles *not exceeding* 1525kg unladen may park without lights on roads where a speed limit is in force (ie on restricted roads) provided they are facing the direction of travel (ie nearside to the kerb) and are not parked within 10 metres (15 yards in Northern Ireland) of a road junction on either side of the road.

Trailers detached from the towing vehicle and vehicles carrying projecting loads must not be parked on roads at night without lights (detached trailers should never be parked on roads or in lay-bys – which are part of the highway).

All parked vehicles must display lights at night when parked on roads where no speed limit is in force.

Loading and unloading

Vehicles may be loaded and unloaded anywhere except where there are signs indicating the contrary. In some areas loading/ unloading restrictions are indicated by yellow lines painted on the kerb at right angles (with relevant times given on nearby plates) as follows:

1. Single yellow right angle lines indicate loading/ unloading restrictions at certain times (eg Mon–Fri 8.00–9.30am 4.30–6.30pm).
2. Double yellow right angle lines indicate loading/ unloading restrictions during working days (eg Mon–Sat 8.30am–6.30pm).
3. Three yellow right angle lines indicate a total ban on loading or unloading during the working day and at additional times (eg at any time) as indicated on the nearby plate.

Loading and unloading in parking meter zones is not allowed during working hours except where a free meter space is available or there is a gap between meter areas. When using a meter bay for loading the meter fee does not have to be paid if the stopping time is 20 minutes or less.

When stopping to load and unload and when leaving the vehicle unattended the engine must be stopped unless it is used for running auxiliary equipment.

Waiting restrictions

Yellow lines painted on the road parallel to the kerb indicate bans on waiting (not to be confused with bans on loading and unloading described above) as follows:

1. A complete ban (ie for at least 8 hours between 7am and 7pm and at other times) is shown by double yellow parallel lines
2. A partial ban (ie for at least 8 hours between 7am and 7pm on at least four days of the week) is shown by a single continuous yellow parallel line
3. A periodic ban is shown by a single broken parallel line.

In every case it is essential to consult the nearby sign (usually on a lamp post or wall) indicating the ban to see the precise times when a particular ban is in operation.

Traffic control

Traffic is controlled by a variety of road signs and signals designed to restrict speed, direct the flow of vehicles, indicate hazardous situations ahead and generally advise the motor vehicle driver on the use of the road. Traffic signs are divided into categories as follows:

Prohibitive	Bordered with red circle (except certain 'no stopping' signs)	Informs the driver what he must or must not do
Compulsory	Blue circles or rectangles	Informs the driver of the direction to be followed
Warning	Mostly bordered with a red triangle	Informs the driver of a variety of traffic situations ahead
Direction	Mostly rectangular with blue, green or white backgrouds. Blue = motorways Green = primary routes White = non-primary routes	Indicates routes, road numbers and general directions
Information	All rectangular	Provides the driver with information about road and traffic situations

In addition to these signs there are road markings to indicate no waiting, no parking, prohibited areas, instructions to give way and lane controls (see the Highway Code for full details). Bus priority schemes (ie bus lanes) are sign-posted (relevant information is sometimes also painted on the road surface) as appropriate and these may only be used by passenger vehicles, taxis and cyclists as indicated on the sign.

Lights are used to control traffic at junctions and on motorways to indicate hazards ahead, speed restrictions and lane closures.

Road traffic offences and legal action

NB: In the following text the procedure for legal action following the commission of road traffic offences has been set out in a logical sequence as likely to be encountered by the road user, namely with the fixed penalty system described first, followed by the prosecution procedure and then the penalties imposed by the Courts in the way of licence disqualification and the endorsement of penalty points and finally dealing with drink driving offences and penalties.

When road traffic related offences are committed alternative procedures may be followed by the police (or traffic wardens where appropriate) in the way of legal action. Depending on the nature of the offence, the offender may be may be issued with a fixed penalty notice or reported for prosecution and required to answer directly to the Court. These various procedures are described here:

Fixed penalty system

Fixed penalty notices (tickets) may be issued for a very large number of traffic, motoring and vehicle offences. Generally these will be issued by the police but traffic wardens are empowered to issue fixed penalty notices for some offences (see pages 104–5). When offences are committed, the driver of the vehicle is given a notice which specifies the offence, an indication as to whether it is a driving licence endorsable or non-endorsable offence (ie by the colour and wording on the notice), and the penalty which has to be paid. If the driver is not available the ticket may be attached to the vehicle windscreen, but the driver is still responsible for paying the penalty. Should the driver of a vehicle fail to pay, responsibility for payment will rest with the registered vehicle keeper (ie the person/company whose name is on the registration document).

Fixed penalty procedure
The fixed penalty system for dealing with road traffic and related offences is operated by the police and, to a certain extent, by traffic wardens. Some 250 motoring offences are included in the scheme divided into driving licence endorsable offences and non-endorsable offences. The former involves the police issuing a yellow penalty ticket for which a penalty is payable and the driving licence is confiscated being returned with the appropriate penalty points added when the penalty is paid.

If the offender does not have his driving licence with him at the time a penalty notice will not be issued on the spot but will be issued at the police station when the driving licence is produced there within seven days. For non-endorsable offences a white ticket (involving a lesser penalty) is issued either to the driver if present or is fixed to the vehicle.

Any driver who receives a fixed penalty notice (yellow or white) can elect to have the matter dealt with by a Court so he can defend himself or put forward mitigating circumstances. Alternatively he can accept that he was guilty of the offence and pay the penalty. However, failure to pay the penalty within the requisite period (28 days) will result in the penalties being increased by 50 per cent. In this case the increased amount becomes a fine and non-payment will lead to arrest and a Court appearance.

Among the offences covered by the scheme are the following:

Yellow ticket (endorsable)
1. Speeding
2. Contravention of motorway regulations
3. Defective vehicle components (brakes, steering, tyres, etc) and vehicle in a dangerous condition
4. Contravention of traffic signs
5. Insecure and dangerous loads
6. Leaving vehicles in dangerous positions
7. Contravention of pedestrian rights.

White ticket (non-endorsable)
1. Not wearing seat belt
2. Driving and stopping offences (reversing, parking, towing, etc)
3. Contravention of traffic signs, box junctions, bus lanes, etc
4. Contravening driving prohibitions
5. Vehicle defects (brakes, steering, speedometer, wipers, etc)
6. Contravening exhaust and noise regulations
7. Exceeding weight limits (overloading, etc)
8. Contravention of vehicle lighting requirements
9. Contravention of vehicle excise requirements.

This is only a summary of a very extensive list of offences included within the scheme.

Failure to pay a fixed penalty within the prescribed period can result in a fine unless a statutory statement of ownership or of fact (to the effect that he was not the legal owner of the vehicle at the time the alleged offence was committed or that, if he was the owner at the relevant time, the vehicle was being used at that time without his permission) has been given to the police in whose area the original offence was committed.

Prosecution

Where one of the following road traffic offences is committed:

1. Dangerous, careless, inconsiderate driving
2. Failure to comply with traffic signs or the directions of a police constable on traffic duty
3. Leaving a vehicle in a dangerous position

the offender must be warned of possible prosecution at the time of the offence (unless an accident occurred at that time or immediately afterwards) or alternatively, within 14 days of the offence, must be served with either a Notice of Intended Prosecution or a summons for the offence.

Notice of Intended Prosecution

The Notice of Intended Prosecution must be in writing and must specify the offence and the time and place where it was committed. It must be served on the driver who committed the offence or the registered keeper of the vehicle. If, after due diligence, the police are unable to trace the vehicle driver or registered keeper within 14 days, action can still be taken to bring about a prosecution. If, as a result of the offence (or immediately after the offence was committed), an accident occurs, there is no requirement to serve a Notice of Intended Prosecution.

The summons

In the case of offences other than those listed above, such as those committed immediately before or at the time of an accident, a summons (to answer the charges before the Court) should normally be issued within six months of the date of the offence but in the case of certain offences (ie obtaining a driving licence while disqualified; driving while disqualified; using an uninsured vehicle; forging a driving licence or test and insurance certificates or making false statements in connection with driving licences, test and insurance certificates) proceedings may be brought to Court up to three years from the date of the offence.

The summons will give details of the offence including when and where it took place. The Court at which the case is to be heard will be named within six months (see also above). The recipient of a summons must respond as follows:

1. Appear in Court in person on the appointed day and make a plea of guilty or not guilty; or
2. Appoint a legal representative to appear in Court and make a plea on his behalf; or

3. Plead guilty in writing* to the Court and allow the case to be heard in his absence (in certain cases the Court may adjourn the hearing and summon the defendant to appear in person).

*NB: A not guilty plea will not (ie cannot) be accepted in writing.

The offender must surrender his driving licence when required to do so to the Court (either by delivering it in person or by sending it by post to arrive on the day prior to the hearing or by having it with him at the time of the hearing). If he fails to do this an offence is committed, the licence will be suspended from the time its production was required and until it is produced (thus to continue driving with it is a further offence). Where a person fails to produce his licence to the Court as required the police will request its production and will seize it and hand it over to the Court.

Court hearing

Depending on the nature of the offence, the Court may hear the case in the absence of the offender and accept a written plea of guilty with a statement of mitigating circumstances. Alternatively, the hearing may be suspended pending the personal appearance of the offender. Following the hearing, a verdict will be reached. If the offender is judged not guilty, there will be no conviction and the matter is ended.

If the offender is found guilty, a summary conviction is made. If the case concerns an indictable offence (ie one which must be tried before a jury) the accused may be bailed or remanded for the case to be heard by the Crown Court. On conviction (indictment) by the Court, a penalty will be imposed (ie a fine or imprisonment or both) as appropriate to the offence. The driver may be disqualified from driving or have his licence endorsed with an appropriate number of penalty points.

Obligatory driving licence disqualification

The following road traffic offences (Road Traffic Offenders Act 1988 Sch 2) carry obligatory disqualification of the driver's licence on conviction:

1. Causing death by reckless driving and manslaughter.
2. Reckless driving within three years of a similar conviction.
3. Driving (or attempting to drive) while unfit through drink or drugs.
4. Driving or attempting to drive with excess alcohol in breath/blood/urine.
5. Failure to provide a specimen (ie breath/blood/urine) for analysis or test.
6. Motor racing and speed trials on public ways (ie the highway).

Where an offence requires obligatory disqualification under the Road Traffic Offenders Act 1988 (34(1)) but for special reasons the Court decides not to impose that penalty it must, as an alternative, endorse a penalty of 4 points (see below for description of penalty point system) on the offender's driving licence (ie on the counterpart under the new 'unified' licence scheme). Further offences (under the Road Traffic Act 1988) allow the Courts a discretionary power of disqualification with the alternative of the obligatory endorsement of a specified number of penalty points on the offender's licence (see below).

12 point disqualification The penalty points system described below does not alter the mandatory disqualification procedure on conviction for serious offences listed above. Also, disqualification of the driving licence will automatically follow, for a minimum of six months, when 12 or more penalty points are endorsed on the licence in a period of three years counting from the date of the first offence to the current offence and not from the date of conviction (but see also below).

Subsequent disqualifications
When a driver has been disqualified once, any subsequent disqualifications within three years (preceding the date of the latest offence – not conviction) will be for progressively longer periods (minimum of 12 months for two disqualifications and 24 months for three disqualifications).

The Court has discretion to disqualify for a period of less than the normal six-month minimum or not to disqualify when 12 points are endorsed on a licence in exceptional circumstances (see below) but in such cases it is required to endorse the driving licence with four penalty points.

Special reasons for non-disqualification
As already mentioned, the Court has discretion in exceptional mitigating circumstances not to impose an obligatory disqualification as described above. However, the mitigating circumstances must not be of a nature which appears to make the offence not serious, and no account must be taken of hardship other than exceptional hardship. Furthermore, if account has previously been taken of circumstances in mitigation of a disqualification, the same circumstance cannot be considered again within three years.

Other reasons for non-disqualification
Where a person is convicted of an offence requiring obligatory disqualification and he can prove to the Court that he did not

know and had no reasonable cause to suspect that his actions would result in an offence being committed the Court must not disqualify him or order any penalty points to be endorsed on his driving licence.

Removal of disqualification
Disqualifications may be removed from a driving licence after the following periods of time:

1. If disqualification for less than four years – after two years.
2. If disqualification for four years to ten years – after half the period.
3. If disqualification for more than ten years – after five years.

Penalty points system (not applicable in Northern Ireland) When drivers are convicted of driving and other road traffic offences where the Court has discretion about imposing a disqualification but is obliged to endorse a licence, the endorsement takes the form of a number of penalty points entered on the driving licence (on the licence 'counterpart' under the system of EU-style driving licences effective from 1991). The number of points endorsed varies according to a scale ranging from two points to ten points depending on the seriousness of the offence (as specified in Schedule 2 of the Road Traffic Offenders Act 1988). When the Court convicts a driver of more than one offence at the same hearing, only the points relative to the most serious of the offences will be endorsed on the licence – the points relative to each individual offence will not be aggregated. The main penalty point offences are listed below.

Section of Road Traffic Act 1988 creating offence	Description	Number of penalty points
2	Reckless driving (1st offence in 3 years) (now replaced by a dangerous driving offence under the RTA 1991 (s 1))	4
3	Careless or inconsiderate driving	3-9
5(2)	Being in charge of motor vehicle when unfit through drink or drugs	10
5(1)(b)	Being in charge of motor vehicle with excess alcohol in breath/ blood/urine	10
6	Failing to provide specimen for breath test	4

Cont...

Cont...

7	Failing to provide specimen for analysis	10
22	Leaving vehicle in dangerous position	3
35/36	Failing to comply with traffic directions and signs	3
42	Contravention of construction and use regulations	3
87(1)	Driving without licence	2
96	Driving with uncorrected defective eyesight or refusing eyesight test	2
97	Failing to comply with conditions of licence	2
103(1)	Driving while disqualified (by order of Court)	6
143	Using motor vehicle uninsured and unsecured against third-party risks	6-8
170(4)	Failing to stop after accident	8-10
178	Taking in Scotland a motor vehicle without consent lawful authority or driving, or allowing oneself to be carried in, a motor vehicle so taken	8

Removal of penalty points

If a driver is convicted for an offence and is disqualified from driving, any existing penalty points on the licence will be erased. The driver will then start again with a 'clean slate' after each disqualification except that, as already mentioned, subsequent disqualifications will be for a longer period.

When the time interval between one offence and the endorsement on a licence of one lot of penalty points and a subsequent offence resulting in endorsement of penalty points is greater than three years (from the date of offence to the date of offence), the earlier points no longer count towards disqualification.

Penalty point endorsements (and disqualifications) shown on driving licences (ie on the 'counterpart' with new EU-style driving licences) can be removed by applying for the issue of a new licence after the following periods of time:

1. For disqualifications and offences other than those below – after four years from the date of the offence (from the date of conviction in the case of a disqualification).

2. For reckless driving offences – after four years from date of conviction.
3. For drink-driving offences – after 11 years.

Other penalties The Courts may also impose fines and, for certain offences, imprisonment or in serious cases both penalties may be imposed. Drivers convicted twice for drink/driving related offences may have their licences revoked altogether. Offenders found with exceptionally high levels of alcohol in their breath/blood will be classed by the Driver and Vehicle Licensing Agency (DVLA) as being of 'special risk' and will have to show that they no longer have an 'alcohol problem' before their licences are restored to them.

Drinking and driving It is an offence to drive or attempt to drive or to be in charge of a motor vehicle when unfit because of the effects of drink or drugs. The maximum permitted level of alcohol in the breath is 35 microgrammes per 100 millilitres of breath. This breath/alcohol limit equates to a blood/alcohol limit of 80 milligrammes of alcohol in 100 millilitres of blood and the urine limit of 107 milligrammes of alcohol in 100 millilitres of urine.

Breath tests A police constable in uniform may arrest any person who is in charge of, driving or attempting to drive a vehicle on a public road (or other public place) while unfit through drink or drugs. A constable may request any person driving or attempting to drive a motor vehicle on a road or other public place to take a breath test if he has reasonable cause to suspect the person of having alcohol in his body or of having committed a traffic offence while the vehicle was in motion or if the person was driving or attempting to drive a vehicle at the time of an accident.

If a breath test proves positive, the person will be requested to provide a further breath sample at a police station (or may be taken there under arrest if appropriate) and may be held there until fit to drive or only released if there is no likelihood of him driving while still unfit to do so. If the second sample exceeds the limit prosecution will follow and on the basis of evidence provided by the breath analysis a conviction may be made by the Court, resulting in mandatory disqualification (see above) from driving plus a possible fine or imprisonment or both.

A person who for health reasons cannot provide a breath sample may request a blood test. So, too, may persons whose breath analyses show not more than 50 microgrammes of alcohol per 100 millilitres of breath.

It is an offence (resulting in arrest and prosecution) to refuse to provide a breath test or a sample of blood or urine.

Drink-driving disqualification Conviction for a drink-driving offence will result in a driving licence disqualification (see obligatory disqualification above) for at least one year.

Conviction for a second or subsequent offence of driving or attempting to drive under the influence of drink or drugs will result in longer periods of disqualification. If the previous conviction took place within ten years of the current offence the driver must be disqualified for at least three years.

Use of duty-free fuel It is an offence to use diesel fuel on which the full applicable rate of duty has not been paid for road vehicles powered by diesel engines (ie heavy oil engines). Fuel used for other non-road-going vehicles (ie contractors' plant) and for space heating may be that which is known as rebated heavy oil, or commonly referred to as gas oil or red diesel, on which no duty is payable. This fuel must not be used in road-going diesel vehicles. Road fuel testing units staffed by Customs and Excise officers may, at any time, examine a vehicle for the purpose of testing its fuel. Such officers may also enter premises and inspect, test or sample any oil on the premises whether in vehicles or not. Powers for this purpose are conferred by the Hydrocarbon Oil Regulations 1973.

Powers of the police, traffic wardens and others
Traffic law enforcement Enforcement of road traffic regulations is carried out by the police and traffic wardens. The latter are concerned mainly with stationary traffic offences and with assisting in traffic control and direction. Most moving vehicle offences are dealt with by the police. The respective legal powers of each are outlined here.

Police constables So far as the law is concerned all policemen are 'constables' irrespective of rank. The police have wide powers to control road traffic and can, in general, direct drivers to follow particular directions, prevent them from following certain routes, can stop them, request the removal of parked vehicles, request the production of driving licences and other documents and so on. Their main powers in this regard are listed below, however it should be noted that space here permits only a summary. Failure to comply with any of these requirements is an offence which could lead to prosecution on a variety of charges including obstructing the police in their duties.

1. A police constable in uniform can stop a moving vehicle on a road. *Note: in GB only a uniformed constable has this power but in Northern Ireland DoE examiners in plain clothes may also stop a moving vehicle.*
2. Where a vehicle has been left on a road causing an obstruction or danger or is in contravention of a parking restriction or has broken down, they can ask the driver

or owner to remove the vehicle. If it appears to have been abandoned they may remove it themselves (even without holding a driving licence covering that category of vehicle) or may arrange for it to be removed.

Note: The local authority is also empowered to remove vehicles which appear to be abandoned.

3. They can require the driver of a vehicle on a road to produce his driving licence and/or to state his date of birth if he fails to provide the licence at the time.

4. They can request an 'L' driver of a vehicle or the person accompanying him to produce his licence.

5. They can request a person believed to have been the driver in an accident or when a traffic offence was committed to produce his driving licence. In both of these cases the licence may be produced immediately or within seven days at a police station nominated by them.

6. They can request a driver to perform the driving test eyesight requirement if they suspect that the driver's vision is deficient.

7. Police constables in uniform can arrest any person driving or attempting to drive a motor vehicle on a road who is suspected of being a disqualified driver.

8. They can arrest a person who takes a breathalyser test indicating that he has an excess of alcohol in the blood, and can also arrest a person who refuses to take a breath test.

9. They can arrest a person driving or attempting to drive a motor vehicle on a road or other public place if he is unfit to drive through the effects of drink or drugs.

10. They can arrest a driver of a motor vehicle who commits an offence of dangerous, careless or inconsiderate driving if the driver will not give his name and address or provide his driving licence for examination.

NB: See also section B4/3 for police powers for testing vehicles and directing vehicles to be weighed or examined.

Traffic wardens Traffic wardens, appointed by the police authority, have powers to enforce the law in respect of: vehicles parking without lights and reflectors; vehicles obstructing a road; vehicles waiting; vehicles parked; vehicles loading or unloading on a road or contravening the Vehicles (Excise) Act; vehicles parked without paying meter charges. They may fulfil duties at street parking places, car pounds, as school crossing patrols and have the power to direct and regulate traffic. They can be empowered to make enquiries about the identity of a driver and, when on duty at a car pound only, can demand to see driving licences. They can request a driver to give his name and address if he is believed to have committed an offence in the list below and can request the name and address of a pedestrian who ignores a traffic direction.

Traffic wardens may also issue fixed penalty tickets for the following non-endorsable driving licence offences:

1. Leaving a vehicle parked at night without lights or reflectors.
2. Waiting, loading or parking in prohibited areas.
3. Unauthorised parking in controlled parking zone areas.
4. Contravention of the Vehicles (Excise) Act 1971 by not displaying a current licence disc.
5. Making U-turns in unauthorised places.
6. Lighting offences with moving vehicles.
7. Driving the wrong way in a one-way street.
8. Over-staying on parking meters or feeding meters to obtain longer parking time than that permitted in the meter zone.

Vehicle owner liability

When a fixed penalty offence has been committed the vehicle owner (ie the registered keeper) is assumed to be the driver unless the real driver was given the ticket at the time the offence was committed. Vehicle owners must give information to the police on request about details of the driver of a vehicle at the time an offence was committed. The vehicle owner is liable to pay any penalty imposed if the driver fails to do so within 28 days. In the case of hired vehicles the hirer becomes the owner for these purposes. Alternatively a statutory statement of ownership may be given (within the same period – 28 days) certifying that at the time of the alleged offence the vehicle was owned by somebody else (in which case the name of the previous or subsequent owner must be given) or, that the vehicle was at the time being used without the owner's knowledge or permission.

Forgery and false statements
Forgery

Forgery means to make an imitation in writing or to produce information in writing to appear (or be passed off) as though it was made by another person (eg by signing somebody else's name) and was genuine. It is an offence to deceive intentionally by means of forgery, alteration or misuse (ie by lending or allowing another person to use), of any document or licence; vehicle test, plating or manufacturer's certificate; maintenance record, driving licence, certificate of insurance or security. Documents altered or obtained by these means are invalid. It is also an offence to have in your possession (with intent to deceive) a forged or false document even if you did not personally perpetrate the forgery or false statement.

False
statements

A false statement is one which is made when it is known to be untrue – in other words it is a lie – and intended to deceive. It is an offence to make false statements knowingly for the purpose of obtaining or preventing the grant of any licence, to produce false evidence or to make false statements knowingly or to make a false entry in any record or to withhold any material information for the purpose of obtaining a certificate of insurance (Road Traffic Act 1988). Any document, record, licence or certificate obtained as a result of a false statement is invalid (see also above about possession of such documents).

National Syllabus
Module B

Part 1: Law

1. Taxation

Vehicle excise duty and registration
The Vehicle Excise and Registration Act 1994 requires that all mechanically propelled vehicles, whether used for business or private purposes, which are driven or parked on public roads in Great Britain (also in Northern Ireland under the Vehicles (Excise) Act (Northern Ireland) 1972) must have and display current and valid excise licences unless they are being driven, by previous appointment, to a place for their annual test.

It is an offence to use or keep (ie park) an unlicensed vehicle (or trade licensed only vehicle) on a road even for a short period of time.

Exceptions apply to certain official vehicles such as those belonging to fire brigades and ambulance services, those operated by the Crown, snow clearance and certain other public utility vehicles.

One other exemption applies when vehicles travel not more than six miles in one week between two sets of premises both belonging to the firm or person who is the registered owner of the vehicle. An 'exempt' disc is provided for display on the vehicle windscreen.

When licensing a vehicle, the following documents must be provided:

1. The registration document (form V5) for the vehicle (in Northern Ireland the log book).
2. A current certificate of insurance (or a temporary cover note, but not the policy).
3. A current MoT or goods vehicle test certificate (where applicable).
4. A completed application form:
   (a) form VE 55 for first registration
   (b) form V 10 for renewal.
5. The type approval certificate (for first registration only).
6. The appropriate amount of duty.

On first registration of the vehicle, a registration number will be allocated. This must be made into plates to be displayed on the front and rear of the vehicle.

A circular windscreen disc is also provided to indicate that duty has been paid (the colouring of these discs is varied to provide ready indication that duty for the current period has been paid). This disc must be displayed on the vehicle windscreen on the nearside, where it can be easily seen. Failure to display the disc (even if the duty has been paid) is an offence.

Rates of excise duty

Vehicle excise duty (VED) is payable either annually or at six-monthly intervals in accordance with scales of duty. Under the present scheme of VED, duty for goods vehicles is payable in accordance with a published scale. The amount of duty payable depends on the vehicle type, its unladen or gross (ie revenue) weight and the number of its axles. For goods vehicles over 3500kg gross weight the duty is based solely on gross weight, and for vehicles over 12 tonnes gvw, also on the number of axles. Vehicles are classed as follows for duty purposes:

1. Private/light goods (PLG), which includes private cars and other privately registered vehicles, and all light goods vehicles up to and including 3500kg gross weight.
2. Goods vehicles not exceeding 7.5 tonnes gross weight.
3. Goods vehicles (ie rigid and articulated vehicles) over 7.5 tonnes but not exceeding 12 tonnes gross weight.
4. Rigid goods vehicles exceeding 12 tonnes gross weight divided into:
   (a) two-axle rigids
   (b) three-axle rigids
   (c) four or more axle rigids.
5. Trailers exceeding four tonnes gross weight (ie drawbar trailers).
6. Special types vehicles and non-plated goods vehicles exceeding 3500kg gross weight.
7. Articulated vehicles exceeding 12 tonnes gross weight divided into:
   (a) two-axle tractive units used with *any* semi-trailer
   (b) two-axle tractive units used with two or more axle semi-trailers only
   (c) two-axle tractive units used with three or more axle semi-trailers only
   (d) three-axle tractive units used with *any* semi-trailer
   (e) three-axle tractive units used with two-axle semi-trailers only
   (f) three-axle tractive units used with three or more axle semi-trailers only.

Dual-purpose vehicles

If a dual-purpose (estate-type) vehicle is used for carrying goods in connection with a trade or business and it is over 3500kg gross weight, the appropriate rate of goods vehicle duty must be paid.

The definition of a dual-purpose vehicle is a vehicle built or converted to carry both passengers and goods of any description, which has an unladen weight of not more than 2040kg and:

1. has four-wheel drive, or
2. (a) has a permanently fitted roof
   (b) is permanently fitted with one row of transverse seats behind the driver which are cushioned or spring and have upholstered backrests
   (c) has a window on either side to the rear of the driver and one at the rear.

The majority of vehicles generally described as estate cars, shooting-brakes, station wagons, land rovers (hard-top version only) and 'hatchback' saloons with fold-down seats are dual-purpose vehicles under this definition, and if these are used in connection with a trade or business (carrying deliveries or trade samples, etc) and are over 3500kg gross weight, the appropriate goods vehicle rate of duty must be paid.

Special rates

Certain vehicles are subject to special and reduced rates of duty, as follows:

1. Recovery vehicles
2. Travelling showmen's vehicles (see note above)
3. Tower wagons
4. Works trucks and trailers, mobile plant, fork-lift trucks and mobile cranes
5. Engineering and digging plant.

Refunds of duty

Paid duty may be reclaimed for each complete month remaining on the licence when it is surrendered. Applications for refunds must be made by the last day of the preceding month and the licence disc must be surrendered.

Alteration of vehicles

If a vehicle is modified, the details must be notified to the Driver and Vehicle Licensing Agency (DVLA) at Swansea.

Fuel duty

Diesel fuel for road-going vehicles is subject to excise duty, whereas the same type of oil used, for example, for use on farms and sites is not. Duty-free diesel is dyed red (legally it is called rebated heavy oil but is generally referred to as red diesel or gas oil) and can easily be detected if used illegally in road-going vehicles. HM Customs and Excise conduct roadside checks of vehicles to ensure that the correct duty-paid fuel is being used.

Trade licences

Trade licences (commonly referred to as trade plates) may be obtained and used by: motor traders (manufacturers, repairers or dealers in motor vehicles including motor vehicle delivery firms) and vehicle testers. The plates may be used on vehicles which are temporarily in their possession as motor traders, and on vehicles submitted for testing. Trade plates must not be used on recovery vehicles.

Applications for trade licences

Application must be made to local Vehicle Registration Offices (VROs) on form VTL 301. The licence is valid for one year (or for a lesser period ie 6 to 11 months). If a trade licence is refused by the VRO an appeal can be made to the Secretary of State for Transport.

Trade plates

Two plates are issued with red letters on a white background; one has the triangular licence affixed to it. This plate must be attached to the front of the vehicle, and the other to the rear.

Use of trade plates

Trade plates may only be used in the following circumstances by bona fide motor traders and testers

1. for test or trial in the course of construction or repair of the vehicle or its accessories or equipment and after completing construction or repair
2. when travelling to or from a weighbridge to check the unladen weight or when travelling to a place for registration or inspection by the Council
3. for demonstration to a prospective customer and when travelling to or from a place of demonstration
4. for test or trial of the vehicle for the benefit of a person interested in promoting publicity for the vehicle
5. for delivering the vehicle to a purchaser
6. for demonstrating the accessories or equipment to a prospective purchaser
7. for delivering a vehicle to, or collecting it from, other premises belonging to the trade licence holder or another trader's premises
8. for going to or coming from a workshop in which a body or equipment or accessories is to be, or has been, fitted
9. for delivering the vehicle from the premises of a manufacturer or repairer to a place where it is to be transported by train, ship or aircraft or for returning it from a place to which it has been transported by these means

10. when travelling to or returning from any garage, auction room or other place where vehicles are stored or offered for sale

11. when travelling to a place to be dismantled or broken up.

Goods may only be carried on a vehicle operating under a trade licence:

1. when a load is necessary to demonstrate or test the vehicle, its accessories or its equipment – the load must be returned to the place of loading after the demonstration or test.

2. when a load consists of parts or equipment to be fitted to the vehicle being taken to the place where they are to be fitted.

3. when a load is built in or permanently attached to the vehicle.

4. when a trailer is being carried for delivery or being taken to a place for work to be carried out on it.

The only passengers permitted to travel on a trade licensed vehicle are:

1. the driver of the vehicle, who may be the trade licence holder or an employee. Other persons may drive the vehicle with the permission of the licence holder but they must be accompanied by the licence holder or his employee – this latter proviso does not apply if the vehicle is constructed to carry only one person.

2. persons required to be on the vehicle by law, such as a statutory attendant

3. any person carried for the purpose of inspecting the vehicle or trailer

4. any person in a disabled vehicle being towed

5. a prospective purchaser or his servant or agent

6. a person interested in promoting publicity for the vehicle.

Trade licensed vehicles must not be left parked on public roads.

Recovery vehicles

Recovery vehicles may not be used for recovery operations on trade plates. A separate class of VED applies to these vehicles. Any vehicle used for recovery work which does not conform to the definition given below must be licensed at the normal goods vehicle rate according to its class and gross weight. Goods must not be carried on a recovery vehicle when in use, except the essential tools or spares.

Definition of
recovery
vehicle

For the purpose of this taxation class, a recovery vehicle is one which is 'either constructed or permanently adapted primarily for the purpose of lifting, towing and transporting a disabled vehicle or for any one or more of those purposes'. A vehicle will no longer be a recovery vehicle under the regulations (ie Vehicle Excise and Registration Act 1994 Schedule 1 Part V) if at any time it is used for a purpose other than:

1. the recovery of a disabled vehicle
2. the removal of a disabled vehicle from the place where it became disabled to premises at which it is to be repaired or scrapped
3. the removal of a disabled vehicle from premises to which it was taken for repair to other premises at which it is to be repaired or scrapped
4. carrying any load other than fuel and any liquids required for its propulsion and tools and other articles required for the operation of, or in connection with, apparatus designed to lift, tow or transport a disabled vehicle.

Plating and
testing of
recovery
vehicles

Recovery vehicles licensed under the recovery vehicle taxation class are not exempt from goods vehicle plating and testing unless they satisfy the definition in the regulations of a 'breakdown vehicle' namely, 'a vehicle on which is mounted permanently fitted apparatus for raising a disabled vehicle from the ground and for drawing that vehicle when so raised, and which is not equipped to carry any load other than articles required for that operation, the apparatus or repairing disabled vehicles'.

Operation of
recovery
vehicles

Licensed recovery vehicles are exempt from 'O' licensing, the EU drivers' hours rules and the tachograph requirements but those persons who drive them must hold driving entitlements of the correct category (eg category C) and must comply with the British Domestic driving hours rules.

Part 2: Road Haulage Business and Financial Management

1. Marketing

What is marketing?

Road hauliers are dependent on marketing skills to win business from their road freight competitors and from other transport modes. Marketing is a function which has been defined in as many ways as it is possible to string words together. However, for the purposes of this text and certainly from the haulier's point of view it is the task of promoting his company and its services to customers (existing and potential) in such a way that the customer wants to use the services offered because the rates are set at the levels he is prepared to pay (ie right price), because the service level offered is what he wants for the delivery of his goods (ie right service), because he is convinced of the reliability and integrity of the haulier (ie right place, right time and right quality of service), because the vehicles are right for his work, because the haulier's drivers are professional in their approach and for many other reasons. It can be summed up as, the function of identifying, anticipating and satisfying customer requirements with profit for his business.

The point about marketing for the haulier is that he has to set out to convince customers that this is the level of service he provides – and more efficiently, more effectively and more economically than his competitors and yet can still make a profit. This is essential because without the profit motive all the marketing skills would be to no avail. It is an unfortunate quirk, of course, that some customers appear only to be interested in obtaining the lowest price and that there is always a haulier who is prepared to work at the lowest (ie clearly uneconomical) rates.

The separate functions of marketing

Marketing is a complex and all encompassing function (having an effect on all aspects of a business) but it can be separated into a number of individual functions, each one inter-related to the others as follows:

1. Market research
2. Marketing planning

3. Sales (including sales promotion)
4. Advertising
5. Public relations (to include customer relations).

It is useful to consider each of these briefly in turn.

Market research
Market research basically means finding potential customers and finding out what they want. The simplest form of market research is for the haulier to merely look in a local telephone directory and identify those firms whom he thinks may be interested in the services he offers. He could then telephone them and ask what services, if any, they require. At the other end of the scale he could employ (if he could afford such a luxury) a market research consultancy that would (with its teams of researchers) conduct surveys of lists of pre-identified potential customers to find out precisely their needs in the way of transport services. In between these two extremes the haulier could obtain lists of firms to whom he could make approaches about the use of his services. The essence of market research is the task of finding out who may be interested in his services, what particular aspects of transport services they require, what special equipment they may need and what levels of price they may be prepared to pay.

Sources of market data
Market data can be obtained from many sources but the most obvious are telephone and trade directories, commercial gazetteers, Chamber of Commerce directories, trade journals, local newspapers and such like. Having identified potential contacts from these sources the next step is to start the data collection process. This involves person-to-person in-depth interviews, telephone interviewing or the use of postal questionnaires to find out what services are required, what aspects of service are important (or orders of priority), what factors influence decisions, who makes the final decision. Importantly too, information is needed on the aspects of service that are not required, not relevant or not important or which would mitigate against a decision.

Marketing planning
Marketing planning is planning to satisfy the requirements (or demands) of potential and existing customers. Having identified from market research what potential customers may want in the way of services, the haulier could plan, firstly, to see whether he could (and how to) offer such services and, secondly, plan his positive methods of approach to those firms by way of advertising, direct selling and sales promotion and indirectly via public relations. He would do this in the same way that a manufacturer of, say, consumer goods would determine what products to make and sell and how to

package and present them and what price levels to set for them bearing in mind his costs and what the market will bear (and in relation to what prices his competitors sell at) and the profit he wants or needs (to satisfy shareholders) to make.

Selling

Selling is the job of actually winning orders. Having identified potential customers and determined that the type, quality and price of service they require can be offered, the haulier has got to go out and 'sell' them. Particularly, without criticising them, he must show that he can improve upon the type, quality and price of service perhaps currently being offered (or provided) by one of his competitors. In other words, the haulier must convince them that what he offers is what they want at the best price with the utmost reliability and so on and get them to agree to use his services. To use salesmanship jargon, this is 'to close the sale'.

Selling techniques are specialised and involve many methods. A common approach is by direct mail, whereby personally addressed letters are sent direct to the relevant person. These letters would set out what the haulier has to offer, an explanation as to why he is better than the competition, and invite the potential client to try the service or at least to ask for a meeting to discuss their precise needs in more detail. Alternatively, the method adopted may be 'cold calling' (or cold canvassing) whereby a salesman calls at a potential customer's premises without prior appointment or introduction and chances getting in to see the relevant person to discuss his business. With a good salesman it can work but otherwise is a difficult task with a high risk of failure because of the turn away rate – by executives who see nobody without an appointment.

Sales promotion
Sales promotion is an extension of the selling effort. It is the business of adding something to the selling message to sway the customer towards deciding to buy your services or your products. It includes the provision of brochures and supporting literature, the staging of exhibitions and other promotional campaigns, the distribution of logo-emblazoned stickers, balloons, hats and T-shirts among other things. We are all familiar with sales promotion methods. In the supermarket they give you free plastic bags (with their name shouting to everybody where you did your shopping). Some firms merely give their customers calendars for the New Year, others give desk diaries, key rings, pens, ties and such like. In the big league, sales promotion may involve bigger and more prestigious gifts or free travel (eg weekend golf matches, trips

to sports events, a day at a grand prix, or visits to factories abroad). All of this would come under the heading of sales promotion – the business of trying to win yet more orders by direct influence.

Advertising

Advertising is the business of trying to attract customers through the media (ie trade papers, journals, newspapers, even by radio or television broadcasting). Generally an advertisement does two things. Firstly, it tells interested firms who you are, what services you offer and where you can be contacted – the basic ingredients of most normal adverts (seeing some magazine and TV adverts you may wonder what is on offer and by whom !). Secondly, the advert may be in the form of an invitation to potential customers to try your services. The added ingredient here is an attraction (bonus offer, eg 'two for the price of one') or an invitation for the reader to telephone (or complete a tear-off strip or send in a reply-paid card) requesting further details or for a sales person to call on him. The latter is known as direct response advertising – that is, the success of the advert can be measured (and its cost effectiveness assessed) by the number of replies in relationship to the circulation (very often this may only be in the region of one or two per cent of a newspaper or magazine readership for example – perhaps four/five per cent for a really successful campaign). The secret of advertising lies in the ability to design a printed (or verbal or filmed in the case of radio and TV) message which catches the eye of the potential customer and holds his attention for sufficiently long for your name and the services you offer to register with him and, if appropriate, to note the telephone number, or fill in and send off the reply slip.

Public relations

To many people this is a complete mystery. It is simply the matter of ensuring that everybody who comes into contact with your firm (customers, the public, the authorities (police, enforcement staffs, local authority etc), neighbours, employees, trade and professional people with whom it has dealings and so on) gains a good impression of it. The concept is for you to make them think that the firm is good, professional and reliable, among other qualities, and not just in its services to customers, but in every other way; for example, with hauliers, being seen as being concerned for the environment and not creating pollution by noise or fumes or obstruction by scruffy lorries parked where they should not be and such like.

Market segments in road haulage

In considering the road haulage industry at large, we are, of course, considering a very broad spectrum of road freighting activities which differ widely in their specialisations and operating methods, and consequently in the equipment they use and the particular skills of the people employed. Therefore they differ considerably in their marketing approach and methods. In examining a list of such market sectors it has to be recognised that there is extensive overlap of specialisations in many firms. Thus, at one end of the scale is the firm (usually running small vans) that promotes the idea that it carries anything for anybody to anywhere at any time. This cannot be strictly true of course, because limitations of weight capacity or suitable vehicles would ensure that they cannot carry 'anything' but the marketing message sounds good and it wins customers. At the other end of the scale, for example, is the specialist bulk road tanker operator who carries only dangerous substances. There is no point in him marketing his services to all and sundry, or of advertising in the mass media or on radio or television because his existing and potential customers, taken all together, may only form quite a small group of chemical manufacturers and suppliers. His marketing efforts would be more effectively directed to public relations; convincing the public that when they see his vehicles they can rest assured they are completely safe, being driven responsibly and operating within the law.

There is a long list of other specialist sectors as follows:

1. Express parcels carriage (eg same-day, next-day services)
2. Bulk carriage in road tankers (ie chemicals/foodstuffs, etc)
3. Carriage of abnormal loads
4. Furniture removals (domestic and industrial and new furniture)
5. Machinery carriage (incl. computers)
6. Livestock carriage
7. Timber haulage
8. Steel haulage (incl. rolled steel, billets and ingots)
9. Boat haulage
10. Contract hire
11. Distribution and storage
12. Refrigerated transport (ie temperature-controlled)
13. International haulage (specialised or general)
14. Groupage operations (plus export packing, labelling and shipment etc)
15. Bulk tipping (minerals/fuels/aggregates/cement/grain/animal feeds)
16. Ready-mixed cement (ie truck-mixers)
17. Container haulage
18. Vehicle/trailer hire/spot rental

19. Distribution of motor vehicles (ie car transporters)
20. Motor parts.

Within these specialisations there are to be found many sub-specialisations. For example hauliers who provide only local or only long distance services, those who cover only certain geographical regions within Great Britain, those who follow only particular routes (eg Glasgow–London–Glasgow), those who serve only particular countries (eg UK–Eire, UK–Spain).

It has to be recognised also that quite a number of haulage firms serve only a single customer either under a specific long-term contract or merely by long-established tradition. With these it becomes questionable as to how much marketing effort is necessary; perhaps very little market research and actual selling (although some sales promotion effort could be worthwhile) but a good public relations image remains essential and should be worked upon.

2. Commercial conduct of the business

Having the ability to calculate vehicle operating costs, road haulage rates plus understand the intricacies of accounting paperwork and dealing with payments, are important attributes for running a haulage business.

Vehicle costing

It is necessary to determine in advance the cost of owning and running commercial vehicles in order to establish the prices to be charged for haulage work and to ascertain whether a particular job can be carried out costing no more than the revenue it will earn and to provide a margin for profit.

In own-account transport operations where profit is not the motive, costing is still necessary to determine whether vehicles are being operated efficiently and within the scope of any pre-budgeted financial limits for transport.

Methods of costing

Vehicle costing comprises a number of separate elements as listed below. These various costs can be further identified as *direct* costs (ie those costs directly attributable to the running of the vehicle such as fuel, maintenance, licences, insurance and so on) and *indirect* costs (ie those costs which relate to the operation of the haulage business rather than specifically to vehicles such as office rent, heating and lighting costs, telephone charges, bank charges, etc). It is important to be able to differentiate between these two types of cost item.

Standing or fixed costs

These are incurred from the time of ownership of a vehicle irrespective of the amount of use to which it is put. They are usually calculated on an annual basis, including the following items:

□ Licences — Vehicle excise licence (ie VED) and 'O' licence

□ Insurance — Compulsory third party plus additional cover

□ Wages — Drivers' wages plus costs of employment (National Insurance, pension, etc)

□ Rents and rates — A proportion of the costs incurred in the provision of land for vehicle parking (alternatively this could be dealt with as an overhead cost item)

□ Interest on capital — Provision for a return on the capital invested in the vehicle on the basis that had the money been invested elsewhere it would have earned a return by way of interest – alternatively this would cover the interest payable if a vehicle was being bought on hire-purchase

□ Depreciation — Provision for a reserve of capital to be built up from the vehicle earnings to pay for its eventual replacement. Usually calculated on a straight-line or on a reducing balance basis as follows:

Depreciation by straight-line calculation method over a fixed period of time (calculation made only once when vehicle is first purchased):

$$\frac{\text{Vehicle original cost} - \text{tyres} - \text{residual value}}{\text{Anticipated life (years)}} = \frac{\text{£}x \text{ depreciation}}{\text{per annum}}$$

To calculate depreciation by the reducing balance method, the amount to be depreciated is reduced by the chosen percentage each year. Say a five year life is expected then the figure can be reduced by 20 per cent in the first year and then each year the carried forward balance is reduced by 20 per cent thereby resulting in a progressively lower depreciation figure for each year. In theory the high early years'

121

depreciation should coincide with low maintenance costs in the vehicle's early life (when there is also warranty protection) and the lower figure with the higher maintenance and downtime costs later in the vehicle life.

Example of calculation:
Total amount to be depreciated, say, £40,000, over 5 years

Year 1	£40,000	×	20%	=	£8,000	=	£32,000
Year 2	32,000	×	20%	=	6,400	=	25,600
Year 3	25,600	×	20%	=	5,120	=	20,480
Year 4	20,480	×	20%	=	4,096	=	16,384
Year 5	16,384	×	20%	=	3,276	=	13,108

Thus after the end of the fifth year the 'written down' value is £13,108.

To depreciate by a current cost accounting method, the calculation would need to be made at least once each year during vehicle life, often more frequently. On each occasion the current (ie as at today) new price for the vehicle would be used instead of the original invoice amount in the straight-line method calculation made above.

Running or variable costs
These are all direct costs incurred through operation of the vehicle. They are usually calculated on a pence per mile/km basis, including the following items:

- Fuel — Fuel consumed at *x* pence per mile/km

- Tyres — The cost of tyre usage, calculated by dividing the tyre costs by their life in miles/km to give a cost in pence per mile/km

- Maintenance — The cost of maintaining the vehicle including regular servicing, safety inspections, oil changes, unscheduled repairs and breakdowns and the annual test.

NB: It may be preferable or even necessary to calculate running costs on a pence/km basis because most heavy goods vehicles now operate tachographs which indicate distance in kilometres only. Similarly, fuel calculations would need to be made on a pence/litre basis since most pumps are now calibrated to record litres only. So, overall, fuel consumption figures may be increasingly referred to on a km/litre basis.

Overheads or establishment costs

These are the indirect costs of operating the business (ie they do not apply directly to the vehicle itself but to the business as a whole) including management and administrative costs, workshop costs, heat and light expenses, telephone and postage charges, salaries, company cars and so on, usually calculated on an annual basis. Every single item of expenditure by the business must be included (ie with a receipt and recorded in the books of account) to produce an accurate reflection of the costs of running the *business* (not the lorries). If any items are missed this can result in distorted cost calculations and lead to incorrect quoting of haulage rates as well as producing inaccurate trading accounts.

Total operating costs

These are a combination of standing costs, running costs and overheads brought together by calculating each item into a common denominator of time or mileage (kms) to give a price per week, per day, per hour or per mile/km. These costs will vary in accordance with the miles run by the vehicle. Less miles/kms means higher cost per mile/km because the fixed costs are spread over fewer miles/kms, while more miles/kms means a reduced overall cost per mile.

Marginal costs

These are the costs of running the vehicle after the fixed and overhead costs have been recovered. For example, once a vehicle route has been costed, if an extra delivery has to be included, its cost would only be the marginal cost of the extra costs incurred after the fixed costs have been recovered (ie fuel and tyre wear etc, plus the driver's extra time).

Profit

With a profit margin added to the total operating cost, this is the amount which a haulier needs to obtain for the operation of vehicles on a profitable basis. A figure of 25 per cent is a useful gross margin to add.

Calculation of haulage rates

Many hauliers accept (or have no choice but to accept) rates quoted to them by their customers. While this may be difficult to avoid, it is important that the operator should work out the cost of the operation by determining how much time it will take, how many miles, etc, and add a profit margin and check whether this falls within the scope of the rates being offered.

Rates are calculated by assessing the cost of operating the type of vehicle needed to carry out the work and adding a margin for profit. The resulting figure can be converted into an appropriate unit price to suit a customer's requirements (ie a rate per day, per hour, per load, per ton, per pallet, per cubic foot, per litre, etc). Rate schedules can be calculated on a mileage/kilometres or tonnage basis with progressively increasing amounts in radial distances and on a tonnage basis starting with 'up to one tonne', increasing to full load prices.

Payment and collection of revenue

In transport operations it is usual for drivers to carry consignment and receipt notes which give instructions regarding collection and delivery of the goods and other relevant information. The receipt copy enables the consignee to acknowledge with his signature the safe receipt of the goods. From these documents the job can be priced according to the nature of the goods carried, the vehicle used, the weight or volume of goods, the distance covered, the waiting time, etc.

When the price has been calculated, an invoice can be sent to the customer identifying the job, enclosing a copy of the receipt note if appropriate to prove delivery – POD – (or this can be retained for the carrier's future reference) and stating the price plus VAT as appropriate. Following the invoice a statement of the account can be sent, on which the customer will base his payment of the account. Some firms pay on receipt of the invoice, others do not pay until a statement is received.

It is becoming more common these days for firms (especially large firms, government departments and other authorities) to pay their suppliers by means of credit transfer whereby amounts owing are paid straight to the payee's bank account (ie direct from the payer's bank account) without the need for preparing, signing and posting individual cheques. This has the added advantage of speeding clearance of the amount into the payee's bank account (ie by avoiding x number of days in the post and sitting on somebody's desk awaiting a trip to the bank). This is also mentioned in module A, section 2/2.

3. Insurance in respect of vehicles and goods in transit

Compulsory insurance

Motor vehicles using the public highway must be covered against third party claims – except those belonging to local authorities; belonging to, used or directed by the police or the armed forces and certain vehicles of the NHS. The cover may be provided by means of a security of £500,000 deposited with the Accountant General of the Supreme Court (subject to the approval of the Secretary of State for Transport) or by means of an insurance policy taken out with an authorised insurer (ie a member of the Motor Insurers' Bureau – MIB) – commonly known as Road Traffic Act (ie of 1988) cover.

The insurance policy must, 'insure such person(s) or classes of person as may be specified in the policy in respect of any liability which may be incurred by him or them, in respect of the death or bodily injury to any person caused by, or arising out of, the use of the vehicle on a road; and must also insure him or them in respect of any liability which may be incurred by him or them relating to payment for emergency treatment'.

The insured person or organisation must have in their possession a current and valid certificate of insurance (the policy is not acceptable proof of cover) showing the cover provided and it must give particulars of any conditions subject to which the policy is issued. It should indicate:

1. The vehicles covered by registration number or by specification
2. The persons authorised to drive the vehicle
3. The dates between which the cover is effective
4. The permitted use of the vehicle.

Claims to MIB Third parties injured in motor vehicle accidents who find subsequently that the vehicle driver/owner was not insured, can seek compensation from the Motor Insurers' Bureau for which purpose it was established.

Passenger liability Passenger liability insurance cover for motor vehicles is compulsory. This requirement includes all vehicles which are required by the Road Traffic Act to have third-party insurance and the cover will extend to authorised passengers, other non-fare paying passengers and also to what may be termed 'unauthorised passengers' such as hitch-hikers and other people who are given lifts. It does not cover employees of the vehicle owner/operator (these are covered under the employers' liability policy).

The display in a vehicle of a sign which says 'No passengers' or 'No liability' does not fully indemnify the owner or driver against claims by unauthorised passengers for injury or damage as a result of negligence even if they agree to travel at their own risk, but the law ensures that such liabilities are covered within the vehicle policy.

Additional voluntary insurance Any insurance cover over the minimum mentioned above is at the vehicle owner's discretion, but in many instances it is advisable for the protection it gives in the event of loss of the vehicle or severe damage to it.

Production of insurance certificate

The owner of a vehicle must produce a certificate of insurance if requested to do so by a police officer or following a road traffic accident. The certificate or a temporary cover note may be produced at any police station nominated by the vehicle owner or driver within seven days (five days in Northern Ireland) from the date of the police officer's request.

Application for an excise licence for a vehicle must be accompanied by a current certificate of insurance or an applicable temporary cover note.

The owner of a vehicle must give the police any information needed to determine whether a vehicle was being driven without third-party insurance in force.

Invalidation of cover

Insurance cover on a vehicle can be invalidated for a number of reasons including the non-payment of premiums, employment of unlicensed or incorrectly licensed drivers, using a vehicle without an excise licence or 'O' licence, the use of a vehicle in an unroadworthy condition, failing to report an accident to the insurers or admitting liability at the scene of an accident or otherwise being in breach of policy conditions (eg operating the vehicle outside the terms of the stated cover).

Cancellation of insurance

When an insurance policy is cancelled the certificate(s) of insurance relating to that policy must be surrendered to the insurer within seven days of the cancellation date.

Insurance for goods carried
Goods in transit (GIT) insurance cover

Vehicle insurance covers risks of loss or damage to the vehicle itself, but not the load it is carrying. This is covered by a goods-in-transit (GIT) policy which provides protection against loss or damage to the load based on a standard valuation of at least £1,300 per ton (ie in accordance with the RHA standard Conditions of Carriage). If the loads carried are of greater value per ton, the cover should be extended as necessary. Usually insurers need to be advised if exceptionally valuable or vulnerable loads are carried (eg spirits, cigarettes, etc). Failure to do so can result in invalidation of the cover or refusal by the insurers to pay out on claims. In any event the firm could lose heavily if it is not adequately covered.

GIT policies usually specify restrictive clauses which require vehicle owners to observe particular conditions as follows:

1. Vehicles must be fitted with anti-theft devices which must be put into operation when they are left – 'immobiliser clause'.
2. Loaded vehicles must be left in a closed building or yard which is locked or guarded – 'night risk clause'.

CMR

For operations within the UK goods-in-transit (GIT) cover applies but when loads are carried on international journeys by professional hauliers the provisions of CMR apply and special insurance cover for loss or damage to goods on such journeys is necessary – normal UK GIT insurance *does not* cover such operations. The amount of cover should be for the current CMR limit per tonne of goods carried plus carriage, Customs and other charges (see page 262 for full details).

4. Methods of operating

Working in road haulage operations will bring the reader into contact with other modes of transport and many other organisations such as freight forwarders, haulage sub-contractors, transport clearing houses and groupage operators. It is important to understand the various different roles fulfilled by these organisations as described below.

Freight forwarder

Many firms with goods to despatch particularly to overseas destinations use the services of freight forwarders. Their role is to provide a complete transport service in connection with the export or import of goods (as well as for inland movements) covering some or all of the following aspects:

1. Advice on the best method of movement (ie road, sea, air).
2. Advice on legal/commercial requirements.
3. Advice on the best services.
4. Making necessary bookings with appropriate transport services.
5. Completing all documentation.
6. Advising on and arranging packing and labelling.
7. Arranging insurance cover as necessary.
8. Arranging for collection and following through until delivery is effected.
9. Arranging Customs clearance for export/import consignments.
10. Ensuring that all charges are reasonable and presenting comprehensive final account.

Clearing house

A clearing house is an organisation which arranges with shippers (ie consignors) of goods to move those goods by sub-contracting the work to road haulage operators (ie it does not normally undertake the carriage itself). The clearing house agrees one price with the customer and another (ie lower) with the haulier and keeps the difference. Alternatively, it advises the haulier of the price to be paid by the customer then deducts a commission for handling and administrative charges from what is due to the sub-contract haulier. Usually the commission is in the region of ten per cent of the original rate but can be less if the rate is poor or substantially more if it is good. Hauliers seeking return loads for vehicles frequently accept loads from clearing houses to save searching around. There are problems on both sides. Unscrupulous clearing houses deduct excessive commission and take a long time to pay the haulier, thereby existing on finance owed to hauliers rather than on their own working capital. Hauliers sometimes pick up loads and deliver to the wrong place, or do not obtain proof of delivery, or take a long time to effect delivery (ie they tranship loads in their own yard for delivery later). Sometimes too, sub-contract hauliers are not adequately covered by goods in transit insurance and if loads are lost or damaged and substantial claims arise, financial problems can result.

Sub-contract hauliers
These are hauliers (often owner-drivers) who have no direct contact with customers but who pick up work from other hauliers and clearing houses. In other words, they undertake work which others have contracted to carry. This method of operating saves them the costs and efforts of marketing but it means they exist always on haulage rates reduced by the main contractor's commission, and they usually have to wait a considerable time for payment since they have no leverage on the customer. There is a significant legal aspect to sub-contract haulage work which is dealt with in detail in module A section 1/1.

Groupage
This is the practice of bringing small consignments together (in industry terminology 'less than container loads' – LCLs) and consolidating them into bulk loads for onward shipment (ie the trunk haul) in a large vehicle or container. Break-bulk is a term used to describe the unloading of consolidated loads ready for delivery of individual consignments to their respective destinations. In the case of import/export groupage, much of this work is carried out at inland clearance depots where HM Customs and Excise have a presence for clearing the necessary documentation for such loads.

Part 3: Access to the Market

1. Operator licensing

The Operators' (ie 'O') licensing system is concerned with safety and this is achieved by regulating the 'quality' of goods vehicle operators entering the industry and is thus a quality licensing system. It is administered by the Licensing Authority (LA) for each of the traffic areas covering England, Wales and Scotland. Northern Ireland is dealt with separately. Its Road Freight Operators' licensing system is administered by the Department of the Environment in the Province.

Quality and quantity licensing

Quality licensing is a system whereby control is exercised on the basis of the quality of licence holders, that is, their ability to operate safely, legally and professionally. Quantity licensing, on the other hand, is based on restricting the number of licence holders or the total volume of freight that licence holders can move. The present UK system of 'O' licensing (and Northern Ireland road freight operators' licensing) is quality-based.

The vehicle user

An 'O' licence is required by the 'user' of an appropriate vehicle (ie one that is not exempt). The 'user' is the person who operates and drives the vehicle in the case of an owner-driver, or who employs a person to drive the vehicle for him in connection with any trade or business which he carries on. Ownership of the vehicle is *not* a relevant factor in determining who is the user. In Northern Ireland own-account users of vehicles are exempt from road freight operators' licensing.

Definition of goods vehicle

For the purposes of 'O' licensing, a goods vehicle is one which is used in connection with the trade or business of the licence holder and as such is a vehicle with a permissible maximum weight (pmw) of over 3.5 tonnes unless it is otherwise exempt.

Exemptions from 'O' licensing

The following small vehicles are exempt from 'O' licensing:

1. Rigid vehicles plated at not more than 3.5 tonnes permissible maximum weight or unplated with an unladen weight of not more than 1525kg
2. Drawbar combinations with plated weights totalling not more than 3.5 tonnes gross or unplated with a total

combined unladen weight of not more than 1525kg (trailers of not more than 1020kg unladen weight need not be included in the calculation to determine whether an 'O' licence is needed).

3. Articulated vehicles with a combined plated weight of not more than 3.5 tonnes gross or, if either is not plated, if the total of the unladen weights is not more than 1525kg.

A number of further exemptions apply to specialised vehicles or vehicles used for specialised purposes, but these are not listed because the Royal Society of Arts does not examine on the exemptions.

Restricted 'O' licences

Own-account operators who only carry their own goods or goods in connection with any trade or business carried on by them (other than that of professional haulier) may hold a *restricted* 'O' licence which allows them to operate both within the United Kingdom and internationally. The licence does *not* permit them to carry any goods for hire or reward, or in connection with a trade or business other than their own.

Standard 'O' licences – national operations

Professional haulage operators and own-account operators who wish to carry goods for hire or reward in addition to their own goods, solely within the UK, are required to hold a *standard* 'O' licence covering *national* transport operations.

The holder of a standard national 'O' licence may also carry his own goods (ie goods in connection with any other trade or business carried on by him) on international journeys as well as on national journeys.

Standard 'O' licences – international operations

Professional haulage (ie hire and reward) operators and own-account operators who wish to carry goods for others in addition to their own goods both nationally and internationally need to hold a standard 'O' licence covering both *national* and *international* operations.

Definition of international operations
For the purposes of the 'O' licence regulations the definition of international operations, which determines whether a standard international licence is required, is as follows:

If the driver or the vehicle is engaged on a journey where the vehicle or part of the vehicle (ie a semi-trailer) leaves the UK in a loaded condition, or the vehicle or part of the vehicle has entered the UK in a loaded condition from another country, then that is an international operation. However, if the driver only takes a loaded trailer or semi-trailer to a British port for unaccompanied onward movement or collects an unaccompanied loaded trailer or semi-trailer from a port and does not leave the country himself, in these circumstances it has been ruled that a standard 'O' licence covering only national operations is required.

Conditions for the granting of restricted/ standard 'O' licences

The conditions which an applicant must meet in order to obtain the grant of a restricted or standard 'O' licence are as follows:

Restricted 'O' licences
The applicant:

1. must be a fit and proper person
2. must be of appropriate financial standing.

Standard national 'O' licences
The applicant:

1. must be of good repute
2. must be of appropriate financial standing
3. must be professionally competent in national transport operations (see page 142).

Standard international 'O' licences
The applicant:

1. must be of good repute
2. must be of appropriate financial standing
3. must be professionally competent in both national and international transport operations (see page 142).

In each case the licence applicant must additionally show he is willing and able to comply with the conditions of the declaration of intent on the 'O' licence application form GV 79. Further, the operating centre at which vehicles on the licence are based must be suitable for the purpose and environmentally acceptable (ie must not be likely to cause environmental discomfort to owners or occupiers of other land in the vicinity).

Number of 'O' licences

Only one 'O' licence may be held by a person/firm in any one traffic area. A separate 'O' licence is required in each traffic area in which goods vehicle operations are based.

Observance of legal requirements

It is a condition of 'O' licensing that operators must observe the law regarding drivers' hours and the keeping of drivers' records (including tachographs); the overloading of vehicles; the maintenance, roadworthiness and use of vehicles; vehicle plating and testing; speed limits and traffic rules (eg motorway driving); drivers' licensing; international road haulage permits;

use of rebated fuel oil; parking restrictions and prohibitions on loading/unloading. They must also comply with the 'O' licensing conditions on the reporting of vehicle defects by drivers, the regular safety inspection of vehicles and the keeping of maintenance records (ie driver defect reports, safety inspection reports and defect repair records).

Declaration of intent
In making an application for an 'O' licence, renewal of an 'O' licence or variation of an 'O' licence, the applicant is required to make a declaration of intent – a legally binding promise that the law regarding all the above mentioned requirements will be strictly observed. This promise must be kept throughout the duration of the licence. Failure to fulfil promises made in the declaration of intent can leave the licence holder open to risk of penalty against the Operator's licence by the Licensing Authority who has the power to curtail, suspend or revoke the licence if such action is considered appropriate.

The precise wording of the promises on Form GV 79 comprising the declaration of intent is shown on page 137

Maintenance
Operators must make proper arrangements, acceptable to the LA, for the maintenance and repair of their vehicles. These arrangements may be the provision by the operator of his own workshop facilities or the use of the services of an outside repairer; the LA would want to see a proper written agreement between the operator and the repairer setting out details of the arrangement and the manner and frequency of the inspection and repairs. Although repairs may be carried out by other repairers, the vehicle user (ie the licence holder) remains fully and solely responsible for the mechanical condition of the vehicles on the road. Blame for faulty work cannot be transferred to the repairers so far as the 'O' licence is concerned.

Maintenance records
Maintenance records, whether prepared in an operator's own workshop or supplied by a repairer (depending on where the repair work is carried out), must be maintained and kept available for inspection for at least 15 months.

Fit persons/
good repute
Applicants for an Operator's licence are required to satisfy the LA that they are fit and proper persons to hold such a licence and in the case of standard 'O' licences are of 'good repute'. In order to determine this fact the LA requires details of any convictions which the applicant, any partners or any other directors of a limited company have had in connection with the operation of goods vehicles.

Rehabilitation of offenders

The convictions that the LA is concerned with are those incurred during the five years prior to the date of the granting of the licence where a fine or community service order was imposed or, if such a conviction resulted in a prison sentence of not more than six months, up to seven years prior to that date and ten years for a longer sentence. If the person concerned was under the age of 17 when any such conviction was made then the respective periods are 2½, 3½ and five years. Convictions for offences prior to these periods are 'spent' under the terms of the Rehabilitation of Offenders Act 1974 and therefore do not count against the applicant. The rehabilitation period where an absolute discharge was granted is six months, where a Detention Centre Order was imposed it is three years and where a Borstal Order was imposed it is seven years.

Financial status

Applicants for an Operator's licence are required to satisfy the Licensing Authority as to their financial status at the time of applying for the licence so that the LA can determine whether there is sufficient money available to enable the applicant to operate and maintain the licensed vehicles to the standards required by law. Detailed questionnaires (form GV 79F) are frequently sent out by LAs for completion, mainly by standard 'O' licence applicants, to obtain details of their financial resources and projected operating expenditure.

Operating centres and parking

When applying for an Operator's licence the applicant is required to give the address of the place where the vehicles will normally be 'kept', which effectively means the place where vehicles are parked when they are not in use. This is termed the 'operating centre'. The LA will need to consider, in view of the facilities available and in conjunction with the local authority, the location and suitability of the premises for the parking of goods vehicles under provisions contained in the Transport Act 1982 (section 52 and schedule 4) amending the Transport Act 1968.

Under these provisions the definition of operating centre includes any place where vehicles are regularly parked, even if this is away from the normal depot. Therefore, when drivers regularly take vehicles home, the place where they park the vehicle may become an operating centre and the subject of an application for use of the place as such – complete with requisite newspaper advertisement (see below). This is then subject to LA approval and to representation by any local resident who is environmentally affected by such parking. This legislation enables representations to be made to LAs about the environmental effects of goods vehicle operating centres on land owned or occupied by the person making the representation in the vicinity of the nominated operating centre.

Advertising of applications

Applicants for new, varied or renewed 'O' licences must place an advertisement in a local newspaper, to appear up to 21 days before or no more than 21 days after their application is received by the Licensing Authority, giving the address of the proposed operating centre or centres for vehicles covered by the licence. The advertisement gives local residents the opportunity to make representations (which must not be vexatious, frivolous or irrelevant) to the Licensing Authority against the grant of a licence (or variation of a licence) on environmental (but no other) grounds, in that it would prejudicially affect their enjoyment of the land they own or occupy. Such representors must write to the LA (within 21 days of the advertisement appearing) setting out their complaint and a copy must be sent to the licence applicant otherwise the representation becomes invalid.

Powers of Licensing Authorities

Applications for Operators' licences have to be made to the LA for the area in which the vehicles to be operated are based.

The LA has the sole power (apart from appeal decisions of the Transport Tribunal – see page 136) of considering applications and of granting or refusing licences, and of placing environmental restrictions on the use of vehicles at operating centres.

The LA requires completion of the appropriate forms and needs to be satisfied of the following:

1. That the applicant is of good repute and is a fit person to hold a licence.
2. That he has suitable facilities or has made satisfactory arrangements for vehicle maintenance.
3. That he has made satisfactory arrangements for ensuring that the law concerning drivers' hours and records and the overloading of vehicles will be complied with.
4. That where appropriate, he is professionally competent or employs somebody who is professionally competent.
5. That he is of adequate financial standing.
6. That the applicant has suitable parking facilities (with appropriate planning permission) for his vehicles.
7. That the operating centre specified for the vehicles is environmentally suitable.

The Licensing Authority has the power to call an operator to public inquiry so he can:

1. Consider the application for an Operator's licence in public.

2. Question an operator about offences which have been committed in contravention of the 'O' licence requirements. This is referred to as a Section 69 Inquiry in recognition of the powers given to LAs in this respect under Section 69 of the Transport Act 1968.
3. Listen to environmental representations by local residents about the suitability of the vehicle operating centre and the use of vehicles at the centre.
4. Listen to statutory objections to the granting of a licence by specified objectors (see below).

Under provisions contained in the Transport Act 1982, LAs have powers to impose conditions on 'O' licences relating to vehicle operating centres, in terms of the number of vehicles parked there, how they are parked, their size, the times when they arrive and depart and the route they must follow in going to and from the operating centre and on other related activities at the operating centre such as maintenance and vehicle loading and unloading activities.

Licence
penalties

The LA also has powers under Section 69 of the Transport Act 1968 to impose penalties on the holder of an Operator's licence as follows:

1. Revocation, whereby the complete licence can be revoked for a stipulated period or (in extreme circumstances) the LA can recommend that the person concerned should never be permitted to hold another Operator's licence.
2. Suspension, where the LA can suspend the complete 'O' licence or a number of vehicles from the licence temporarily.
3. Curtailment, where the LA reduces the number of vehicles which may be operated under the licence.

In the case of curtailment or suspension the LA can rule that the vehicles concerned must not be used under any other 'O' licence for a period of up to six months.

Objections to
an 'O' licence
application

The bodies listed below may object – not to be confused with environmental representations mentioned above – within 21 days of publication of the application in the booklet *Applications and Decisions* (commonly referred to as A's and D's), to the granting of an 'O' licence on the grounds that the applicant does not meet the necessary qualifications, because:

1. the applicant is not of good repute
2. he is not of appropriate financial standing
3. he does not meet the requirements of professional competence

4. he is not likely to comply with the law regarding drivers' hours and records and the overloading of vehicles

5. there are not satisfactory arrangements or facilities for maintaining the vehicles

6. the applicant does not have suitable facilities for parking vehicles when they are not in use.

The bodies are:

- A chief officer of police
- A local authority
- A planning authority
- The Freight Transport Association (FTA)
- The Road Haulage Association (RHA)
- The British Association of Removers (BAR)
- The General and Municipal Workers' Union (GMWU)
- The National Union of Railwaymen (NUR)
- The Transport and General Workers' Union (TGWU)
- The Union of Shop, Distributive and Allied Workers (US-DAW)
- The United Road Transport Union (URTU)

If an objection is to be raised by any of the listed bodies against an application, the objector is required to provide the applicant with a copy of the objection.

Appeals to the Transport Tribunal
An applicant for an Operator's licence whose application is refused or an existing operator whose licence is revoked, suspended or curtailed has the right of appeal to the Transport Tribunal which will consider his appeal and rule for or against him in the light of information provided at the Appeal. An operator may also appeal against the decision of an LA following representations on environmental grounds or against conditions placed on a licence in such circumstances.

An objector can appeal against an LA's decision but people making environmental representations have no such rights of appeal.

Appeals must be made within one month of the LA's decision being published in *Applications and Decisions*.

The Tribunal has three members: the Chairman, who is a QC, plus two other eminent and experienced people from industry.

Applications for 'O' licences
Applicants for 'O' licences are required to complete form GV 79, which should be sent to the Traffic Area Office in which the vehicles to be specified on the licence are based at least nine weeks in advance of the date when operation of the vehicles is required to commence.

In addition, form GV 79A (ie list of vehicles to be specified on the licence) must be completed. The LAs also usually require further information about the applicant's financial standing, which must be provided initially by the submission of accounts, accountant's letter, bank statements or other evidence of resources. Applicants are sometimes required to complete form GV 79F giving details of their projected expenditure and earnings.

If there are environmental representations against a licence application, following publication of the newspaper advertisement, form GV 79E (dealing with environmental matters) must be completed.

Form GV 79
Form GV 79 is the basic application for an 'O' licence – it requires the name, trading name, address, telephone and telex numbers of the applicant together with the following information:

1. Details of any subsidiary companies whose vehicles are to be included on the licence.
2. Details of the previous experience of the applicant, his partners or fellow directors in operating or driving goods vehicles.
3. Details of any other Operator's licence held or previously held.
4. Details of the operating centres for the vehicles to be included on the licenceand the number of vehicles and trailers in possession or to be acquired.
5. Details of any previous convictions which the applicant or his partners or fellow directors may have had during the past five years relating to the roadworthiness of vehicles, overloading offences or drivers' hours and records offences which have resulted in a fine or imprisonment.
6. Details about the financial status of the business proprietor, his partners or the directors of the business, and whether any of them have been made bankrupt in the past three years.
7. Details about the professionally competent person in the case of applications for standard operator's licences.

Declaration of intent: In addition to these basic questions form GV 79 requires the applicant to make a declaration of intent regarding his ability and willingness to comply with the law. The points included in the declaration are as follows:

'I declare that the statements made in this application are true. I understand that the licence may be revoked if any of the statements are false or I do not fulfil the statement of intent made below.

I will make proper arrangements so that:

□ the rules on drivers' hours are observed and proper records are kept
□ vehicles are not overloaded
□ vehicles are kept fit and serviceable
□ drivers will report safety faults in vehicles as soon as possible
□ records are kept (for 15 months) of all safety inspections, routine maintenance and repairs to vehicles, and make these available on request

I will:

□ have adequate financial resources to maintain the vehicles covered by the licence
□ tell the Licensing Authority of any changes or convictions which affect the licence
□ maintain adequate financial resources for the administration of the business (applies to standard licence applicants only)

Vehicles mentioned above include any trailers.'

The applicant is required to sign form GV 79 declaring that the information provided and the statements of fact are true.

Form GV 79E (environmental information)
Form GV 79E is sent to licence applicants if the Licensing Authority receives representations from local residents following publication of details of the applicant's operating centres in local papers. The form requires details of the applicant and his proposed operating centre, the vehicles normally to be kept at the place and the number and types of trailer to be kept there. Information must be given of any other parking place in the vicinity of the centre used for parking vehicles specified on the licence. If the licence applicant is not the owner of the premises he must send evidence to show that he has permission or authority to use the place for parking vehicles.

Questions must be answered about the operating times of authorised vehicles (ie those on the licence or licence application – not others). In particular, what time will lorries arrive at and leave the centre, will they use the centre on

Saturdays or Sundays, what times will they arrive and leave on these days, will maintenance work be carried out there and between what hours, and will any of this work take place on Saturdays or Sundays and, if so, between what hours? Information must be given about any covered buildings at the centre in which this work is carried out.

A plan must be sent showing the parking positions for authorised vehicles, entry and exit points, main buildings, surrounding roads with names. Details must be given of any application for or any planning permission granted for use of the site as a vehicle operating centre.

Form GV 79F (financial information)
Form GV 79F may be sent to new standard licence applicants when the LA requires additional financial information to enable him to consider whether the applicant meets the extra financial requirements for this type of licence (ie to run a professional haulage business and not be dependent on any other trading activity). An application will be refused unless the LA is satisfied that the applicant has sufficient financial resources to set up and run the business.

Answers have to be given on the form about the vehicles to be included on the licence, their average annual mileage and the estimated running cost for each individual type of vehicle.

Details must be given about the funds available to start up the business and where these are held (eg in a bank as savings, or overdraft or loan facilities, or share capital, or a deposit elsewhere) and about the starting up costs for the business including the purchase price or down payment on the vehicles and on the premises (advance rents etc, or purchase of the freehold or leasehold) and the sum to be held in reserve as working capital. The applicant is required to give a forecast of the annual expenditure and income for his road haulage operations for a financial year. The LA expects this information to give a clear indication of the business finances for the year ahead.

Form GV 79A
Form GV 79A is a supplementary sheet to form GV 79, requiring the applicant to provide details of the vehicles currently in possession to be included on the licence as follows:

1. Registration number.
2. The DoT plated maximum permissible weight or gross train weight.

3. Body type, eg van, tipper, tanker, platform, etc, and whether articulated.

This document will eventually become part of the Operator's licence, if granted, and the Traffic Area Office will place its stamp in the right-hand column of the form alongside authorised vehicles. This stamp will be cancelled when the vehicles are removed from the licence. In some instances a new style of computerised form is being used.

Form GV 80

Application to make changes within the total number of vehicles already authorised on an existing 'O' licence should be made on form GV 80. The form requires details of the applicant and of the vehicles to be added to or removed from the licence. A period of one month is allowed in which to notify the Traffic Area Office of details of vehicles added to a licence within the margin (ie the total number authorised).

Form GV 81

Application to vary an 'O' licence by increasing the total number of vehicles authorised on the licence should be made on form GV 81. It is also used to make other variations of the licence such as a change of operating centre, a change of maintenance arrangement, to add or delete other operating centres, to change the type of licence (eg from restricted to standard or vice versa), to request a change or removal of conditions from the licence. This form requires details of the applicant and any convictions against the applicant, his partners or co-directors. It also requires the applicant to repeat the declaration of intent made on the original application form GV 79 and place an advertisement in a local newspaper as previously described.

Renewal of 'O' licence
When an existing 'O' licence expires, application for a new licence (ie it is not a renewal) to replace it is made (at least nine weeks in advance) on forms GV 79 (and GV 79E where appropriate) and GV 79A as with the original application.

Publication of applications
Applications for new 'O' licences or for variations of existing licences are published by the LA in the booklet *Applications and Decisions*, so that potential objectors can see details of the applications and, if they wish, make objection within 21 days (see also page 134). Similarly, decisions to grant licences or variations of licences or refusal to grant applications may also be published in this document, copies of which are obtainable from Traffic Area Offices.

Subsidiary/associate companies

The vehicles of any subsidiary company (ie one in which more than a 50 per cent shareholding is held) may be included in the application for an 'O' licence by a holding/parent company but those of an associate company (ie where there is less than 50 per cent share holding) may not.

Transfer of vehicles

If vehicles are transferred to another traffic area for more than three months they must be specified on an 'O' licence in that area. If a licence is not held in that area then a new application must be made at least nine weeks before the vehicles are to start operating. It is illegal to operate goods vehicles (ie over 3.5 tonnes maximum permissible weight) from a base in a Traffic Area in which *no* 'O' licence is held.

Licence margin

Application may be made and granted for more vehicles than are initially required in order to provide a 'margin' of surplus vehicles on the licence in case extra vehicles are needed at any time during the currency of the licence (ie normally five years) to cover for maintenance, vehicles off the road for other reasons and to cater for peaks of trade.

Adding vehicles

Additional vehicles within the total number authorised on an 'O' licence may be added at any time. The LA must be advised of details of the vehicles added within one month by submission of form GV 80.

Notification of changes

Licence holders must notify the LA of any changes in the legal entity of their business (eg change of name, partners, or if a limited company is formed) because the existing licence will no longer be valid and application will have to be made for a new one. Any change of business address must be notified within three weeks and other changes which must be notified are changes affecting a nominated professionally competent person or where such a person dies or becomes physically disabled or mentally disordered and unable to work, or where the licence holder or a partner or director is declared bankrupt or the company goes into insolvent liquidation. Failure to notify the LA can result in a fine and he can revoke, suspend or curtail the 'O' licence.

Fees and validity

The fee for an 'O' licence is calculated on a per vehicle per quarter basis plus a licence fee. Licences are normally valid for five years but shorter-term licences may be granted in certain circumstances, for example when the LA wishes to review an operator's activities and conduct in less than the normal duration of a licence. An existing licence will automatically continue in force after its expiry date provided an application has been made for a new licence before the old one expired.

Interim licences

An LA may grant an interim 'O' licence pending consideration of an application for a full licence. Issue of an interim licence does not guarantee that a full licence will be granted.

Temporary derogation

Holders of a standard 'O' licence may operate without a professionally competent person if the person dies or becomes physically or mentally incapacitated (the LA must be notified in writing) for no more than 12 months, after which time the licence will be revoked unless the LA accepts that there are exceptional circumstances and permits an extension of this period (the maximum is 18 months).

Licence discs

Licence discs for display in vehicle windscreens are issued when a licence is granted or when vehicles are added to a licence. The discs are coloured for easy identification as follows:

- □ Restricted licence – orange
- □ Standard national – blue
- □ Standard international – green
- □ Interim licence – yellow

The discs show the type of licence, the operator's name, the 'O' licence number, the licence expiry date and the vehicle registration number.

Production of 'O' licences

The LA, a certifying officer, examiner, police constable or other authorised person (ie by the LA) can demand production of an 'O' licence for examination within 14 days either at an operating centre covered by the licence or at the main place of business of the holder or, in the case of a demand by a police constable, at a police station selected by the holder.

Admission to the occupation – professional competence

Applications for a standard Operator's licence must be supported by the name of a person (the applicant himself/herself or one partner or a director of the applicant's company or a full-time employee) who is professionally competent in either national or international transport operations (depending on whether a standard national or international 'O' licence is required), in accordance with The Goods Vehicles (Operators Licences Qualifications and Fees) Regulations 1984 (as amended).

Methods of acquiring competence

There are various methods by which a person can or could have become professionally competent.

Grandfather Rights
Any person who was employed by an 'O' licence holder in responsible road transport employment or who held an 'O' licence in his own name prior to 1975 could obtain a Certificate of Professional Competence based on past experience (known as Grandfather Rights) by applying to the LA for the traffic area in which he lived by 30 November 1979. All certificate issues under this scheme have now ceased.

Temporary Grandfather Rights
Any person who took up a position of responsibility for the operation of goods vehicles on an 'O' licence between 1 January 1975 and 31 December 1977 or who became the holder of an 'O' licence during that time was considered to be professionally competent until 31 December 1979. After that date professional competence had to be confirmed either by passing the appropriate examination or by gaining exemption.

Definition of responsible road transport employment

The legal definition of the 'responsible road transport employment' an applicant for a Certificate of Professional Competence under the Grandfather Rights scheme had to have was as follows:

> 'employment in the service of a person or a company who has held an 'O' licence where that employment was such that the person had responsibility for the operation of goods vehicles under that 'O' licence and where that employment was prior to 1 January 1975'.

NB: It should be understood that it is no longer possible to qualify for professional competence under the Grandfather Rights scheme. This item is included here for information only.

Exemption
Certain members of professional transport institutes in specified grades qualify for professional competence by exemption by virtue of their continuing valid membership, and therefore do not need to meet the experience requirement mentioned above or pass the official examination. The institutes and membership grades are as follows:

For both international and national operations:
1. Membership of the Chartered Institute of Transport (CIT) in the grade of Fellow or Member (in the road transport sector).
2. Membership of the Institute of Transport Administration (IoTA) in the grade of Fellow, Member or Associate Member (in the road transport sector).
3. Membership of the Institute of Road Transport Engineers (IRTE) in the grade of Member or Associate Member.
4. Membership of the Institute of Furniture Warehousing and Removing Industry (IFWRI) in the grade of Fellow or Associate.

For national operations only:
1. Membership of the Chartered Institute of Transport (CIT) in the grade of Associate (in the road transport sector).

2. Membership of the Institute of Road Transport Engineers (IRTE) in the grade of Associate (by examination).
3. Membership of the Institute of Transport Administration (IoTA) in the grade of Graduate or Associate must be a holder of the NEBSS Certificate (road transport sector), must be at least 21 years of age and have 3 years' practical experience.
4. Holder of the General Certificate in Removals Management issued by the Institute of Furniture Warehousing and Removing Industry (IFWRI).
5. Holders of the RSA Certificate in Road Goods Transport gained by examination since May 1984.

Examination

Those people who do not qualify for professional competence by other means can do so by examination. The official examination is conducted at various centres throughout the country four or more times per year on behalf of the official examining body (the Royal Society of Arts – RSA). Copies of the examination syllabus can be obtained from the RSA. For further details see p15 of this manual.

Fees and validity

Certificates of Professional Competence were granted on a once-only basis with no renewal, and they were free of charge. Similarly, gaining or holding the professional competence qualification costs nothing beyond the price of studying for and sitting the examination or payment of Institute annual subscriptions. Once acquired, the professional competence qualification will remain valid, without renewal, so long as the scheme remains in existence.

Issue of Certificates of Professional Competence

Certificates of Professional Competence were issued *only* to those persons who qualified under the Grandfather Rights scheme. Where the qualification is achieved under the exemption arrangements through membership of the professional institutes a valid membership is sufficient indication that the person is professionally competent although the institutes listed will issue a confirmatory certificate if required.

Where professional competence is obtained by passing the official RSA examinations a pass certificate from the examination board will indicate that the person is professionally competent. This certificate will not be exchanged for a Certificate of Professional Competence of the type issued to those people who qualified under the Grandfather Rights.

Part 4: Technical Standards and Aspects of Operation

1. Weights and dimensions of vehicles and loads

Definition of vehicle weights
Vehicle weights are specified by different means for different purposes. The following definitions generally apply:

Unladen weight (ULW)
The weight of the vehicle inclusive of body and parts normally used in operation (the heavier of any alternative body being counted), but exclusive of weight of water, fuel, loose tools and equipment and batteries where these are used for propelling the vehicle.

Kerb weight
The weight of a vehicle in road-going condition inclusive of oil, water and fuel but without its load and without driver and any passengers on board.

Tare weight
The weight of a vehicle in road-going condition including the weight of the driver and any passenger carried, prior to loading. This is the weight deducted from the gross weight to determine the actual or potential 'payload'.

Maximum laden weight (MLW)
The actual total weight of a vehicle and its load including the weight of fuel, driver and passenger, if carried. This weight should not exceed the limits specified by law for the vehicle - see below.

Gross vehicle weight (GVW)
The maximum weight at which a rigid vehicle is designed and permitted to operate as indicated on the vehicle plate (ie manufacturer's plate showing the design weight) or the DoT plate and plating certificate (showing the permitted maximum weight to be transmitted to the road by *all* the wheels of the vehicle in Great Britain). This is sometimes called the gross plated weight (gpw) - or gross mass - but, more correctly, is the permissible maximum weight (pmw).

Gross train weight (GTW)
The total weight of a drawbar combination (eg a rigid vehicle and drawbar trailer) including its load, fuel and driver and as defined above for gross vehicle weight.

Gross combination weight (GCW)
The total weight of an articulated vehicle with its load, fuel and driver and as defined above for gross vehicle weight.

Permissible maximum weights (PMW)

Permitted maximum weights (ie the total weight allowed on the road in the UK for the vehicle and load, including fuel and driver, plus passenger if carried) for goods vehicles and trailers depend on their wheelbase, the number of axles, the outer axle spread (the distance between the centre of the wheels on the front and rear axles) or the relevant axle spacing in the case of articulated vehicles. All goods vehicles over 3500kg gross weight (and trailers over 1020kg ulw) should be fitted with a 'Ministry' plate showing the permissible maximum axle and gross weight (or for articulated vehicles, the gross train weight) for that vehicle in Great Britain. These weights must not be exceeded.

The current permissible maximum weights for different types of vehicle are as follows:

Vehicle type	Permissible maximum weight (kg)
Two-axled rigid vehicles	17,000
Three-axled rigid vehicles	26,000
Rigid vehicles with four or more axles	32,000*
Articulated vehicle with three axles	25,000
Articulated vehicle with four axles	35,000*
Articulated vehicle with five or more axles	38,000**
Articulated tractive unit with two axles	17,000 (if vehicle has a gross train weight over 32,520)
Articulated tractive unit with three or more axles	24,390
Lorry and trailer (ie draw-bar) combinations	38,000**
Maximum drive axle weight	10,500
Maximum weight on tandem-axle bogie	20,000
Maximum weight on tri-axle bogie	7500 on each axle 8000 if fitted with air suspension*

Cont...

Cont...

All the above maximum weights are dependent upon the vehicle/trailer meeting relevant plated weights.

> * Certain weights are dependent upon the fitment of road-friendly suspensions.
>
> ** *6-axle articulated vehicles and drawbar combinations may operate at up to 44 tonnes pmw in combined transport operations only - subject to meeting all relevant conditions (see below).*

Combined Transport Vehicles

New rules were introduced in March 1994 by the Government to boost rail freight prior to rail privatisation. These permit swap-body and container-carrying lorries running to and from rail terminals to operate at up to 44 tonnes gross weight. This increased weight limit applies only to articulated vehicles and drawbar combinations equipped with at least six axles and road-friendly suspensions (or those that have no axle exceeding 8.5 tonnes), and to articulated vehicles comprising specially-built bi-modal semi-trailers (ie capable of running on road or rail), used in combined road-rail transport operations.

When operating at this weight (ie above 38 tonnes) the driver must carry with him documentary evidence to show that the swap-body or container load is on its way to a rail terminal (the document must show the name of the rail terminal, the date of the contract and the parties to it), or is on its way back from a rail terminal (in which case the document must show the terminal and the date and time that the unit load was collected). There is no restriction on the distance that may be travelled to or from a rail terminal for the purposes of complying with this legislation.

Gross weight calculation

The gross weight of a goods vehicle is the unladen weight of that vehicle plus the weight of its driver, any passengers carried, fuel, (ie the tare weight) plus the load and load-securing devices - in other words, when the vehicle is laden and 'ready for the road' .

The permissible maximum weight is that shown on the DoT plate and plating certificate. Vehicles may only be operated up to the maximum legal limit as shown on this plate which is not necessarily that which is shown on the manufacturer's plate.

Axle weight calculation

In order to calculate front or rear axle weights for vehicles when given certain information, the following formula is used:

1. Determine the vehicle wheelbase.
2. Determine the weight of the load (ie payload).
3. Calculate the front loadbase (ie centreline of front axle to centre of gravity of load); or, calculate the rear

loadbase (ie centreline of rear axle to centre of gravity of load).

4. Apply the formula as follows:

$$\frac{\text{Payload (P)} \times \text{Loadbase Distance (D)}}{\text{Wheelbase (W)}} = \text{(see items 1 and 2 below)}$$

ie for simplicity, remember formula $\dfrac{P \times D}{W}$

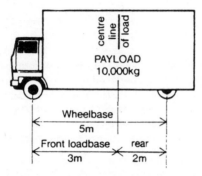

1. If *front* loadbase distance is used the answer will be the weight on the *rear axle.*

2. If the *rear* loadbase distance is used the answer will be the weight on the *front axle.*

1. Rear axle weight calculation:

$$\frac{\text{payload} \times \text{front loadbase}}{\text{wheelbase}} = \text{payload weight on rear axle}$$

$$\frac{10{,}000 \times 3}{5} = 6000\text{kg}$$

2. Front axle weight calculation:

$$\frac{\text{payload} \times \text{rear loadbase}}{\text{wheelbase}} = \text{payload weight on front axle}$$

$$\frac{10{,}000 \times 2}{5} = 4000\text{kg}$$

Overloading and GV 160 procedure

It is an offence to overload a goods vehicle. A police constable, DoT examiner (ie of the Vehicle Inspectorate -VI) or trading standards officer may require a goods vehicle to be driven to a weighbridge to determine whether or not the vehicle is overloaded. In the event of an overloading offence being detected, both the vehicle driver and the 'user' (ie the driver's employer) are liable for prosecution and penalty on conviction.

When weighed, a certificate will be issued which shows the weight and which exempts the vehicle from further weighing on that journey with that load - whether the vehicle is overloaded or not. If the weight of the vehicle and load exceeds legal limits and appears unsafe or to be a danger a prohibition notice (Form GV 160) will be issued. This requires the excess weight to be off-loaded and reduced to within the legal limit before the vehicle proceeds. The driver may be directed to take the vehicle to a specific place to remove the excess load.

A vehicle may be sent up to five miles to a weighbridge without the owner being able to claim compensation for the costs incurred should the weight prove to be within legal limits. If sent beyond this distance, and the vehicle is found to be within legal limits, a claim for any losses incurred can be made to the Highway Authority (on whose behalf the direction for weighing would have been made).

Dynamic weighing

Under the Weighing of Motor Vehicles (Use of Dynamic Axle Weighing Machines) Regulations 1978, vehicles can be weighed at roadside checks on dynamic weighing machines. Vehicles are driven slowly across the machine allowing each axle to be separately weighed and the weight printed out or manually recorded by an authorised examiner. The weights shown by a dynamic weighing machine are presumed to be accurate to within plus or minus 150kg per axle (unless proved otherwise).

Overall length and width of vehicles

The overall length and width of a motor vehicle is the total distance between two vertical planes passing through its extreme projecting points but exclusive of the following items of equipment:

- □ driving mirror
- □ starting handle
- □ hood
- □ fire escape or turntable
- □ snow plough
- □ container for Customs seal.

Maximum overall lengths for vehicles/ trailers

1. Rigid goods vehicles   12m
2. Articulated vehicles (except those constructed to carry indivisible loads of exceptional length, low loaders and those with semi-trailers complying with item 10 below)   15.5m

3. Articulated vehicles with semi-trailers complying with item 10 below and satisfying conditions as to turning circles*   16.5m
4. Articulated low-loader type vehicles   18m
5. Lorry and drawbar trailer combinations   18.35m**
6. Drawbar trailers (with four wheels and over 3500kg gross weight)   12m
7. Composite trailers (comprising towing dolly plus semi-trailer)   14.04m
8. Other trailers not exceeding 3500kg gross weight   7m
9. Semi-trailers built since 1 May 1983 (not of a type in item 10 and not a low-loader) (internal loadspace dimension)   12.2m†
10. Semi-trailers used in combinations up to 16.5m (see item 3 above):

    kingpin to rear   12m
    kingpin to rear (car transporters)   12.5m
    kingpin to front‡   2.04m
    kingpin to front‡ (car transporters)   4.19m

* Articulated vehicles exceeding 15.5 metres overall length must be capable of turning within minimum and maximum swept circles with radii of 5.3 metres and 12.5 metres respectively (ie no part of the vehicle must pass outside concentric circles of these radii). This does not apply to articulated vehicles which are car transporters, low-loaders or step-frame low-loaders and those constructed and used for the carriage of indivisible loads of exceptional length.

** This dimension must comprise a minimum driving cab length of 2.35m and a minimum coupling distance of 0.35m. This leaves a potential loadspace of 15.65m within a 16m 'envelope' measured from the back of the cab to the rear of the trailer.

† This dimension does not apply when such semi-trailers are used in international operations.

‡ Front in this context means the dimension is measured to the furthest point of the semi-trailer forward of the kingpin (ie the front corners).

Maximum overall widths for vehicles/ trailers

1. Locomotives (see page 154 for definition)   2.75m
2. Motor tractors (see page 154 for definition)   2.5m
3. Heavy motor cars   2.5m
4. Motor cars   2.5m

5. Trailers   2.5m
6. Trailers when drawn by a vehicle not exceeding 3500kg gross weight   2.3m
7. Specially designed refrigerated vehicles with insulated side walls at least 45mm thick   2.6m

Overhang

The overhang of a vehicle is the distance measured between the centreline of the rear axle and the extreme rear projection of the body or chassis. The overhang distance must not exceed 60 per cent of the vehicle wheelbase.

OVERHANG

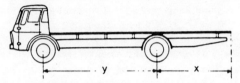

Four wheeled vehicles: overhang 'x' must not exceed 60 per cent of length 'y'

In the case of vehicles with twin rear axles, the overhang distance to the extreme rear projection is measured from a point 110mm to the rear of the centre of the two rear axles (see diagram below).

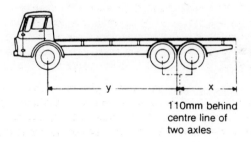

110mm behind centre line of two axles

There is no overhang limit for trailers and the overhang limit does not apply to tipping vehicles if the distance from the centre of the rear axle to the rearmost point of the vehicle does not exceed 1.15 metres.

Dimensions of vehicles and loads

Apart from the actual maximum length and width limitations on vehicles and trailers already covered, additional regulations specify the maximum dimensions for vehicles and the loads they are carrying. These apply to:

1. vehicles operating under the Construction & Use Regulations
2. vehicles which comply with the Regulations but which are constructed and normally used for carrying indivisible loads of exceptional length
3. vehicles operating under the provision of the Special Types General Order (STGO) carrying abnormal indivisible loads (see module B 4/4).

The relevant dimensions together with the requirements which must be met (such as police notification* and carrying statutory attendants†) are as follows:

Where notification of the police is required, this means notification of the police for every district through which the vehicle and load is to pass. The notification must be given at least two clear working days (ie excluding weekends and Bank holidays) in advance of the movement. In the interests of road safety, the police have power to delay the movement or direct that particular routes should or should not be used.

† Where three or more vehicles and loads requiring statutory attendants travel in convoy, attendants are only required on the first and last vehicles in the convoy.

Length

Vehicle type	Two days' police notification	Attendant to be carried
Rigid vehicle and load		
over 18.3m	yes	yes
Articulated vehicle and load over 18.3m	yes	yes
Articulated vehicle for carrying long loads over 18.3m (excluding length of tractive unit)	yes	yes
Combination of vehicles and load (excluding the length of the drawing vehicle) over 25.9m	yes	yes
over 27.4m (excl length of drawing unit)	*only by Special Order (from Secretary of State for Transport)*	

Width

Vehicle type	Two days' police notification	Attendant to be carried
Vehicles and trailers		
over 2.9m	yes	no
over 3.5m	yes	yes
over 4.3m (on C & U vehicle but operating under STGO*)	yes	yes
over 5.1m up to 6.1m (under STGO*)	*only by Special Order (from Secretary of State for Transport)*	

See note above about attendants on vehicles travelling in convoy.
* See module B 4/4 for details of operation under STGO

Projecting loads

A projecting load is one which extends beyond the foremost and/or rearmost points of a vehicle. Depending on the length of the projection, certain requirements (such as police notification, carrying attendants and displaying side and/or end marker boards - see Highway Code for coloured illustration of these) have to be met.

Forward Projections

If a vehicle carries a load which projects to the front:

1. more than 2m - side and end markers and attendant required
2. more than 3.05m - side and end markers, attendant and two days' notice to the police
3. more than 4.5m - as in 2 above plus additional side markers within 2.5m of first and subsequent sets.

Rearward projections

If a vehicle carries a load which projects to the rear:

1. more than 1m - it must be made clearly visible
2. more than 2m - end marker boards required
3. more than 3m - side and end markers, attendant and two days' notice to the police
4. more than 5m - as in 3 above plus additional side markers within 3.5m of the first and subsequent sets.

Side projections

If a vehicle carries a load* which projects to the side:

1. more than 400mm beyond the existing front or rear position lamps - extra position lamps must be carried within 400mm of the outer edges of the load (This is a requirement of The Road Vehicles Lighting Regulations 1989)
2. more than 305mm on either side or more than 2.9m overall - two days' notice to the police

*See overleaf

3. more than 3.5m - two days' notice to the police and an attendant is needed
4. more than 5m - see note above about need for approval from Secretary of State for Transport.

* For these purposes, unless the load comprises loose agricultural produce or is indivisible it must not be carried if the side projection exceeds the dimensions given in item 2 above.

2. Vehicle selection

Definition of vehicle types

Motor vehicles of various types have specific legal definitions laid down in regulations. The Road Traffic Act 1988 defines vehicles as follows:

Goods vehicle: A vehicle (or trailer) constructed or adapted for use in the carriage of goods.

Motor car: A vehicle constructed to carry goods or passengers with an unladen weight not exceeding 3050kg. (*NB:* 3050kg *not* 3500kg). Otherwise any other vehicle with an unladen weight not exceeding 2540kg.

Heavy motor car: A vehicle constructed to carry goods or passengers with an unladen weight exceeding 2540kg.

Motor tractor: A vehicle which is not constructed to carry a load and which has an unladen weight not exceeding 7370kg.

Light locomotive: A vehicle which is not constructed to carry a load and which has an unladen weight of more than 7370kg but not exceeding 11,690kg.

Heavy locomotive: A vehicle which is not constructed to carry a load and which has an unladen weight exceeding 11,690kg.

Articulated vehicle: (As defined in the Construction and Use Regulations) a motor car or heavy motor car with a trailer so attached that when the semi-trailer is uniformly loaded at least 20 per cent of the weight of the load is imposed on the drawing vehicle.

Definition of other relevant vehicles (defined elsewhere in legislation)

Small vehicles (eg for 'O' licensing purposes):

1. *rigid vehicles* which have plated weight of not more than 3.5 tonnes
2. *vehicle and trailer outfits* which have a total combined plated weight of not more than 3.5 tonnes *(Note: for 'O' licensing purposes only, trailers with an unladen weight of less than 1020kg should not be included)*

3. *articulated vehicles* which do not exceed 3.5 tonnes. The weight is calculated as follows: 'the plated weight of the semi-trailer plus the unladen weight of the tractive unit'.

Medium-sized goods vehicle: A vehicle constructed or adapted for the carriage of goods, which has a maximum gross weight between 3.5 and 7.5 tonnes.

Heavy goods vehicle: A vehicle constructed or adapted for the carriage or haulage of goods, which is an articulated vehicle or has a maximum gross plated weight exceeding 7.5 tonnes (this definition is used in determining whether or not an LGV driving entitlement is required).

Rigid vehicle: Under C&U regulations - a vehicle not constructed or adapted to form part of an articulated vehicle. In practical terms, a vehicle where the driving cab and the load carrying space are mounted on a rigid chassis.

Tractive unit: A motor vehicle which forms the towing unit of an articulated vehicle with a semi-trailer attached by a coupling in such a way that when the semi-trailer is uniformly loaded, at least 20 per cent of the weight of the load is borne by the tractive unit. It is *not* designed to carry a load other than when a semi-trailer is attached and should not be confused with a 'tractor' as described below.

Tractor: See motor tractor. A towing unit which does not have part of the weight of the trailer superimposed upon it (as described above for articulated tractive units). Usually tractors are employed in heavy haulage operations and carry ballast to give them sufficient traction for pulling very heavy loads at low speeds.

Semi-trailer: A trailer drawn by a tractive unit in a manner where at least a proportion of its weight is superimposed on the tractive unit (ie at least 20 per cent of the weight of the load when uniformly loaded - see also above) and connected by means of a kingpin and fifth wheel mounting plate or by an automatic-type coupling.

Drawbar trailer: One which has axles on both the front and the rear and the steerable front axle is connected to the rear of the rigid towing vehicle by means of a solid drawbar with flexible brake and electrical connections between the vehicle and the trailer. No part of the weight of the trailer is imposed on the towing vehicle.

Composite trailer: A semi-trailer connected to a towing dolly to comprise a drawbar trailer.

Choice of
vehicle

An operator's choice of vehicle is governed by many factors but the initial consideration will relate to the weight and volume of loads to be carried and the nature of the loads which will determine the size of the vehicle and its type (for example platform truck, box van, refrigerated vehicle, tipping vehicle, etc). The choice will also be significantly affected by the need for the vehicle to be specified on an Operator's licence (ie 3.5 tonnes gross weight threshold) and to employ LGV licensed drivers (ie currently 7.5 tonnes gross weight threshold).

Selection for
operational
needs

Efficient operation of goods vehicles starts with the selection of the right vehicle for the job. A badly chosen vehicle which is unsuited to its work will prove costly in terms of:

1. inefficient use
2. under-use
3. repeated breakdowns
4. excessive downtime
5. driver discontent
6. disruption of delivery schedules
7. customer discontent
8. reduced vehicle life.

The operator needs to take account of operational and economic factors such as that savings in initial capital cost are frequently more than offset by higher operating costs and shorter life so the ideal approach is to buy on the basis of likely 'total life cost' (ie purchase price plus operating costs throughout the vehicle life, less its residual value).

3. Vehicle condition, fitness and maintenance

Goods
vehicle
plating and
testing (in
Northern
Ireland,
goods vehicle
certification)

Goods vehicles are required to display (in a conspicuous position where they can be readily seen) plates showing the permissible maximum weight at which they may be operated and the respective maximum weights for any axle. The statutory provisions for these requirements are to be found in The Road Traffic Act 1988 and the Goods Vehicles (Plating and Testing) Regulations 1988 (as amended).

These regulations also require that goods vehicles must be tested annually at a Department of Transport goods vehicle test station with the first test being due no later than 12 months from the date of original registration. Trailers are due for test no later than 12 months from the date on which they were first supplied or sold retail. Because trailers have no identification by registration, they are given a DoT serial number indicating when they are due to be tested. This number must be permanently fixed to the trailer -usually by welding it on to the chassis side frame on the nearside.

Vehicles
covered -
plating

The following vehicles are required to be plated:

1. by the manufacturer (showing the vehicle design
   weights or legal weights, whichever are the lower):
   (a) all goods vehicles
   (b) trailers over 1020kg unladen.
2. by the DoT (ie 'Ministry plating' showing permissible –
   ie legal – maximum weights):
   (a) articulated vehicles
   (b) rigid goods vehicles over 3500kg gross weight
   (c) trailers over 1020kg unladen.

Vehicles
covered -
annual testing

The following vehicles are required to be tested:

1. at MoT-approved garages (by the third anniversary of
   the date of their original registration and annually
   thereafter);
   (a) private cars and dual-purpose vehicles
   (b) goods vehicles up to 3500kg gross weight.
2. at DoT goods vehicle test stations (annually from the first
   year):
   (a) articulated vehicles
   (b) rigid goods vehicles over 3500kg gross weight
   (c) trailers over 1020kg unladen.

Manufacturers'
plates

Manufacturers of all goods vehicles, and trailers over 1020kg
unladen, must, by law, fit a plate on the vehicle or trailer
showing the maximum weights at which the vehicle or trailer is
designed to operate. Where such weights exceed current legal
limits in Great Britain, the legal maxima will normally be shown
(see also below).

The information to be shown on the plate is as follows:

1. Manufacturer's name
2. Date of manufacture
3. Vehicle type
4. Engine type and power rating
5. Chassis or serial number
6. Number of axles
7. Maximum weight allowed on each axle
8. Maximum gross weight for the vehicle (including the
   weight imposed on the tractive unit by a semi-trailer in
   the case of articulated vehicles)
9. Maximum train weight.

In the case of a trailer, the following information is required:

1. Manufacturer's name
2. Date of manufacture
3. Chassis or serial number

4. Number of axles
5. Maximum weight allowed on each axle
6. Maximum weight imposed on the drawing vehicle if it is a semi-trailer
7. Maximum gross weight for the trailer.

DoT (ie 'Ministry' plates

When a goods vehicle or trailer is first registered it is issued with a plate and plating certificate showing the maximum weights at which it is *legally permitted to operate* in Great Britain.

The gross weight and axle weight figures shown on the DoT plate and certificate may coincide with those shown on the manufacturer's plate or they may be lower if the maximum legal limit for the class in which that vehicle falls is lower than the weight at which the particular vehicle is *designed* to operate (eg where a 44 tonnes gtw articulated vehicle is permitted to operate at only 38 tonnes gtw in Great Britain under current legal weight limits) - see also above.

The DoT plate will show the following information:

1. Registration/identification mark
2. Chassis/serial number
3. Year of original registration
4. Make
5. Model
6. Axle weights (not to be exceeded in Great Britain)
7. Gross weight (not to be exceeded in Great Britain)
8. Train weight (not to be exceeded in Great Britain)
9. Design weights (where these are greater than those indicated in 6, 7 and 8 above).

It is an offence to use a vehicle on a road loaded to a weight in excess of the gross, train and axle weights shown on the DoT plate or, if the vehicle is not plated, in excess of the maximum legal limits for that class of vehicle.

Standard lists

In determining the relevant plated weight for vehicles or trailers, DoT testing stations use information contained in published 'standard lists' which identify by type, code and serial number every make and model of vehicle/trailer produced and the appropriate gross and axle weights in accordance with the vehicle specification. Copies of standard lists can be obtained from HMSO.

Notifiable alterations

If the structure of a vehicle is altered, the Goods Vehicle Centre, Swansea, must be advised (on form VTG 10) before the vehicle is used on the road. The items which constitute alterations for this purpose are as follows:

1. Alterations to the structure or fixed equipment of a vehicle which vary its carrying capacity, including:
   (a) chassis frame or structure
   (b) steering, suspension, wheels and axles (including stub axles and wheel hubs)
   (c) fitting an alternative body of a different design, construction or type.
2. Alterations to the braking system.
3. Other alterations to the structure or fixed equipment.

Annual testing Operators of vehicles subject to testing must apply to the Goods Vehicle Centre, Swansea, on the following forms:

1. VTG 1L: first test of vehicle
2. VTG 2L: first test of trailer
3. VTG 40L: subsequent annual tests of vehicles and trailers.

Application should be made not less than one month but not more than three months before the last date when the vehicle can operate *without* a test certificate. An appointment for the test will generally be made at the testing station of the operator's choice unless that station is over-booked.

The test

Goods vehicle annual tests are categorised as follows:

1. First test (ie first annual test of a goods vehicle or trailer).
2. Part 2 re-test (ie examination of a vehicle/trailer which fails its first test).
3. Periodical test (ie the annual test applicable to all vehicles/trailers after the first test).
4. Part 3 re-test (ie examination of a vehicle/trailer which fails its periodical - annual test).
5. Part 4 test (ie examination of a vehicle/trailer following a notifiable alteration).
6. Re-test following appeal (ie examination of vehicle/trailer after an appeal to the DoT Area Mechanical Engineer).

NB: Additionally, the reader should be aware that goods vehicle test stations carry out the 'Group V' test, which is the light vehicle MoT test for large passenger vehicles which cannot get into normal MoT test garages because of their size.

On arrival at the test station, the vehicle will be subjected to a rigorous inspection covering all the points listed in the *HGV Inspection Manual* (copies available from HMSO). The inspections are carried out in four main areas: out-of-doors, where the external aspects of the vehicle cab and bodywork, lights, equipment and fittings are examined and the engine is tested for smoke emission; inside the station, over the pit, where the underside is inspected including the vehicle's steering, suspension, transmission, wheels and tyres, wiring and pipework; in the next area, where headlamp beam settings are checked; and finally on the roller brake tester, where the vehicle's braking efficiency is checked.

Test certificate
If the vehicle or trailer is found to be in a satisfactory mechanical condition a test certificate (form VTG 5), valid for one year, will be issued. Test certificates must be produced to a police constable on request.

A vehicle must not be operated on the road unless it has a valid and current test certificate except where it is being driven to a place to be tested by prior appointment. The certificate is required in order to re-tax the vehicle when its excise licence expires.

Refusal to test
The test station may refuse to test a vehicle on the following grounds in which case they will issue form VTG 12 (Refusal to Test):

1. Arrival after the appointed time.
2. If the appointment card or vehicle registration document is not produced.
3. If it is found that the vehicle brought to the test station does not conform to the details given on the application form.
4. If the vehicle was booked for the test with a trailer but the trailer is not taken to the test station.
5. If the chassis number cannot be found by the examiners or if the serial number given for the vehicle by the DoT is not stamped on it.
6. If the vehicle is in a dirty or dangerous condition.
7. If the vehicle does not have sufficient fuel or oil to enable the test to be carried out.
8. If the test appointment card specifies that the vehicle should be loaded for the test and it is taken to the test station without a load (normally, the decision as to whether the vehicle is to be tested loaded or empty is left to the operator but in some circumstances the Goods Vehicle Centre may ask for the vehicle to be submitted with a load or part load to enable the brakes to be accurately checked).

9. With a trailer, if the vehicle submitted with it is not suitable to draw it.
10. If a vehicle breaks down during the test.
11. If the vehicle is submitted for its annual test (not the first test) or a re-test and the previous test and plating certificates are not produced.

Test failure and re-test
If a vehicle undergoing a test is found to have defects it will not pass the test; the necessary repairs need to be carried out and the vehicle submitted for re-test.

If the re-test is booked at the same test station within 14 days of the failure, a reduced test fee will be charged.

Temporary exemption
Temporary exemption from the test for up to three months can be granted by the test station manager if for special reasons the test cannot be conducted (eg because of bad weather, fire, epidemic, industrial dispute, etc). A Temporary Exemption Certificate (form VTG 33) is issued.

The three months' exemption can be extended by the Secretary of State for Transport for up to 12 months.

Appeals against test decisions
An appeals procedure is laid down for operators not satisfied with a test station decision.

Appeals must be made to the DoT Area Mechanical Engineer at the Traffic Area Office within ten days of the test. If no satisfaction is achieved with this appeal, a further appeal to the Secretary of State for Transport may be made within 14 days.

Goods vehicle type approval The Motor Vehicles (Type Approval) Regulations 1980 - as amended - make provision for vehicles and their components to be 'Type Approved'. This means that manufacturers of vehicles and components can submit examples of their products, which conform to an established specification, for 'Ministry' approval and if such products meet all the necessary requirements a Type Approval Certificate (Certificate of Conformity) will be issued. Once such a certificate is issued all subsequent identical products which meet the same specification are therefore of the same 'type' and as such are legally approved for sale and for use. The manufacturer issues a certificate to purchasers confirming that the product conforms to that approved type -this is required for production when first registering a Type Approved vehicle.

Once a new vehicle is first registered, the operator has no legal obligations under Type Approval but must conform to the detailed requirements of the construction and use regulations in respect of the vehicle and all its component parts.

Construction and use of vehicles

The Road Vehicle (Construction & Use) Regulations 1986 and their subsequent amendments regulate;

1. The manner in which motor vehicles and their components, accessories and equipment are constructed, adapted and used to ensure the safety of vehicles/trailers on roads, and
2. the legal standards regarding the weights, dimensions, design and construction of vehicles/trailers.

The Construction & Use Regulations for motor vehicles (see above) specify many aspects of vehicle construction and use in considerable detail, of which the following requirements are the important items as identified in the CPC examination syllabus. In general terms it is illegal to use any vehicle or trailer on a road when these specific conditions (and indeed any of the requirements) are not complied with. Conviction for such offences can result in heavy fines, the endorsement of driving licence penalty points (for both the driver and his employer - but not if a company), and penalty against LGV driving licences and 'O' licences.

Brakes

Goods vehicles must be fitted with efficient braking systems which provide specified braking efficiencies on the primary (ie service) and the secondary braking systems; a parking brake meeting specified efficiency standards must also be provided. Goods vehicles first used since 1 April 1983 must meet technical requirements laid down in EU Directive 489/1979. Vehicles first used prior to this date can comply with the EU requirements or with the requirements of the C&U regulations broadly as described in the following text.

Where a vehicle has dual-circuit brakes (ie a split braking system) , the system must provide emergency braking in the event of one part of the system failing. If one part of a split braking system fails, the rest of the system must provide a minimum braking efficiency of not less than that specified for the secondary brake - namely 25 per cent.

Braking efficiency
The specified braking efficiencies are as follows:

Vehicles first used on or after 1 January 1968

Service brake   50 per cent

Secondary brake   25 per cent

Parking brake   must be capable of holding the vehicle on a gradient of at least 1 in 6.25 (ie 16 per cent) without the assistance of stored energy (eg compressed air in a reservoir – air tank).

Trailers constructed before 1 January 1968 must have an efficient braking system on half the number of wheels.

Trailers constructed after 1 January 1968 must be fitted with brakes operating on all wheels which can be applied by the driver of the drawing vehicle, having maximum efficiencies matching the braking requirements for the drawing vehicle, emergency brakes operating on at least two wheels and a parking brake capable of holding the trailer on a gradient of at least 1 in 6.25 (ie 16 per cent).

Post-1977 trailers which have a gross weight of not more than 3500kg can be fitted with over-run brakes.

Trailers weighing less than 102kg unladen, agricultural trailers and broken-down vehicles being towed are exempt from the braking requirements.

Vehicle combinations in which either the vehicle or the trailer conforms to EU braking requirements are exempt from the C&U braking provisions.

Speedometers   Motor vehicles must be fitted with a speedometer which indicates to the driver the speed of the vehicle in miles per hour and kilometres per hour simultaneously, or by operating a switch.

Speedometers are not required on vehicles with a maximum speed not exceeding 25mph or which it is unlawful to drive in excess of this speed. On vehicles to which the relevant law applies (ie EU 3821/85), a tachograph instrument replaces the speedometer.

It is a good defence to a charge of having a defective speedometer to show that the defect occurred during the course of the journey during which the offence was detected, or to show that at the time when the contravention was detected steps had been taken to have the defect repaired 'with all reasonable expedition'.

Speed Limiters   UK legislation requires certain heavy vehicles to be fitted with speed limiter devices restricting their top speed to 60mph (ie 96.5kph). Separate EU legislation also requires certain vehicles to be fitted with speed limiters restricting top speed to a maximum of 90kph (56mph).

UK Regulations

The UK regulations limiting relevant vehicles to a maximum
speed of 60mph (ie 96.5kph) apply:

1. from 1 August 1992, to newly registered goods vehicles
   over 7.5 tonnes gross weight and capable of more than
   60mph on the flat when unladen;
2. from 1 August 1993, to existing vehicles over 16 tonnes
   gross weight capable of more than 60mph on the flat
   when unladen, first registered on or after 1 January
   1988 and which are:
   (a) rigid vehicles constructed to draw trailers, having a
       difference between the plated gross weight and
       gross train weight of at least five tonnes
   (b) articulated tractive units.

Vehicles which cannot exceed 60mph (eg refuse collection
and certain highway maintenance vehicles) are exempt from
the regulations, as are vehicles:

1. being taken to a place to have a speed limiter device
   fitted or calibrated;
2. owned and being used by the navy, army or airforce;
3. being used for military purposes or while under military
   orders;
4. being used for fire brigade, ambulance or police
   purposes;
5. exempt from excise duty under the Vehicles Excise and
   Registration Act 1994.

Speed limiter equipment must comply with BS AU 217 Part 1
1987 (or an acceptable equivalent), be calibrated to a set
speed not exceeding 60mph and be sealed by an 'authorised
sealer'. A speed limiter plate must be fitted (see below).

Existing speed limiters, fitted to vehicles on a voluntary basis
prior to 1 August 1992, are permitted and do not have to be
sealed by an 'authorised sealer'. In this case no speed limiter
plate is required.

Speed limiters must be maintained in good working order, but
it is a defence to show that where a vehicle is driven with a
defective limiter the defect occurred during that journey, or that
at the time it was being driven to a place for it to be repaired.

Speed Limiter Plates

Vehicles required to have speed limiter equipment must also
carry a plate (fitted in a conspicuous and readily accessible
position in the vehicle cab) showing the words SPEED
LIMITER FITTED, the standard with which the installation

complies, the speed setting in mph/kph and the name/trade-mark of the calibration firm. Normally these plates are provided by the authorised sealer.

EU Requirements

The speed limiter requirements of EU Directive 6/92 (which came into force from 1 January 1994) apply to newly registered goods vehicles over 12 tonnes gross weight which must have speed limiter devices set to a maximum of 90kph (56mph). Vehicles over 12 tonnes first registered between 1 January 1988 and 1 January 1994 should have been fitted by 1 January 1995, but those used exclusively in national transport operations have until 1 January 1996 to comply.

Mirrors

Goods vehicles and dual-purpose vehicles must be fitted with at least two mirrors; one of these must be fitted externally on the offside and the other may be fitted either in the driver's cab or driving compartment, if it can provide an adequate view to the rear or, otherwise, externally on the nearside. Mirrors must show traffic to the rear or on both sides rearwards.

Goods vehicles exceeding 12 tonnes pmw and first used since 1 October 1988 must be fitted with additional mirrors which provide close proximity and wide angle vision in accordance with EU Directive 562/1986

Safety glass

Goods vehicles must be fitted with safety glass (ie toughened or laminated) for windscreens and windows in front and on either side of the driver's seat. The windscreen and all windows of dual-purpose vehicles must be fitted with safety glass. Glass should be maintained in good condition and should be clean; it is an offence for the driver's vision to be obscured while driving on a road.

Windscreen wipers and washers

All vehicles must be fitted with one or more efficient automatic windscreen wipers capable of clearing the windscreen to provide the driver with an adequate view of the road. The wipers must be maintained in good and efficient working order and must be properly adjusted. Windscreen washers must also be fitted which are capable of cleaning the area of the windscreen swept by the wipers of mud or dirt. Vehicles must not be driven on the road with defective windscreen washers or wipers.

Audible warning devices

All vehicles must be equipped with an audible warning device (ie a horn). Gongs, bells, sirens and two-tone horns are prohibited on all vehicles except emergency vehicles and those from which goods are sold (eg mobile shops and ice-cream vans). Such devices must not be sounded in built-up areas between the times of 11.30pm and 7.00am (ie

23.30 - 07.00 hours). Reversing alarms (see also page 170) come within the same restriction.

Fuel tanks
Vehicles first used since 1 July 1973 which are propelled by petrol engines must have metal fuel tanks fitted in a position to avoid damage and prevent leakage. This requirement does not apply if the petrol tank complies with EU Directive 221/70.

Silencers
Adequate means of silencing exhaust noise must be fitted to all vehicles. Silencers must be maintained in good condition at all times when a vehicle is on a road.

Tyres
Most goods vehicles must be fitted with pneumatic tyres and they must be maintained in good condition at all times* when on the road. In particular:

1. They must be inflated to the vehicle or tyre manufacturer's recommended pressure to be fit for the use to which the vehicle is being put.
2. No tyre must have a break in its fabric or a cut which is deep enough to reach the body cords or is more than 25mm or 10 per cent of its section width in length, whichever is the greater.
3. There must be no lumps or bulges caused by separation or partial fracture of the tyre structure, nor must any portion of the ply or cord structure be exposed.
4. All tyres on goods vehicles (over 3.5 tonnes gross weight††) must have a tread depth (excluding any tie bars or tread wear indicators) of at least 1mm across three-quarters of the breadth and around the entire circumference of the tyre. Across the remaining section width, the base of the original tread pattern grooves must still be visible.

NB: Exemptions apply to vehicles used solely on rough ground.

† *NB: For light goods vehicles not exceeding this weight, plus cars, the relevant minimum tread depth is 1.6mm.*

Recut tyres may be fitted to goods vehicles of over 2540kg unladen weight which have wheels of at least 405mm rim diameter. The use of a mixture of cross-ply tyres on the rear axle and radial-ply tyres on the front axle is prohibited on goods vehicles which have single rear wheels (ie light/medium vans/trucks) but such mixtures are permitted where the vehicle has twin rear wheels. It is an offence to have tyres of different structure (ie cross-ply and radial-ply) fitted to opposite wheels of the vehicle or on the same axle.

Seat belts

Seat belts for the driver and one front seat passenger must be fitted to goods vehicles of not more than 1525kg unladen weight registered since 1 April 1967 and goods vehicles of not more than 3500kg gross weight registered since 1 April 1980. The belts must be maintained in good condition, must be secured so they do not lie on the floor, and must be worn by the driver and the front seat passenger for whom they are provided. Where, for example, a van has a dual passenger seat, the requirement is for a belt to be fitted only for the occupant of the outer part of the seat (ie furthest from the driver) so a person sitting in the middle section need have no belt. However, where only one person occupies such a seat they must sit in the part for which a belt is provided - they cannot choose to sit in the middle and not wear the belt, as this is illegal.

Wings

Vehicles and trailers must be fitted with wings capable of catching mud or water thrown up by the wheels of the vehicle unless adequate protection is provided by the vehicle bodywork. See also details of anti-spray requirements on page 170.

Noise

It is an offence to use, cause or permit to be used a motor vehicle or trailer which emits excessive noise due to a defect, lack of repair or faulty adjustment of its components or of its load or which could have been reasonably avoided by the driver.

Maximum permissible noise levels for vehicles first used since 1 October 1983 in use are as follows:

1. Vehicles not exceeding 3500kg gross
   plated weight   - 81dB(A)
2. Vehicles exceeding 3500kg gross
   plated weight   - 86dB(A)
3. Vehicles over 12,000kg gross weight
   with engine power of 200hp (DIN) or
   more   - 88dB(A)

Smoke

Vehicles must not emit smoke, visible vapour, grit, sparks, ashes, cinders or oily substances which may cause damage to property or injury or danger to any person.

Excess fuel devices must not be used on diesel-engined vehicles while they are in motion.

Diesel-engined vehicles first used since 1 April 1973 must comply with smoke opacity limits specified in BS AU 141a/1971.

Towing

Goods vehicles (ie motor cars and heavy motor cars as defined in law) may draw only one trailer. Motor tractors may draw one laden or two unladen trailers; locomotives (ie both light and heavy) may draw three trailers.

A rigid goods vehicle (ie a heavy motor car) can legally tow a trailer which comprises a towing dolly and an articulated semi-trailer supported on that dolly because under the regulations this is defined as a composite trailer and counts as one trailer only.

Similarly, a rigid goods vehicle (ie a motor car or heavy motor car) is permitted to tow a broken-down rigid vehicle partially raised on a towing dolly, although this would normally be considered to be two trailers. Also, a heavy motor car can tow a broken-down articulated vehicle provided it is unladen because it counts as one trailer only; if the broken-down articulated vehicle is laden it counts as two trailers and can only be towed by a light locomotive or heavy locomotive (see page 154 for definitions of these vehicles).

When one vehicle is towing another with the aid of a rope or chain (or with a modern-style webbing towing strap) the distance between the two vehicles must not exceed 4.5m. If the distance exceeds 1.5m the tow rope/chain/strap must be made clearly visible from both sides of the vehicles. If a rigid towbar is used no minimum distance limit or marking requirements are specified.

When a vehicle is on tow the registration number of the towing vehicle must be clearly displayed to the rear and additional lights must be provided if the towed vehicle's rear lights are not working.

Rear underrun bumpers

Rear underrun bumpers (referred to in legislation as rear underrun protection) must be fitted to most rigid vehicles over 3.5 tonnes gross weight which are manufactured from 1 October 1983 and first used from 1 April 1984.

Trailers, including semi-trailers, over 1020kg unladen weight manufactured since 1 May 1983 must also be fitted with bumpers.

Certain specialised vehicles and trailers are exempt from the fitting requirements.

Strength of bumpers
Rear underrun bumpers must be capable of withstanding a force equivalent to half the gross weight of the vehicle or trailer or a maximum of 10 tonnes whichever is the lesser without deflecting more than 400mm from the rearmost point of the vehicle or trailer.

Fitment of bumpers

Usually only one bumper will be fitted but, where a tail-lift is fitted or the bodywork or other parts of the vehicle make this impracticable, two or more bumpers may be fitted.

Bumpers must be fitted as near as possible to the rear of the vehicle and the lower edge must not be more than 500mm from the ground.

Sideguards

Sideguards must be fitted to the following goods vehicles and trailers:

1. Goods vehicles exceeding 3.5 tonnes maximum gross weight which are manufactured from 1 October 1983 and first used from 1 April 1984.
2. Trailers exceeding 1020kg unladen weight which are manufactured from 1 May 1983 and which, in the case of semi-trailers, have a distance between the foremost axle and the centreline of the kingpin (or rearmost kingpin if there is more than one) exceeding 4.5 metres.

Sideguards are *not* required on vehicles and trailers, other than semi-trailers, where the distance between any two consecutive axles is less than 3 metres.

Strength of sideguards

Sideguards must be capable of withstanding a force of 200kg (two kilo-newtons) over their length, apart from the last (or rear) 250mm of their length, without deflecting more than 150mm. Over the last 250mm of their length the deflection must not be more than 30mm under such force.

Ground clearance for trailers

Minimum ground clearances are specified for goods-carrying trailers manufactured from 1 April 1984. They must have a minimum ground clearance of 160mm if the trailer has an axle interspace of more than 6 metres and not more than 11.5 metres. If the interspace is more than 11.5 metres the minimum clearance is 190mm.

Measurement of the axle interspace is taken from the point of support on the tractive unit in the case of semi-trailers, or the centreline of the front axle in other cases, to the centreline of the rear axle or the centre point between rear axles if there is more than one.

In determining the minimum ground clearance no account should be taken of any part of the suspension, steering or braking system attached to any axle, any wheel and any air skirt. Measurement of the ground clearance is taken in the area formed by the width of the trailer and the middle 70 per cent of the axle interspace.

Reversing
alarms

Voluntary fitment of reversing alarms (bleepers) to certain goods and passenger vehicles is permitted. It is a condition that the sound emitted must not be capable of being confused with the 'sound emitted in the operation of a pedestrian crossing' and such alarm sounds must not be emitted in a built-up area between the hours of 23.30 and 07.00 (the same as with audible warning instruments).

The only vehicles legally permitted to use such alarms on the road are the following:

1. Goods vehicles over 2 tonnes permissible maximum weight
2. Large passenger-carrying vehicles
3. Engineering plant
4. Works trucks.

Anti-spray

Certain heavy goods vehicles and goods-carrying trailers are required to be fitted with anti-spray equipment which conforms to British Standard Specification BS AU 200 Parts 1 and 2 1984 and 1986. The following are the vehicles and trailers to be fitted and the relevant dates:

1. Motor vehicles over 12 tonnes gross weight made on or after 1 October 1985 and first used on or after 1 April 1986.
2. Trailers over 3.5 tonnes gross weight made on or after 1 May 1985.
3. Trailers over 16 tonnes gross weight with two or more axles:
   (a) made before 1 January 1975 - fitment required from 1 October 1987.
   (b) made on or after 1 January 1975 but before 1 May 1985 - fitment required from 1 October 1986.
   (c) made on or after 1 May 1985 - fitment required from 1 May 1985.

In order to comply with the legislation, relevant vehicles and trailers must be fitted with anti-spray systems which fall into one or other of two main categories:

1. A straight valance across the top of the wheel and a flap hanging vertically behind the wheel all made from approved spray suppressant material; or
2. A semi-circular valance following the curvature of the wheel with either:
   (a) air/water separator material round the edge, or
   (b) a flap of spray suppressant material hanging from the rear edge.

All devices fitted to comply with the legal requirement (and every part of such device) must be maintained, when the vehicle/trailer is on the road, so that they are free from 'any obvious defect which would be likely to affect adversely the effectiveness of the device'.

Maintenance of parts

It is a general condition of the C&U regulations that all parts and equipment required to be fitted to vehicles (eg brakes, lights, wipers, safety glass, etc) must be maintained in clean, fit and serviceable condition and must be correctly adjusted where appropriate. It is illegal to use (ie drive) a vehicle on a road if any of these requirements are not met.

Safety

All vehicles and trailers, their parts and components and the weight distribution, packing and adjustment of their load must be such that no danger is caused or is likely to be caused to any person in or on the vehicle or the road. A vehicle must not be used for any purpose for which it is so unsuited as to be likely to cause danger to persons in or on the vehicle or the road.

Lighting and marking of goods vehicles

Between sunset and sunrise vehicles used on a public road must display obligatory lights indicated thus * in the list below. Other lights and reflectors should also be shown:

1. Two dipped-beam headlamps showing white (or yellow) lights to the front (when driven on unlit roads between the hours of darkness - ie defined as being from half an hour after sunset to half an hour before sunrise).
2. Two front position lamps* (ie sidelights) showing white (or yellow if part of a yellow headlamp) lights to the front.
3. Two rear position lamps* showing red lights to the rear.
4. Two rear red reflex retro reflectors.
5. The rear registration plate must be indirectly illuminated*.
6. One or two red rear fog lights (on post-1 April 1980 vehicles).
7. Certain goods vehicles and trailers must be fitted with side and end marker lights.*

Vehicles must not show red lights to the front or white lights to the rear (with the exception of reversing lights when reverse gear is engaged).

Lights in poor visibility conditions

Vehicles must display front and rear position lights and headlamps during daylight hours if visibility is poor due to fog, mist, rain, spray, hail, snow and similar conditions. Rear fog lamps, if fitted, should also be used under these conditions.

Headlamps   Vehicles must be fitted with two headlamps showing white or yellow lights to the front which are permanently dipped or fitted with dipping devices.

Further, vehicles must also be fitted with main-beam headlamps (any number so long as they comply with the regulations) capable of illuminating the road a long distance ahead. They must be mounted so as not to cause dazzle and be capable of being dipped. Main-beam headlamps on pre-1 April 1986 vehicles must have a light intensity of at least 30 watts.

When driving on roads where there are no street lamps or the street lamps are more than 200 yards apart (the definition of unlit roads), headlamps must be illuminated. When stationary, except at traffic stops, (ie when parked) the headlamps must be switched off.

Front fog lamps   Front fog lamps (any number for pre-1 April 1991 vehicles but only two for vehicles first used after this date) should be fitted and used in pairs (ie symmetrically mounted and emitting light of substantially the same colour and intensity). They may be used only in conditions of poor visibility, without headlamps, provided the vehicle front and rear position lights are also illuminated. If such lamps are used singly (and then only in seriously reduced visibility conditions), the vehicle headlamps must also be switched on. In any case they should not cause dazzle or discomfort to other road users.;

Such lamps should be fitted not more than 1200mm from the ground (with certain exceptions) and not more than 400mm from the outer edge of the vehicle.

Stop lamps   Vehicles registered since January 1971 must be fitted with two red stop lamps. Vehicles registered before that date need only one stop lamp which should be fitted in the centre or on the offside of the vehicle.

Number plate lamps   Rear registration number plates on vehicles must be indirectly illuminated by a white light which must be shielded so it does not show to the rear.

Reversing lamps   One or two white reversing lamps may be fitted to a vehicle provided that:

1. they are only used when the vehicle is reversing
2. they operate automatically when the reverse gear is selected or they may be operated manually provided they are on a separate switch and the driver has a warning light showing when they are in use
3. they do not dazzle other road users.

Rear fog
lamps

Vehicles and trailers manufactured on or after 1 October 1979 and first used after 1 April 1980 must be fitted with rear fog lamps as follows:

1. One lamp on the off-side or two lamps (maximum) fitted as an equal pair
2. Fitted not less than 250mm and not more than 1m from the ground except certain special vehicles (ie agricultural vehicles, engineering plant and motor tractors) when the maximum height may be 1.9m – or if the body shape makes this impossible, 2.1m
3. The lights must only operate when the other lights of the vehicle are switched on
4. They must not be connected to the brake light circuit
5. The driver must be provided with an indication that the lights are switched on
6. The lights must be used only in poor visibility conditions (ie fog, rain, snow, smoke, spray, etc) when the vehicle is moving or during a traffic stop
7. The lights must not dazzle other road users.

Vehicles first used before 1 October 1979 which have such lights fitted voluntarily must comply with the above requirements and the lights must be fitted so that no part of the illuminating surface is within 100mm of the illuminating surface of the vehicle stop lamps.

Direction
indicators

All goods vehicles must be fitted with direction indicators positioned between 350mm and 1500mm from the ground.

The following indicators are required:

1. one front and one flashing amber rear indicator on each side, or
2. one shoulder and one flashing amber rear indicator on each side, or
3. one flashing amber side indicator on each side.

Where front and rear indicators are more than 6m apart an additional flank indicator must be fitted on each side of the vehicle, within one third of the vehicle's length from the front.

Indicators must flash between 60 and 120 times a minute. A visible or audible warning must indicate to the driver when they are in operation.

Emergency (ie
hazard) warning

Direction indicators operating on both sides of the vehicle simultaneously may be used in hazardous situations and emergencies, if a vehicle is stationary on a road due to a breakdown or if the vehicle is causing a temporary obstruction while loading or unloading. A tell-tale in the cab must indicate to the driver when the lights are in use.

Roof-mounted lamps

Amber rotating lamps (called beacons in legislation) mounted on vehicle roofs or cab tops may be used on vehicles used in connection with road clearance, breakdowns, road maintenance, Special Types operation and Customs and Excise for fuel testing.

White swivelling spot lamps may be used on vehicles at the scene of an accident or breakdown, providing the vehicle carrying the lamp also has an amber rotating lamp and this is in use.

Blue rotating lamps may only be used on the following vehicles:

Fire, police or ambulance service vehicles

1. Vehicles carrying human tissue for transplanting
2. Forestry Commission vehicles
3. Bomb disposal vehicles
4. Blood transfusion vehicles
5. HM Coastguard and Coast Lifesaving Corps vehicles
6. National Coal Board vehicles used for mines rescue
7. RAF mountain rescue vehicles
8. Royal National Lifeboat Institution vehicles used for launching lifeboats.

Green rotating lamps (beacons) may be used on vehicles in an emergency by a medical practitioner registered by the General Medical Council (GMC).

Side marker lamps

Side marker lamps (on each side) must be fitted on long vehicles and trailers as follows:

1. vehicles (including a combination of vehicles) exceeding 18.3m long (including the length of the load):
   (a) one lamp within 9.15m of the front (of the vehicle or load)
   (b) one lamp within 3.05m of the rear (of the vehicle or load)
   (c) additional lamps at 3.05m intervals between front and rear side marker lamps (see items (a) and (b) above).
2. Vehicles in combination between 12.2m and 18.3m long carrying a supported load:
   (a) one lamp within 1530mm of the rear of the rearmost vehicle in the combination
   (b) one lamp within 1530mm of the centre (ie mid-way point) of the load, if the load extends further than 9.15m to the rear of the drawing vehicle.

3. Trailers more than 9.15m long (excluding the length of the drawbar):
   (a) one lamp within 1530mm of the centre (ie mid-way point) of the trailer length.

For vehicles first used from 1 April 1991 side marker lamps are required if they have a maximum speed exceeding 25mph and are more than 6 metres long. Trailers built since 1 October 1990 must also be fitted with such lamps if they exceed 6 metres overall length. The lamps must be positioned no more than 4 metres from the front and no more than one metre from the rear and at not more than 3 metre intervals in between.

Side marker lamps may show a white light to the front and a red light to the rear on pre-1 October 1990 trailers but on all other vehicles and trailers they must show an amber light (unless fitted within one metre of the rear of the vehicle/trailer when they must be red). They must be positioned not more than 2300mm from the ground.

End-outline marker lamps
Vehicles first used from 1 April 1991 and exceeding 2.1 metres overall width and trailers built from 1 October 1990 and exceeding this width must be fitted with at least two end-outline marker lamps visible from the front (showing white lights) and at least two visible from the rear (showing red lights). Additional such lights may be fitted as required so long as they show only white lights to the front and red lights to the rear. They must be positioned not more than 400mm in from the outer edges of the vehicle/trailer and mounted at the front at least level with the top of the windscreen.

Rear reflectors
Vehicles and trailers must be fitted with two red reflex retro reflectors facing squarely to the rear.

Triangular rear reflectors
Trailers (including articulated semi-trailers, drawbar trailers, small trailers drawn by private cars and dual-purpose vehicles, caravans and boat trailers) *may* be fitted with two red triangular rear reflectors - they are not a mandatory requirement of law. Such reflectors must not be fitted to other vehicles.

Side-facing reflectors
Vehicles more than 8 metres long (6 metres if first used since 1 April 1986) and trailers more than 5m long must be fitted with two or more amber* side-facing reflectors on each side. One must be fitted not more than one metre from the extreme rear end of the vehicle (* this one can be red instead of amber) and the other not more than 4 metres from the front with further reflectors on each side at 3 metre intervals. The reflectors must be mounted between 350mm and 1500mm from the ground.

Vehicle marking
The unladen weight of goods vehicles over three tons unladen must be marked on the nearside of the vehicle where it can be

easily seen. This is not necessary where the vehicle is fitted with a DoT plate showing the *unladen* weight of the vehicle.

Height marking

Goods vehicles and trailers carrying containers constructed mostly of metal and greater than 8 cubic metres capacity (including demountable bodies) and engineering equipment or which itself is engineering plant must have the overall travelling height marked in the cab for the driver to see to within plus or minus 1 inch if such height exceeds 12ft (3.66m). The figures must not be less than 40mm tall.

The overall travelling height is defined as the distance from the ground to the highest point of the vehicle or its load measured when the vehicle is standing on a reasonably flat surface, and is in normal road-going condition (ie with tyres complying with legal requirements, etc).

Plates

A DoT plate must be displayed on goods vehicles over 1525kg unladen (unless the vehicle is exempt from plating and annual testing) after the end of the first anniversary month of the date of their original registration. Other vehicles must be fitted with a manufacturer's plate (see page 157).

Number plates

Motor vehicles must be fitted with registration plates which can be clearly read. On vehicles first registered after 1 January 1973 (except goods vehicles fitted with rear reflective markers - see below) the plates must be made of reflecting material, white at the front and yellow at the rear, with black letters and numerals.

Rear reflective markings

The following goods vehicles and trailers must be fitted with rear reflective markers:

1. Goods vehicles first used before 1 August 1982 which are over 3000kg unladen weight.
2. Goods vehicles first used from 1 August 1982 which are over 7500kg gross weight.
3. Trailers first used before 1 August 1982 which are over 1020kg unladen weight.
4. Trailers first used from 1 August 1982 which are over 3500kg gross weight.

The rear reflective markers are described as follows (see also illustration in colour in the Highway Code):

1. Vehicles not exceeding 13m in length and trailers in combinations not exceeding 11m in length - a single or pair of diagonally striped markers - the long one mounted horizontally or the pair mounted horizontally or vertically.
2. Trailers in combinations between 11m and 13m in length - markers as above or a single or pair of 'long vehicle' markers.

3. Vehicles more than 13m in length and trailers in combination more than 13m in length - a single or pair of 'long vehicle' markers.

Markers must be fitted so that the lower edge is between 400mm and 1700mm from the ground. They must be parallel to the ground and facing square to the rear.

Fleet inspections and roadside checks

DoT authorised examiners (ie of the Vehicle Inspectorate -VI) conduct regular mechanical inspections on vehicles both at roadside checkpoints set up specially for the purpose (where the police are in attendance to stop moving vehicles and often enforcement officers of the VI also check drivers' records – tachographs), and on operator's premises where they have certain legal rights of entry (see below).

These examiners have statutory powers to impose prohibition notices on goods vehicles found to be defective (or overloaded or unsafely loaded) - in the circumstances mentioned above or when a vehicle is presented for its annual test - to prevent them from being driven on roads until the specified defects have been rectified. The prohibition notices take account of the severity of the defects found and may give the operator a specified time in which to carry out the necessary repairs (delayed prohibition) or they may have instant effect (immediate prohibition - plus the prospect of prosecution for an offence under the C&U regulations).

When a prohibition notice has been received, the operator must arrange to effect the repairs and must then submit the vehicle for further inspection by VI examiners (at a goods vehicle test station) who may give a clearance notice, or if the defect has not been satisfactorily rectified, they may issue a further notice (see below).

It is a serious offence to use a goods vehicle on a road contrary to the provisions of a prohibition notice. However, it is permissible to drive the vehicle (unladen) to a testing station, by appointment, for re-examination after repair. It may also be road tested after repair but only within three miles of the repair location.

Prohibition notices

A number of official forms as described below are used by DoT (ie VI) examiners in the process of inspecting vehicles, recording defects and prohibiting the use of those which are defective:

Form GV 3

This form is authorisation for the VI examiners to direct a vehicle to proceed to a specified place to be inspected (normally not more than five miles away).

PGDN 35 (Vehicle Inspection Notice)

Following an inspection of a vehicle, this form may be issued to indicate to the user one or more defects which it is in his interest and the interests of other road users to have rectified at an early date - it is not actually a prohibition.

Form PG 9

When an inspection by a VI examiner reveals defects of a serious nature form PG9 will be issued, specifying the defects and stating the precise time at which the prohibition preventing further use of the vehicle comes into force (which could be the time when the notice is written out - ie immediate effect - or later).

When form PG 9 has been issued, a copy is given to the driver and this must be carried on the vehicle until the prohibition is removed. A further copy of the notice is sent to the vehicle operator (ie the 'O' licence holder) as well.

If the PG 9 has immediate effect, this means that the vehicle cannot be driven or towed away at least until the vehicle has been unloaded (see below).

Form PG 9A

This form (Variation in the Terms of a Prohibition ...) is issued if the VI examiner wishes to vary the terms of a PG 9 notice by either suspending the PG 9 until a future time (eg midnight on the day of issue), altering the time (which is effectively the same thing as suspending the notice as mentioned above) or altering the list of defects shown on the PG 9 notice.

Form PG 9B

A VI examiner may, after issuing a PG 9, exempt the vehicle (Exemption from a Prohibition ...) from the terms of the prohibition and permit its movement on certain conditions, as follows:

1. that the vehicle is unladen
2. that the vehicle proceeds at a speed not in excess of a specified figure
3. that the vehicle does not tow a trailer
4. that the vehicle is towed on a rigid tow-bar
5. that the vehicle is towed on a suspended tow
6. that the vehicle is not used after lighting up time (if it has lighting defects)

7. that the vehicle proceeds only between two specified points.

Form PG 9C

When a vehicle which is subject to a PG 9 notice is presented to a VI examiner for clearance of the defect and the examiner is not satisfied that it is fit for service he may issue form PG 9C (Refusal to Remove a Prohibition ...), which means that the original PG 9 notice remains in force until the defects are satisfactorily rectified.

Form PG 10

If the defects specified in a PG 9 notice have been repaired to the satisfaction of the VI examiner to whom the vehicle is presented for clearance and the examiner is satisfied that the whole vehicle is in a satisfactory condition for use on the road, he will issue a PG 10 notice (Removal of Prohibition...) which removes the prohibition.

Form GV 160

This notice relates to prohibition on the use of overweight vehicles. It effectively requires the driver of the vehicle to take the vehicle to a weighbridge and, if found to be overloaded, reduce the gross weight to legal limits before proceeding on his journey.

NB: It is a defence to a charge of overloading that the vehicle was on its way to the nearest practicable weighbridge or that at the time of loading the weight was within legal limits and was subsequently not more than five per cent heavier despite not having any additions to the load en route.

Appeals against the issue of prohibition notices

There is no appeal against the imposition of a PG 9 prohibition notice but there is a right of appeal against refusal to remove a prohibition after repair.

Powers of police and DoT examiners and certifying officers

The Road Traffic Act 1988 gives authorised examiners (specifically, Department of Transport (VI) examiners, London taxi examiners, authorised police officers and persons appointed for the purpose by a chief officer of police and certifying officers appointed under the Public Passenger Vehicles Act 1981) powers to test and inspect vehicles (and examine vehicle records), on production of their authority, as follows:

1. They can test any motor or trailer on a road to check that legal requirements regarding brakes, silencer, steering, tyres, lights and reflectors, smoke and fumes

are complied with, and may drive the vehicle for this purpose.

2. They can test a vehicle for the same purposes on premises if the owner of the premises consents or has been given at least 48 hours' notice, except where the vehicle has been involved in a notifiable accident, when there is no requirement to give notice. If the notice is given in writing it must be sent by recorded post and the time limit is extended to 72 hours.

3. They may at any time enter and inspect any goods vehicle and goods vehicle records, and may at a reasonable time enter premises on which they believe a goods vehicle or goods vehicle records are kept.

4. They can request a driver of a stationary goods vehicle to take the vehicle to a place for inspection up to five miles away.

5. They can at any reasonable time enter premises where used vehicles are sold, supplied or offered for sale or supply or exposed or kept for sale or supply to ensure that such vehicles can be used on a road without contravening the appropriate regulations. They may drive a vehicle on the road for this purpose.

6. They may enter at any reasonable time premises where vehicles or vehicle parts are sold, supplied, offered for sale or supply, exposed or kept for sale or supply.

7. They may require the person in charge of any vehicle to take it to a weighbridge to be weighed. If the vehicle is more than five miles from the place where the request is made and the vehicle is found not to be overloaded the operator can claim against the highway authority for any loss sustained.

8. When a goods vehicle has been weighed and found to exceed its weight limit and its use on a road would be a risk to public safety, they can prohibit its road use by the issue of form GV160 until the weight is reduced to within the legal limit.

9. If they find that a goods vehicle is unfit or likely to become unfit for service they can prohibit the driving of the vehicle on the road either immediately or from a later date and time by the issue of a prohibition notice (form PG 9 see above).

10. Where a prohibition order has been placed on a vehicle for various reasons, they are empowered to remove the prohibition (by the issue of form PG10 when they consider the vehicle is fit for use.

11. They can ask the driver of a goods vehicle registered in an EU member state, fitted with a tachograph, to

produce the tachograph record of the vehicle when it is used in this country and ask to examine the official calibration plaque in the instrument. They can at any reasonable time enter premises where they believe such a vehicle is to be found or that tachograph records are kept and may inspect the vehicle and records (ie tachograph charts).

Police constables

1. A police constable *in uniform* can stop a moving vehicle on a road ('constable' includes any rank of uniformed police officer). *Note: in GB only a uniformed constable has this power but in Northern Ireland DoE examiners in plain clothes may also stop a moving vehicle*. They can test any motor vehicle or trailer on a road to check that legal requirements regarding brakes, silencer, steering, tyres, lights and reflectors, smoke and fumes are complied with. They may drive the vehicle for this purpose.

2. They can test a vehicle for the same purposes on premises if the owner of the premises consents or has been given at least 48 hours' notice (or 72 hours if given by recorded post) except that consent is not necessary where the vehicle has been involved in a notifiable accident.

   NB: This authority applies to all constables even if not specially authorised under the Road Traffic Act 1988 as mentioned above.

Trading standards officers

Trading standards officers (ie employed by local authorities) can request the driver of a vehicle which is carrying goods that need an official conveyance note (ie ballast which includes sand, gravel, shingle, ashes, clinker, chippings, including coated material, hardcore and aggregates) to take that vehicle to a weighbridge to be weighed. Goods may have to be unloaded if necessary.

Mechanical conditions - vehicle maintenance

An important aspect of vehicle operation is the need for a comprehensive system of preventive maintenance to ensure that vehicles are kept fully serviceable and do not suffer unexpected mechanical problems between regular safety inspections or manufacturer's recommended scheduled services. Also, it is vital to ensure that the mechanical condition of vehicles complies at all times with the C&U regulations so they are both legally sound and safe to operate on the road.

Breakdowns on the road are costly in terms of the use of breakdown services and of lost time plus the annoyance suffered by customers awaiting delivery of their goods.

Further, being found on the road with a legally defective vehicle can result in the issue of a prohibition notice possibly followed by prosecution for contravention of the C&U regulations. This can lead to the vehicle being off the road for a period until repairs are satisfactorily carried out and cleared with the enforcement authorities (the DoT Vehicle Inspectorate), a costly business on its own without the fines which could be imposed when the prosecution is brought to court plus the further risk of penalty to the firm's 'O' licence.

For these reasons every care should be taken when a vehicle is being inspected and serviced to ensure that all visible and potential defects are identified and remedied to reduce the risks described above. It is much cheaper to deal with these items in the workshop (even replacing certain parts prematurely) than to have a failure when the vehicle is perhaps on a motorway many miles from base or for it to be found defective in a roadside check.

Systems of preventive maintenance

Vehicle maintenance operations may be carried out by the owner in his own workshop or he may contract the work out to a garage or repair specialist.

Responsibility for contracting out

In the latter circumstances, the Licensing Authority will expect the vehicle owner, as the 'O' licence holder, to have a proper arrangement with the repairer for regular inspection and repair of his vehicles to an established timetable or schedule of time or mileage. Further, although the repair work may be carried out by a contractor, the vehicle owner or operator (ie the 'user') is still responsible for ensuring that the work is properly carried out and that the vehicles comply fully with the law regarding their mechanical condition. Copies of all documents which relate to the regular inspection and repair of vehicles, including drivers' defect reports and details of action taken in response to drivers reporting defects must be obtained from the repairer.

Safety inspections

It is a requirement (as a condition upon which the 'O' licence is issued) that vehicles and trailers are inspected at regular intervals of time or mileage (some Licensing Authorities prefer a time-based inspection system). These inspections are intended to ensure that they meet all legal requirements and are safe to operate on the road. A written report of the inspection (usually in the form of a pre-printed check list of all relevant components to be inspected) and any defects found should be made and a written record kept of the action taken to rectify any defects found.

Driver defect reporting

It is a further requirement of 'O' licensing (again a condition of the licence) that goods vehicle operators must provide drivers with a means of reporting defects in their vehicles. This is best done by issuing pads of defect reports so that any problem can easily be noted during the day while the driver has it in his mind. Ideally (and preferred by some LAs), if there is nothing wrong with the vehicle, the driver should write 'nil' so that the operator knows there were no defects in that vehicle on that day.

Once a driver has reported a defect, positive action should be taken to have it rectified and a note of the action, when it was taken and by whom, should be made either on the defect report or on another record filed with the defect report.

Regular servicing

Regular manufacturers' recommended services (such as oil changes and other lubrication tasks and regular replacement of certain components - such as diesel fuel injectors) should also be carried out. These may coincide with safety inspections, which will reduce vehicle downtime.

Maintenance records

It is a condition upon which 'O' licences are issued that records of inspections, defects, repairs and other maintenance work on vehicles should be kept for at least 15 months. To comply with this requirement, record systems should ideally consist of the following:

Wall charts: To indicate 'at a glance' when vehicles/trailers are due for safety inspections, service or annual test, etc and, subsequently, when the work was done.

Vehicle history files: To contain all relevant details of the vehicle, ie date of purchase, price, specification, engine/chassis numbers, supplier, body manufacturer, etc. All other records such as those relating to regular inspections, driver defect reports, servicing and repair should be kept in this file.

Safety inspection reports: As described above, these should be completed at regular intervals of time or mileage in accordance with promises made to obtain the 'O' licence. Ideally, the check list used should cover all the items shown in the *HGV Inspection Manual* (available from HMSO).

Driver defect reports: As described above, these are important records which the LAs are very anxious for operators to keep, as promised, when obtaining their 'O' licences. They should be made by drivers in writing, ideally with a 'nil' report when no defects are found, and should be acted upon immediately.

Repair sheets: These are a record of the work carried out to rectify defects identified on safety inspection reports and as reported by drivers' on their defect reports as well as other necessary repairs.

Service records: A record should be kept of manufacturers' recommended services carried out, eg lubrication, adjustments, replacements, etc.

Tyre records: A separate record may be kept of tyres on the vehicle, tyre repairs and changes.

Repair invoices: When work is carried out by outside repair garages a copy of the repair invoice should be kept in the vehicle history file as evidence of maintenance work done, together with a record of the replacement components fitted and the cost. The garage should also provide copies of their safety inspection, servicing and defect repair reports to accompany the invoice - the invoice alone does not satisfy the legal requirement relating to maintenance record keeping (see above).

4. Loading of vehicle and transit of goods

Legislation on safe loading and carriage of goods

The Road Vehicles (Construction & Use) Regulations 1986 state that every motor vehicle and trailer and all parts and accessories of the vehicle and trailer and the weight, distribution, packing and adjustment of the load on the vehicle or trailer shall, at all times, be such that no danger is caused or is likely to be caused to any person in or on the vehicle or trailer or on the road.

Further, the Regulations state that the load carried by a vehicle or trailer shall at all times be so secured or be in such a position that danger or nuisance is not likely to be caused to any person by reason of the load or any part of the load falling or being blown from the vehicle or as a result of movement of the load on the vehicle. The load must be secured by physical restraint if necessary.

It is an offence under these regulations to use a vehicle which is so unsuitable as to cause, or be likely to cause, danger. Further, it is an offence to load a vehicle so that the permitted maximum individual axle or gross vehicle weights are exceeded.

Liability

Both the driver and his employer as 'users' of the vehicle are liable for prosecution in the event of a load or part of a load falling from a vehicle or otherwise causing danger, and for overloading offences. If such an occurrence results in injuries to another road user, claims for compensation could be made against both the driver and the employer. Conviction for offences under these provisions can result in very heavy fines, imposed by the Courts, and to further penalty by the Licensing Authority against the driver's LGV driving entitlement and the vehicle operator's 'O' licence.

Code of Practice - Safety of Loads

The Department of Transport (DoT) Code of Practice 'Safety of Loads on Vehicles' (available from HMSO) explains the legal requirements for the safe loading of vehicles and identifies the problems concerned with the safety of loads on vehicles. It describes methods of load restraint and load distribution and covers the strength requirements of restraint systems and load securing equipment. The Code identifies a variety of particular types of load and shows how such loads should ideally be secured to the vehicle and the restraining equipment which should be used. It mentions the possible hazards connected with carrying certain types of load and lists the precautions to be taken to reduce such hazards.

The basic principle upon which the Code of Practice is based is that the combined strength of the load restraint system must be sufficient (under normal road-going circumstances -not accident situations) to withstand a force: 'not less than the total weight of the load forward and half the weight of the load backwards and sideways'.

Do's and don'ts
The Code lists some advisory do's and don'ts for drivers as follows:

Do's
1. Do make sure your vehicle's load space and the condition of its load platform are suitable for the type and size of the load.
2. Do make use of load anchorage points.
3. Do make sure you have enough lashings and that they are in good condition and strong enough to secure your load.
4. Do tighten up the lashings or other restraining devices.
5. Do make sure that the front of the load is abutted against the headboard, or other fixed restraint.
6. Do use wedges, scotches, etc so that your load cannot move.
7. Do make sure that loose bulk loads cannot fall or be blown off your vehicle.

Don'ts
1. Don't overload your vehicle or its individual axles.
2. Don't load your vehicle too high.
3. Don't use rope hooks to restrain heavy loads.

4. Don't forget that the size, nature and position of your load will affect the handling of your vehicle.
5. Don't forget to check your load:
   (a) before moving off
   (b) after you have travelled a few miles
   (c) if you remove or add items to your load during your journey.
6. Don't take risks.

Carriage of hazardous substances

Strict legislation is applied to the carriage of dangerous (ie hazardous) substances by road. The legislation is grouped under three headings as follows:

1. Packaging and labelling regulations - *The Carriage of Dangerous Goods by Road and Rail (Classification, Packaging and Labelling) Regulations 1994* (commonly referred to as the CDG - CPL regulations).
2. Tanker regulations - *The Dangerous Substances (Conveyance by Road in Road Tankers and Tank Containers) Regulations 1992.*
3. Package regulations - *The Road Traffic (Carriage of Dangerous Substances in Packages etc) Regulations 1992* (commonly referred to as the PGR regulations).

Additionally, there are regulations governing the carriage of explosives by road namely, *The Road Traffic (Carriage of Explosives) Regulations 1989.*

These regulations (and associated Codes of Practice -available from HMSO) are made by the Health and Safety Commission and enforcement is the responsibility, variously, of the police, the Health and Safety Executive and local authorities depending on particular circumstances. Trading standards departments also play a role in this matter as does the Pharmaceutical Society of Great Britain (in regard to packaging and labelling).

The CPC student will be mainly concerned with the tanker regulations and those relating to the carriage of dangerous substances in packages and the carriage of explosives because these are the ones principally applicable to transport operators. The essential elements of the legislation concern vehicle and load marking, the issue and carrying of information in writing, the training and certification of drivers and safety matters. These are described in the following text.

Carriage of dangerous goods in tanks and road tankers

The tanker regulations referred to above apply where dangerous substances identified in the Health and Safety Executive (HSE) 'Approved List' are carried or where any substance which 'by reason of its characteristic properties creates a risk ... comparable with the risk created by substances specified in the approved list'.

The regulations *do not* apply to a vehicle carrying dangerous goods when it is:

1. engaged in international transport under the International Convention for the Conveyance of Goods by Rail (CIM)
2. engaged in international transport under the European Agreement concerning the International Carriage of Dangerous Goods by Road (ADR)
3. under the control of the armed forces of the Crown or of visiting forces
4. exempted from excise duty (VED) under the Vehicles Excise and Registration Act 1994
5. A road construction vehicle (other than a road tanker) used for conveying liquid tar (ie substance identification number 1999 in approved list).

Tanker/tank 'operators'

Operators of road tankers and other vehicles are defined in the regulations along with operators of tank containers, who are the tank owner or his agent or, in the absence of either of these, the operator of the vehicle (ie the 'O' licence holder) on which the container is conveyed. In the case of leased or hired tanks the operator is the person to whom the tank is leased or hired. The significance of the definition of 'operator' is that it is he who is fully responsible for ensuring that the regulations are met.

Tanks/tankers

For the purposes of the regulations a tank container is one which has a cubic capacity exceeding three cubic metres.

A vehicle or tank container must not be used for the conveyance of dangerous goods unless it is properly designed; is of adequate strength and good construction from sound and suitable material; is suitable for the purpose for which it is being used; is designed, constructed and maintained so that the contents cannot escape; and is constructed of material which would not be adversely affected by contact with the substance being carried.

Information

An operator must not convey dangerous substances by road in a road tanker or tank container, unless he has obtained from the consignor information which, first, enables him to comply with the regulations and, second, enables him to be aware of the risks created by the substance to the health and safety of any person. It is the responsibility of the person supplying such information to ensure that it is accurate and sufficiently detailed.

In regard to the supply of information about substances, the requirement is to ensure that the vehicle driver is given information in writing to enable him to know the identity of the substance and the nature of the dangers which may arise with that substance and the emergency action he should take.

The regulations place a duty on drivers to ensure that the written information they are given is kept in the cab of the vehicle and is available at all times while the substance in question is being conveyed on the vehicle. Furthermore, it is an important requirement that written information about substances which are *not* being carried at the time is removed from the vehicle or destroyed or placed in a 'securely closed container clearly marked to show that the information does not relate to a substance then being conveyed'.

Generally, the requirement to provide this written information is met by the use of TREMCARDS. These are pre-printed (usually laminated) pocket-sized 'Transport Emergency Cards' on which details of the substance and the emergency procedures for dealing with it in the event of spillage or leakage are shown.

Safety
Safety measures about observing the precautions for preventing fire and ensuring that tanks are not overfilled are included in the regulations and another safety measure requires vehicles to be parked in a safe place and be supervised at all times by the driver or another competent person (ie trained - particularly in emergency procedures) over 18 years of age. This applies to tankers displaying hazard warning panels on which the emergency action code ends with the letter E. However, it does not apply if the driver can show that the tank is empty or that, if the identification code number 1270 is displayed, no petrol is being conveyed and the tank is empty; or if the number 1268 is displayed that no toluene or petroleum distillate (flash point less than 21°C) is being conveyed and the tank is empty.

Driver training
The vehicle operator must ensure that the driver receives adequate instruction and training to enable him to understand 'the nature of the dangers to which the substance being carried may give rise and the emergency action he should take'. The instruction must also ensure that he fully

understands these regulations. A record of driver instruction and training must be kept and a copy made available to the driver.

Under the Road Traffic (Training of Vehicles Carrying Dangerous Goods) Regulations 1992, drivers must carry, and produce on request, a Vocational Training Certificate relevant to the dangerous goods being carried. Fleet operators are free to provide their own training for drivers in whatever manner they think is appropriate and sufficient to satisfy the regulations (eg by in-house training or by the use of approved courses such as those run under The National (Dangerous Substances) Driver Training Scheme – NDSDTS).

Tanker labelling
The regulations impose requirements for notices (commonly referred to as Hazchem labels) to be displayed on road tankers which are being used to carry prescribed dangerous substances . The relevant substances are specified in the approved list, together with:

1. an internationally recognised substance identification number
2. an emergency action code:
    (a) by numbers 1 to 4 indicating the equipment suitable for fire-fighting (1 = jets, 2 = fog or spray, 3 = foam, 4 = dry agent)
    (b) by letters indicating the appropriate precautions to take (eg Full = fully protective clothing, BA = breathing apparatus, E = evacuate, V = can be violently explosive or reactive, Dilute = may be washed into drains with plenty of water, Contain = must not enter drains or water courses)
    (c) the hazard warning symbol to be used as follows:

□ flammable liquid	□ corrosive substance
□ toxic substance	□ harmful substance
□ non-flammable compressed gas	□ toxic gas
	□ oxidising substance
□ flammable gas	□ other hazardous
□ organic peroxide	substance.

All relevant vehicles must be labelled with 'notices' (ie Hazchem labels), in accordance with the regulations depending on whether a single or multi-load is carried (see illustrations p 190).

For a *single load*, a warning label must contain the following details:

1. Emergency action code for the substance.
2. Substance identification number.
3. Appropriate hazard warning symbol.
4. Telephone number where specialist advice can be obtained plus, if required, the name of the substance and the name of the manufacturer.

For a *multi-load,* a warning label must contain the following details:

1. Appropriate multi-load emergency action code.
2. The word 'multi-load'.
3. The appropriate hazard warning symbol.
4. Telephone number where specialist advice can be obtained plus, if required, the name of the manufacturer.

Additionally, on each tank or each compartment a label must show:

1. The appropriate substance identification number (and the name if desired)
2. The hazard warning sign applicable to the contents of that tank or compartment where this is different from other hazards from any other substance on the vehicle.

The warning label must be orange with black borders, figures and letters, except for the space where the individual hazard warning sign is placed, which is white (an illustration in full colour is to be found in the Highway Code, which also contains the individual hazard warning symbols).

Hazard warning label for full/single load.

Hazard warning label for multi-load.

Carriage of
dangerous
goods by road
in packages

The regulations controlling the carriage of dangerous goods by road in packages, referred to above, apply as follows:

1. When any quantity of self-reactive organic peroxides or flammable solids are conveyed at controlled temperatures or when dangerous substances are carried in small tank containers and tipper lorries.
2. When substances identified as being in United Nations Packing Group 1 (high risk - and other substances of similar risk - ie toxic gases, flammable gases, organic peroxides, asbestos or asbestos waste) are carried in receptacles with a capacity of 5 litres or more.
3. When UN Packing Group 2 (ie medium risk) substances are carried in receptacles with a capacity of 200 litres (ie approx 44 gallons) or more.
4. When notionally empty receptacles (ie having previously carried specified substances) are carried.

The substances covered by the regulations are those included in the 'Approved List' relating to these particular regulations plus any other substances which are not specified in the list but which have similar chemical properties and present similar hazards to those in the list, and mixtures of both types of substance (ie listed and non-listed similar substances).

General requirements
The reader should be aware that in general terms the legal requirements relating to the carriage of dangerous substances in packages duplicate those already described above in relation to the carriage of such substances in road tankers and tank containers. This applies particularly in regard to the need for the supply of relevant information and the use of Tremcards, driver training and the supervision of vehicles.

Driver training
Drivers of vehicles carrying relevant (ie approved list) dangerous substances in packages must have received proper instruction in handling the products carried and training in emergency procedures in the event of accident or dangerous occurrence, as well as instruction about their duties under the regulations; they must also carry Vocational Training Certificates relevant to the dangerous goods being carried. While training by official sources is not required, nevertheless driver employers will have to establish some form of adequate training scheme to cover all the products likely to be encountered by drivers or arrange training with specialist training firms (see also p 196).

Supervision of vehicles

Similar requirements apply for the supervision of vehicles loaded with dangerous substances to those already mentioned for tanker vehicles (see pages 186–91). In particular, if the products carried amount to 3 tonnes or more, the vehicle must be parked in a safe place or must be supervised by the driver at all times or by some other competent person (ie over the age of 18 years).

Information

Vehicle operators have responsibility under the regulations for ensuring that they receive from consignors adequate information about the substances to be carried to enable them to comply with the regulations in giving the driver instruction, in marking vehicles correctly, and in being aware of the risks created by the substances to the health or safety of any person.

Drivers must carry in the vehicle cab written details of the substances on board at the time. The provision of Tremcards will satisfy this requirement (see page 188). Similar provisions to those already described in regard to tanker operations for ensuring that written notices for substances no longer on board the vehicle are removed, destroyed or locked securely away, must be observed. Information carried on vehicles must be given to the police and traffic examiners on request.

Vehicle marking

Vehicles used for carrying dangerous goods in packages must be correctly marked with reflectorised orange-colour plates at both the front and rear. These plates are rectangular and plain orange in colour surrounded by a broad black border. When the vehicle is no longer carrying relevant substances the plates must be removed or covered.

Carriage of explosives by road

The Road Traffic (Carriage of Explosives) Regulations 1989 (SI 615/1989) control the movement of explosives by road. For the purposes of the regulations the term 'explosives' means explosive articles or substances which have been classified under the Classification and Labelling of Explosives Regulations 1983 (SI 1140/1983) as being in Class 1 or those which are unclassified. An 'explosive article' is an article which contains one or more explosive substances and an 'explosive substance' is a solid or liquid substance or a mixture of solid or liquid substances, or both, which is capable by chemical reaction in itself of producing gas at such a temperature and pressure and at such speed as could cause damage to surroundings, or which is designed to produce an effect by heat, light, sound, gas or smoke or a combination of these as a result of non-detonative self-sustaining exothermic chemical reactions.

The term 'carriage' means from the commencement of loading explosives into a vehicle or trailer until they have all been unloaded, whether or not the vehicle is on a road at the time, but it is not applied where explosives are loaded on an unattached trailer or semi-trailer; carriage begins and ends when the trailer is attached to and later is detached from the towing vehicle or when the explosives have been unloaded, whichever is the sooner.

Explosives must not be carried in any vehicle being used to carry passengers for hire or reward except that a passenger in such a vehicle may carry explosives under the following conditions:

1. The substance carried is an explosive listed in Schedule 1 to the regulations (eg certain cartridges, fireworks, distress-type and other signals, certain flares, fuses, igniters, primers and other pyrotechnic articles, gunpowder, smokeless powder or any mixture of them).
2. The total quantity of such explosive carried does not exceed 2kg.
3. The explosives are kept by that person and are kept properly packed.
4. All reasonable precautions are taken by the person to prevent accidents arising from the explosives.

The person carrying the explosives on the vehicle remains totally responsible for them and no responsibility for them is legally attached to the driver or the vehicle operator.

Suitability of vehicles and containers
Any vehicle or freight container used for the carriage of explosives must be 'suitable' to ensure the safety and security of the explosives carried. The operator is responsible for ensuring that the specified maximum quantities of any particular class of explosive carried on a vehicle or in a freight container are not exceeded and that no greater quantity of explosive is carried than that for which the vehicle or container is 'suitable'.

The limits on quantities of explosives permitted to be carried are shown below:

Type of explosives		Maximum quantity
Division	Compatibility Group	
1.1	A	500kg
1.1	B, F, G or I	5 tonnes

Cont...

Cont…

1.1	C, D, E or J	16 tonnes
1.2	Any	16 tonnes
1.3	Any	16 tonnes
Unclassified explosives carried solely in connection with an application for their classification		500kg

---

Marking of vehicles

Vehicles used for the carriage of explosives must be marked at the front and rear with a rectangular reflectorised orange plate with black border. Additionally, a square placard set at an angle of 45 degrees must be displayed on each side of the vehicle container or trailer containing the explosives. The placard must conform to minimum dimensions and have an orange-coloured background with a black border and with a 'bomb blast' pictograph and any figures or letters denoting classification and Compatibility Group shown in black. Certain exemptions apply to the display of markings where the quantities of explosives of particular categories carried are below certain limits.

Markings on vehicles and containers must be clearly visible, be kept clean and free from obstruction and must be completely covered or completely removed when all explosives have been removed from the vehicle or container. Both the vehicle driver and operator are responsible for ensuring these marking provisions are complied with.

Duty to obtain information

Operators must obtain information in writing from consignors of explosives which enable them to comply with the regulations. The consignor's duty is to ensure the information given is both accurate and sufficient to allow the operator to comply.

Information to be given to drivers

The operator must give the driver or the vehicle attendant the following information in writing:

1. The division and Compatibility Group for classified explosives.
2. The net mass (in tonnes or kg) of each type of explosive carried (or the gross mass if the net mass figure is not available).
3. Whether the explosives carried are explosive articles or explosive substances (in the case of Group C,D or G explosives).

4. The name and address of the consignor, the operator of the vehicle and the consignee.
5. Such other information as necessary to enable the driver to know the dangers which may arise and the emergency action to be taken.

This information must be carried on the vehicle at all times during the carriage from the start of the journey and must be shown on request to a police officer or goods vehicle traffic examiner. It must also be shown to a fire brigade officer if required. Information must not be carried on a vehicle when the explosives it refers to are no longer on that vehicle. It must be removed, destroyed or placed in a securely closed container marked to show that the contents do not relate to explosives then being carried. If the necessary information is not available to the driver or vehicle attendant the explosives must not be carried.

Safe and secure carriage
The operator and the driver must take all reasonable steps to prevent accidents and minimise the harmful effects of any accident. They must also prevent unauthorised access to, or removal of, all or part of the load. A competent person must be constantly in attendance with the vehicle whenever the driver is not present except during stops in a safe and secure place and when the vehicle is on a site where adequate security precautions are taken.

The operator and driver of a vehicle used to carry more than 5 tonnes of explosives in Division 1.1 must follow a route agreed with the chief officers of police for each area through which it is to pass.

Procedure in the event of accident
The driver or vehicle attendant must contact the police, fire brigade and vehicle operator as quickly as possible in the event of the following circumstances:

1. Spillage of explosives such as to constitute a safety risk.
2. Damage to the explosives or their packaging such as to constitute a safety risk.
3. If the vehicle overturns.
4. If a fire or explosion takes place on the vehicle.

When such circumstances arise the driver, vehicle attendant and the operator must take all proper precautions to ensure the security of the explosives and the safety of persons likely to be affected and the vehicle operator must immediately notify the Health and Safety Executive.

Duration of carriage and delivery

The operator and the driver are responsible for ensuring that the carriage of explosives is completed within a reasonable period of time having regard to the distance involved, that explosives are unloaded as soon as reasonably practicable on arrival, that the explosives are delivered to the consignee or his agent or to another person who accepts them in custody for onward despatch provided they are delivered to a safe and secure place or a designated parking area in an airport , a railway transhipment depot or siding, a harbour or harbour area. If they cannot be delivered as required they must be returned to the consignor or his agent. If loaded in a trailer the trailer must not be detached except in a safe place or in an emergency.

Training of drivers and attendants

Drivers and vehicle attendants must have received adequate training and instruction to enable them to understand the nature of the dangers which may arise from the carriage of the explosives, the action to be taken in an emergency and their duties under these regulations and under the Health and Safety at Work etc Act 1974.

The operator must keep a record of his own training and instruction if he is a driver or attendant and that given to drivers and attendants in his employment. A copy of the training record must be made available to the employees concerned.

Minimum ages

A minimum age of 18 years applies to those engaged in the carriage of explosives as a driver or vehicle attendant, for being made responsible for the security of explosives or for travelling in a vehicle carrying explosives unless in the presence of and supervised by a competent person over 18 years of age.

Delivery of food in road vehicles

Vehicles used for the delivery of food must be constructed and maintained to keep the food carried clean and fresh. Under the Food Hygiene (Markets, Stalls and Delivery Vehicles) Regulations 1966 the driver of a food vehicle should wear clean overalls and if meat or bacon sides are transported, which the driver has to carry over his shoulder, a hat should be worn to prevent the meat touching his hair. He must not smoke while loading or unloading or serving the food and any cuts or abrasions on hands must be covered with waterproof dressings.

Food vehicles must show the owner's name and address on the nearside and the address at which the vehicle is garaged, if this is different. If a vehicle based in England or Wales has a fleet number clearly shown and is garaged at night on company premises then the garage address is not required to be shown.

A wash-hand basin and a supply of clean water must be provided on vehicles which carry uncovered food (eg mobile shops) except bread, unless the driver can wash his hands at both ends of the journey before handling the food. When meat is carried, soap and clean towels and a nailbrush must be provided on the vehicle.

An authorised officer of a Council may enter and detain any food-carrying vehicles except those owned by British Rail or those operated by haulage contractors.

Waste food vehicles

Vehicles used to collect unprocessed waste food intended as food for livestock and poultry must be drip-proof, covered and enclosed with material capable of being cleansed and disinfected. Vehicles must be thoroughly cleansed and disinfected on the completion of unloading.

Carriage of livestock

The Welfare of Animals during Transport Order 1994, requires livestock hauliers to ensure that animals in transit do not suffer distress or discomfort. Nor must they be loaded or unloaded in a manner likely to cause injury or suffering.

Depending on their species, they must be given food and water both before and during the journey, as well as rest. For most species feeding, watering and rest intervals must not exceed 15 hours. Written instructions on feeding and watering must be given to the person responsible. Animals must be entrusted only to persons who know how to care for them in transit.

Journey plans must be made by the haulier transporting cattle, sheep, goats, pigs and horses if the journey is likely to exceed 15 hours, and in the case of any other animal if it is likely to exceed 24 hours. The journey plan must set out the arrangements for the animals to be rested, fed and watered; to be unloaded and accommodated (only if necessary); and the feeding and watering arrangements should the planned journey change.

The journey plan must accompany the vehicle and be adhered to. Following the journey the person who drew up the plan should certify in writing that it was carried out, or if not, the extent of any material differences and send it to the divisional veterinary officer. Copies of the plan must be kept for six months from the end of the journey and produced on request to an inspector. False certification of journey plans is an offence, as is failure by a driver to comply with a journey plan.

197

Where animals are transported for less than 15 or 24 hours, a journey plan is not required. Instead, an Animal Transport Certificate, signed by the haulier, must accompany the consignment. Certificates must be kept for six months from the end of the journey and produced on request by an inspector. Exceptions apply when cattle, sheep, goats, pigs or horses are transported for 50km or less.

Besides the specific provisions of this order, it is an offence for any person to transport, or permit to be transported, animals for more than 50km, except as follows:

1. Animals must be able to lie down (unless that would cause them harm or injury).
2. Horses must wear halters (except unbroken foals or those in individual boxes).
3. Tethers must be of a type to eliminate injury.
4. Animals must not be tied by a nose ring.
5. Animals of different species must be segregated, except where that would cause distress to a companion animal.
6. Stallions must not be transported in the same vehicle unless they are used to each other, or are effectively separated.
7. Domestic animals (ie horses, cattle, sheep, goats and pigs) must not be suspended by mechanical means, lifted or dragged by the head, horns, legs, tail or fleece.
8. Electric prods must be avoided as far as possible.
9. Vehicle floors must be covered with sufficient litter unless droppings are regularly removed.
10. Animals must be loaded only in to vehicles which have been thoroughly cleaned and, where appropriate, disinfected.
11. Road vehicles must have a weatherproof roof.

Inspectors (ie official veterinary officers) may prohibit unfit animals being carried for a period of time or indefinitely, or may set conditions (with their reasons) under which they may be transported. Animals may be marked for these purposes.

If an inspector finds that animals are suffering unnecessarily during a journey or are being caused injury, he may require them to be returned to their place of departure, specify conditions under which they may be transported, require them to be held in suitable accommodation until the problem is solved or require their humane slaughter. Failure to comply (besides being an offence), may lead the inspector to carry out the necessary action himself, or cause another person to do so (at the haulier's expense).

Carriage of abnormal indivisible loads

The provisions of the Construction and Use Regulations regarding length, width and weight do not apply to vehicles specially designed, constructed and used solely for the carriage of abnormal indivisible loads (these are known as 'Special Types vehicles'). Such vehicles come within the scope of The Motor Vehicles (Authorisation of Special Types) General Order 1979 as amended.

An abnormal load is defined as one which cannot, without undue expense or risk of damage, be divided into two or more loads for a journey by road and which cannot be legally carried by a vehicle complying with the Construction and Use Regulations (ie one having a permissible maximum weight not exceeding 38,000kg and complying with the dimensional limitations and all other requirements for such vehicles).

Certain conditions apply to these vehicles when abnormal indivisible loads are carried. To ensure the safe carriage of large loads, such vehicles (locomotives and trailers) may if necessary be up to a maximum of 6.1m wide (including the width of the load). The overall length of a Special Types vehicle and its load or a combination of vehicles/ trailers and the load must not exceed 27.4m.

Special Types vehicles

Special Types vehicles used for carrying abnormal indivisible loads are divided into three categories according to their total laden weight. Such vehicles must observe varying speed limits. Details of categories, weights and speed limits are as follows:

| | | **Speed Limits** | | |
Category	Laden weight not exceeding	Motorways	Dual carriageways	Other roads
1	46,000kg	60	50	40
2	80,000kg	40	35	30
3	150,000kg	30	25	20

Vehicles operating under this order must display an identification sign at the front with white letters on a black background reading as follows:

STGO	Letters 105mm high
CAT	Letters and figures 70mm high

A figure 1, 2 or 3 must follow the word 'CAT' as appropriate.

Additionally, such vehicles falling in categories 2 and 3 must display 'Special Types Plates' (under the provisions of the Road Vehicles (Marking of Special Weights) Regulations 1983) showing the maximum operational weights recommended by the manufacturer when travelling on a road at varying speeds as follows: 12, 20, 25, 30, 35, 40mph. The weights to be shown are the maximum gross and train weights and weights for each axle. Plates on trailers (including semi-trailers), will show maximum gross weight and the maximum weights for each axle.

Attendants

An attendant must travel on Special Types vehicles where:

1. the vehicle or its load is more that 3.5m wide
2. it is more than 18.3m long (excluding the drawing vehicle), or in combination with other vehicles is more than 25.9m long
3. the load projects more than 1.83m to the front or more than 3.05m to the rear of the vehicle.

If three or more vehicles carrying abnormal loads or other loads of dimensions requiring statutory attendants to be carried travel in convoy, attendants are only necessary on the first and last vehicles in the convoy.

Police notification

The police of every district through which a Special Types vehicle combination is to be moved must be given two clear working days' notice (ie excluding Saturdays, Sundays and Bank holidays):

1. if the vehicle or its load is more than 2.9m wide, or
2. if it is more than 18.3m long (excluding the drawing vehicle), or in combination with other vehicles is more than 25.9m long, or
3. if the load projects more than 3.05m to the front or rear, or
4. if the weight of the vehicle combination and the load is more than 80,000kg.

When notice has been given to the police of the movement of an abnormal load, they have the power to delay the vehicle during its journey if it is holding up other traffic or in the interests of road safety.

Extra wide loads

Application for approval must be made to the Secretary of State for Transport when the width of a vehicle and its load exceeds 5 metres. Form VR1 (movement order) is used for the application and must be carried on the vehicle at all times during the authorised movement.

Notification to
Highway and
Bridge
Authorities

If a vehicle and its load weighs more than 80,000kg or in other ways does not comply with C&U regulations five clear days' notice must be given to the Highway and Bridge Authorities for the areas through which the vehicle is to pass. The operator of such a vehicle is also required to indemnify the Authorities against damage to any road or bridge over which it passes. An appropriate form for this purpose is set out in Schedule 2 to the Special Types General Order.

Two days' notice must be given to these authorities in any case where a vehicle exceeds the overall C&U weight limit (ie 38,000kg) or a maximum axle weight.

A Special Types vehicle must not knowingly be driven onto a bridge at the same time as any other such vehicle or parked on a bridge (apart from in circumstances outside the driver's control). If such a vehicle, weighing more than 38,000kg, has to stop on a bridge for any reason it must be moved off as soon as possible. If it has broken down, the advice of the Bridge Authority (usually the Highways department of the local authority) must be sought before the vehicle is jacked up on the bridge.

Part 5: Road Safety

1. Drivers' hours and records

Drivers' hours regulations

Goods vehicle drivers in Great Britain are restricted in the number of hours they may drive and work and must observe minimum requirements relating to breaks during the driving day and rest periods between working days and weeks. These requirements are specified in EU Regulation 3820/85 on drivers' hours and the Transport Act 1968 (as amended). The rules that apply in particular circumstances are as follows:

1. International driving (ie journeys within the EU) – EU hours' rules apply.
2. National driving (ie journeys exclusively within UK) – EU hours' rules apply.
3. Domestic driving (ie exempt from EU provisions) – 1968 Transport Act rules apply.
4. Mixed driving (ie a combination of any two or three driving categories mentioned above in the same week) – a set of mixed rules apply.
5. International journeys outside the EU – AETR rules apply (see text for module D/1).

Exemptions to EU rules

Certain vehicles and specialised transport operations as listed below are specifically exempt from the EU rules. However, it should be noted that exemption from these rules does not mean total exemption; the British Domestic rules may apply instead (see page 207). Also, there is no exemption for short period or short distance driving operations. If the EU rules apply, because there is no exemption, then they must be followed from the moment a vehicle is driven on the road.

NB: Examination candidates should note that while it is not necessary to learn this list of exemptions 'parrot fashion', it is important for them to have a sound understanding of the type of operation that is exempt and that which is not.

Exemptions in international transport operations
1. Vehicles not exceeding 3.5 tonnes maximum permissible weight including the weight of any trailer drawn.
2. Passenger vehicles constructed to carry not more than nine persons including the driver.

3. Vehicles on regular passenger services on routes not exceeding 50 kilometres.
4. Vehicles with legal maximum speed not exceeding 30kph (approximately 8.6mph).
5. Vehicles used by armed services, civil defence, fire services, forces responsible for maintaining public order (ie police).
6. Vehicles used in connection with sewerage; flood protection; water, gas and electricity services; refuse collection and disposal; highway maintenance and control; telephone and telegraph services; carriage of postal articles; radio and television broadcasting; detection of radio or television transmitters or receivers.
7. Vehicles used in emergencies or rescue operations.
8. Specialised vehicles used for medical purposes.
9. Vehicles transporting circus and funfair equipment.
10. Specialised breakdown vehicles.
11. Vehicles undergoing road tests for technical development, repair or maintenance purposes, and new or rebuilt vehicles which have not yet been put into service.
12. Vehicles used for non-commercial carriage of goods for personal use (ie private use).
13. Vehicles used for milk collection from farms and the return to farms of milk containers or milk products intended for animal feed.

Exemptions in national transport operations
1. Passenger vehicles constructed to carry not more than 17 persons including the driver.
2. Vehicles used by public authorities on or after 1 January 1990 to provide public services which are not in competition with professional road hauliers. This exemption applies only if the vehicle is being used by:
   (a) a health authority in England and Wales or a health board in Scotland;
      i)   to provide ambulance services in pursuance of its duty under the NHS Acts
      ii) to carry staff, patients, medical supplies or equipment in pursuance of its general duties under the Acts
   (b) a local authority to fulfil social services functions, such as services for old persons or for physically and mentally handicapped persons
   (c) HM Coastguard or lighthouse authorities
   (d) harbour authorities within harbour limits
   (e) airports authorities within airport perimeters

    (f)   British Rail, London Regional Transport, a Passenger Transport Executive or local authority for maintaining railways

    (g) British Waterways Board for maintaining navigable waterways.

3. Vehicles used by agricultural, horticultural, forestry or fishery undertakings* for carrying goods within 50 kilometres radius of the place where the vehicle is normally based including local administrative areas, the centres of which are situated within that radius.

To gain the exemption the vehicle must be used to carry live fish or to carry a catch of fish which has not been subjected to any process or treatment (other than freezing) from the place of landing or to a place where it is to be processed or treated.

4. Vehicles used for carrying animal waste or carcasses not intended for human consumption.

5. Vehicles used for carrying live animals from farms to local markets and vice versa or from markets to local slaughterhouses.

6. Vehicles specially fitted for and used:
- as shops at local markets and for door-to-door selling
- for mobile banking, exchange or savings transactions
- for worship
- for the lending of books, records or cassettes
- for cultural events or exhibitions.

7. Vehicles not exceeding 7.5 tonnes maximum permissible weight carrying materials or equipment for the driver's use in the course of his work within 50 kilometres radius of base, providing the driving does not constitute the driver's main activity and does not prejudice the objectives of the regulations.

8. Vehicles operating exclusively on islands not exceeding 2300 sq km not linked to the mainland by bridge, ford or tunnel for use by motor vehicles.

9. Vehicles not exceeding 7.5 tonnes maximum permissible weight used for the carriage of goods propelled by gas produced on the vehicle or by electricity.

10. Vehicles used for driving instruction (but not if carrying goods for hire or reward).

11. Tractors used after 1 January 1990 exclusively for agriculture and forestry work.

12. Vehicles used by the RNLI for hauling lifeboats.

13. Vehicles manufactured before 1 January 1947.

14. Steam propelled vehicles.

EU rules covering national and international transport operations

EU Regulation 3820/85 (effective from 29 September 1986) applies to drivers of relevant (ie non-exempt) vehicles on both national and international transport journeys within the EU. The provisions of the regulations are as follows:

Maximum daily driving	9 hours – which may be increased to 10 hours on two days in a week
Maximum driving before break	4½ hours in aggregate
Breaks	45 minutes after 4½ hours' driving or other breaks of at least 15 minutes each spread throughout the driving period to equal 45 minutes minimum
Minimum daily rest	11 hours (normally)
Reduced daily rest	Daily rest may be reduced to 9 hours on three occasions in a week (reduced time to be made up by end of next following week)
Split daily rest	Daily rest taken in 2 or 3 periods; – one minimum 8 hours – other periods minimum 1 hour each – total rest 12 hours in 24 hours
Interrupted daily rest (ie on ferries and trains)	Daily rest may be interrupted provided – part of rest taken in terminal and part on board ferry or train – not more than 1 hour between parts – driver to have access to bunk/couchette for both parts of rest – total rest period in a day to be increased by 2 hours
Maximum weekly driving	6 driving shifts in a week
Maximum driving in two weeks	90 hours
Minimum weekly rest	45 hours (normally)
Reduced weekly rest	Weekly rest may be reduced to – 36 hours when vehicle/driver at base – 24 hours when taken elsewhere – reduced time to be made up *en bloc* by the end of the third following week

Double-manned vehicles

When a vehicle is double-manned each driver must have had 8 hours of continuous rest in each period of 30 hours. One driver must not be taking his *rest* period while the vehicle is being driven by the other (see point below about rest) but he may take a *break* .

Day/week
For the purposes of these regulations a 'day' is any period of 24 hours (ie rolling period) and a 'week' is a fixed week starting at 00.00 hours Monday to 24.00 hours (midnight) on the following Sunday.

Breaks
Where a break period is due after 4½ hours' driving the driver may forgo this if immediately following the driving period he commences a daily or weekly rest period. At no time during the driving day must 4½ hours be exceeded without a full 45 minutes break having been taken. This is critical when drivers take a number of 15 or 30 minute breaks rather than a full 45 minutes. If total daily driving does not amount to 4½ hours then no break is required by law. During break periods the driver must not carry out 'other work' but waiting time and time spent riding passenger in a moving vehicle or time spent on a ferry ship or train is not counted as 'other work'. Breaks must not be counted as part of daily rest periods.

Rest periods
A daily rest period must be taken once in each 24 hours. Weekly rest must be taken after 6 daily driving periods or may be postponed until the end of the sixth day so long as the weekly driving limit is not exceeded. Weekly rest commenced in one fixed week and continuing into the next may be attached to either week.

During rest periods the driver must be 'free to dispose of his time as he wishes'. The driver may take his rest period in a vehicle so long as it is fitted with a bunk and is stationary for the whole of the time.

Made-up rest
Made-up (ie compensated) rest must be attached to other rest periods of at least 8 hours duration. Made-up *daily* rest can be split when adding to other daily or weekly rest periods (eg if 4 hours to be made up from previous week this could be taken as 2+2 or 3+1) but when making up for reduced *weekly* rest periods the time must be added *en bloc* to other daily or weekly rest periods. Compensated rest must be taken at the place chosen by the driver (ie at home or away), not as dictated by the employer.

Emergencies
Under the EU regulations there is an exemption from the need to follow the stated requirements in emergency situations. In such circumstances, drivers may depart from the rules to the extent necessary to enable a suitable stopping place to be reached when emergencies arise where the driver needs to ensure the safety of persons, the vehicle or its load providing

road safety is not jeopardised. The nature of the emergency and the reasons for departing from the rules should be shown on the tachograph chart.

Prohibition on payments

It is prohibited under the EU rules to make any payment to wage-earning drivers in the form of bonus or wage supplement related to distances travelled and/or the amount of goods carried unless the payments are such that road safety is not endangered.

Employers' responsibilities

Employers have a duty under the regulations to organise drivers' work in such a way that the hours' law is not broken. They must also make regular checks to ensure the regulations are complied with and take appropriate steps to prevent any repetition if the law is found to have been broken.

British rules applicable to domestic driving

Drivers of vehicles not exceeding 3.5 tonnes maximum permissible weight (including the weight of any trailer drawn) and of other vehicles which are exempt from the EU regulations (see list above) must follow the British Domestic drivers' hours rules set out in the Transport Act 1968 as amended unless they are exempt as shown below.

Exemptions

Total exemption from the rules (ie the daily driving and duty limits) is given to the following:

1. Drivers of vehicles used by the armed forces, the police and fire brigades.
2. Drivers who always drive off the public highway.
3. Private driving not in connection with any trade or business or with any employment.
4. When the driving does not amount to more than 4 hours on each day of the week.

Driving and duty limits under British Domestic rules

(a) Maximum daily driving   10 hours
(b) Maximum daily duty   11 hours

Driving and duty

For the purposes of these regulations, driving means time spent behind the wheel actually driving and the limit applies to such time spent driving on public roads. Driving on off-road sites and premises such as quarries, civil engineering and building sites and on agricultural and forestry land is counted as duty time not driving time. The daily duty limit does not apply on any day when a driver does not drive.

Special Note: Readers should note that under the Domestic rules there are no limits on continuous duty, weekly duty or on daily spreadover times. There are also no break period and no daily or weekly rest period requirements.

Light vehicle driving

Drivers of light goods vehicles not exceeding 3.5 tonnes maximum permissible weight (including the weight of any trailer drawn) must conform to the British Domestic limits stated above (although there are no record-keeping requirements – see below – so the enforcement authorities have no sure means of verifying whether the limits are observed) but where such vehicles are driven in connection with the following activities only the 10 hour maximum daily driving limit need be observed:

1. by doctors, dentists, nurses, midwives or vets
2. for any service of inspection, cleaning, maintenance, repair, installation or fitting
3. by a commercial traveller and carrying only goods used for soliciting orders
4. by an employee of the AA, RAC or the RSAC
5. for the business of cinematography or of radio or television broadcasting.

Emergencies

Daily driving and duty limits may be suspended when an emergency situation arises. This is defined as an event requiring immediate action to avoid danger to life or health of one or more individuals or animals, serious interruption in the maintenance of essential public services, for the supply of gas, water, electricity, drainage, or of telecommunications and postal services, or in the use of roads, railways, ports or airports, or damage to property. Details of the emergency should be entered in the record sheet when the rules are exceeded.

Postal vehicles

Special requirements apply to postal vehicles which carry parcels traffic and which are over 3.5 tonnes maximum permissible weight. Drivers of such vehicles must comply with the British Domestic driving hours rules on daily driving and duty limits although their vehicles are required to be fitted with tachographs under the EU rules.

Mixed driving

In certain circumstances a driver may, in a day or a week, drive vehicles or be engaged in operations which come within the scope of both the EU rules and the British Domestic hours' rules. When this arises he may chose to conform strictly to the EU rules or alternatively take advantage of the more liberal Domestic rules. If he decides on the latter and combines the two sets of rules he must watch the following points:

1. Time spent driving under the EU rules cannot count as an off-duty period for the Domestic rules.
2. Time spent driving or on duty under the Domestic rules cannot count as a break or rest period under the EU rules.

3. Driving under the EU rules counts towards the driving and duty limits for the Domestic rules.
4. If any EU rules' driving is done in a week the driver must observe the EU daily and weekly rest period requirements for that day and that week.

Penalties for drivers' hours offences

Drivers who are found to be in breach of any of the various hours' rules provisions (ie EU or British) are liable to face prosecution and heavy fines on conviction in Britain. On the continent such breaches may incur heavy on-the-spot fines which must be paid immediately otherwise the vehicle may be impounded and the driver held until the fine is paid. The employer is also likely to face prosecution for failing to cause the driver to observe the law and heavy fines on conviction. Also, convictions for such offences may result in penalty against the driver's LGV driving entitlement and the employer's goods vehicle 'O' licence.

Hours of work records
Vehicles covered

Official records of hours worked, driving time, rest and break periods must be kept by drivers of all goods vehicles except the following, who are exempt:

1. Drivers of goods vehicles not exceeding 3.5 tonnes gross weight.
2. Drivers who, on a working day, do not drive a vehicle to which the driving hours' regulations apply.
3. Drivers engaged on domestic work who, on any day, do not drive for more than four hours *and* who do not travel outside a 50 kilometre radius of the vehicle operating centre.

Type of record

Drivers engaged in Domestic transport operations, must keep written records in a simplified record book issued by the employer. Drivers engaged in national and international transport operations within the scope of the EU rules (ie EU regulations 3820/85 and 3821/85) must keep records by means of a tachograph.

Record keeping under the British Domestic rules

Where the driver has only one employer, that employer must issue him with a record book. Where the driver has two employers, it is the first employer who must issue the book. In this case, each employer must make available to the other details of the driver's working and rest times.

When a record book is issued the employer must:

1. complete the details on the front of the book;
   - the company name
   - address
   - telephone number
   - operator's licence number.

2. give the driver instructions about the use of the book (instructions for use are printed in the book).

On receipt of a record book the driver must:

1. write his name (surname and first name(s)) on the cover
2. fill in his address
3. record the date when the book was first used.

When the book is completed, the driver must write the date of the last sheet on the cover and then return the book to his employer after retaining it for 14 days for inspection by an authorised examiner if required.

There is space on the front cover of the record book for the name, address and telephone number of any other employer of the driver to be entered (where employers have an official stamp this can be used in the space provided).

Method of completion
A new record sheet must be used for each week covering the period from 00.00 hours Monday to 24.00 hours on the following Sunday. A duplicate record must be made by means of 'carbon paper or otherwise' and entries in the record must be made in ink or with a ball-point pen. The driver must enter his name in box 1 and the dates when the week commences and ends in box 2 at the top of the weekly sheet. He must then complete the following information on the sheet (in boxes 3–9) for each day on which he drives making the entries at the beginning and end of the day as appropriate:

1. Registration number of vehicle(s)
2. Place where vehicle(s) are based
3. Time of going on duty
4. Time of going off duty
5. Time spent driving
6. Time spent on duty
7. Signature of driver.

When the week's sheet has been completed, the driver must return the book to the employer who issued it within seven days to enable the employer to examine and sign the records. The employer signs in box 10 to the effect that he has examined the entries, adds his signature (to both top copy and the duplicate) and the position he holds (eg Transport Manager). He must detach the duplicate sheet and return the book to the driver 'before he is next on duty'.

Owner-drivers
Owner-drivers (provided they are operating under the British Domestic rules – and there are not many of them) should complete the details on the front cover of the book putting their business address in section four where employers enter their

information and this is the address where their duplicate record sheets should be returned after completion. They should complete the record sheets in the same way as employed drivers. On completion, record books should be retained by owner-drivers for 12 months counting from the date when the book was completed or ceased to be used.

Signatures Weekly record sheets must be signed by the driver against each day's entry and later by the employer after they have been checked.

Examination of records The employer must collect the duplicates of used weekly record sheets from drivers within seven days of completion, check them for accuracy, sign them, and retain them for inspection for 12 months counting from the date when the sheets were returned by the driver. Used record books must also be retained for the same period.

Police constables and other authorised Department of Transport officials may request a driver to produce a current weekly record sheet and record sheets for the previous two weeks for inspection.

Delays In the event of exceptional delay during a journey caused by unforeseen circumstances, a driver should enter full details on the record sheet for future reference. Despite delays, the driver is still bound by the driving and working hours' regulations unless the reason comes within the category of 'emergency'.

Summary of employers' obligations Employers must issue their drivers with record books, enter appropriate details on the front cover of the book, collect, check and sign completed duplicate weekly sheets and collect completed books 14 days after the date of the last entry.

All records must be retained, available for inspection, for 12 months counting from the date when they were returned by the driver.

Employers must give their drivers specific instructions as to the use of record books and the hours of work and rest periods.

A record book, issued to a driver who subsequently leaves the employer's service, or who no longer has any use for it, may be re-issued to another driver if it contains a supply of unused sheets.

If discrepancies or false entries are found by an employer on a driver's record sheet a written notice and a warning should be given to the driver in advance of any disciplinary proceedings.

Record-keeping offences It is an offence for a driver to fail to keep records and for an employer to fail to cause a driver to keep records. The employer can avoid conviction if he can show to the Court that

211

he took all reasonable steps to ensure that the driver did keep proper records. On conviction for such offences heavy fines may be imposed and both the driver's LGV driving entitlement and the employer's 'O' licence are put in jeopardy.

Record
keeping by
tachograph

Drivers of vehicles operating within scope of the EU drivers' hours rules must keep records of their driving times, breaks and rest periods by means of a tachograph under the provisions of EU Regulation 3821/85.

Vehicles
covered

Tachographs must be fitted to all vehicles used for the carriage of goods by road and registered in member states except those vehicles exempt from the EU driving hours' law specified in Regulation 3820/85 (see page 202).

Types of
tachograph

The tachographs referred to in these regulations are those which meet the detailed specifications laid down in the EU regulations and no other type.

Installation and
inspection

Tachographs must be fitted and repaired only by fitters or workshops approved by the official authority in each member state. In Britain this authority is the Department of Transport which requires tachograph centres to be quality approved to BS 5750 standard.

On inspection (calibration) by an approved fitter or workshop, a plaque must be fixed to the vehicle and the instrument must be sealed and specially marked. Details of these markings must be recorded and given, together with a list of approved fitters and workshops, to other member states.

When presented for calibration, vehicles must be in normal road-going trim complete with body and fixtures. They must be unladen and the tyres must be inflated to manufacturers' recommended pressures.

Calibration and
sealing

Tachographs are calibrated and sealed to firstly ensure the accuracy of the recordings on the charts in respect of the vehicle in which the instrument is fitted, and secondly, so that any tampering with the instrument to give false readings can be readily detected.

Permitted
tolerances

The EU regulations specify permitted limits of accuracy for tachograph equipment as follows:

	During Bench Tests	On Installation	In Use
1. Speed	±3 kph	±4 kph	±6 kph
2. Distance	±1 per cent	±2 per cent	±4 per cent
3. Time	±2 minutes per day or ±10 minutes per seven days		

These tolerances are based on real speed and real distance of at least one kilometre.

Breakage of seals

The regulations are specific about where seals must be located and which ones may be broken in an emergency.

Seals must be fitted at:

1. the installation plaque
2. the two ends of the link between the recording equipment and the vehicle
3. the adaptor and its point of insertion into the circuit
4. the switch mechanism on vehicles with two or more rear axle ratios
5. the links joining the adaptor and switch mechanism to the rest of the equipment
6. the instrument casing to protect its internal parts from tampering.

Only the seals at points 2, 3 and 5 may be broken in an emergency and a written record of the reason for breakage should be made.

Tachograph checks and recalibration

Vehicles must be submitted to a DoT approved tachograph centre for a statutory tachograph 'check' or 'inspection' every *two years* and a full recalibration every *six years* unless these have been carried out following repair or re-sealing in the interim. The two-year and six-year periods count from the previous 'check' or 'calibration' date.

Use of equipment

Both the employer and the driver are responsible for ensuring that a tachograph functions properly and that the seals remain intact. The seals may be broken only in a case of absolute necessity, which must be proved (see above).

The employer is responsible for issuing drivers with tachograph charts – called record sheets in law. These must be of a type which are 'type approved' for the particular make/model of instrument in use. It is an offence to use charts which are not type approved for a particular instrument.

A sufficient number of sheets (charts) must be issued by the employer and when they are returned to him (no later than 21 days after use) they must be retained for one year and produced at the request of any authorised inspecting officer.

Drivers must not use dirty or damaged charts, but if one chart becomes damaged it must be attached to the sheet/chart which replaces it.

Time

The driver must ensure that the time recorded on the sheet agrees with the official time in the vehicle's country of registration (ie tachographs fitted in British registered vehicles operating in Europe where the time difference applies should show British time, not the local European time).

Use of mode switch

Drivers must operate the mode switch on the tachograph to indicate the activity in which they are engaged while recordings are being made, as follows:

Activity	Symbol
Driving	
Break/rest period	
Active work (not used officially in UK)	
Passive work (attendance at work in the UK)	

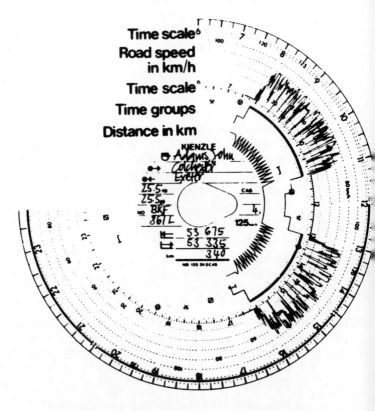

Time scale[6]
Road speed in km/h
Time scale[6]
Time groups
Distance in km

A typical tachograph chart showing recording areas

Continuous records

The tachograph must be kept running continuously from the time the driver takes over the vehicle until finishing the day's work with the vehicle. A continuous record for a 24-hour period must be made and, while drivers are away from the vehicle, their activity must still be recorded either automatically or manually.

Entries on charts

Drivers must enter the following information on the chart:

1. Their surname and first name
2. The date and place when use of the chart begins and ends
3. The registration number of each vehicle driven
4. The distance recorder (odometer) reading:
   (a) at the start of the first journey on the chart
   (b) at the end of the last journey recorded on the chart
   (c) in respect of any other vehicles driven
5. The time of any change of vehicle.

Production of charts

Drivers must be able to produce to an authorised inspecting officer on request a chart or charts giving full details of all relevant periods (eg driving times, other work, breaks and rest periods) for not less than the current week and the last day of the previous week in which they drove (but not going back more than 21 days).

Drivers must return used charts to their employer no later than 21 days after use.

Breakdowns

If the tachograph breaks down it must be repaired by an approved fitter or at an approved workshop as soon as reasonably practicable. If the vehicle does not return to base within one week (seven consecutive days), the necessary repairs must be carried out *en route* at an authorised tachograph repair and calibration station (ie by the seventh day).

While the tachograph is broken, drivers must manually enter details of their driving times, other work, breaks and rest periods on the charts.

Retention of charts

Charts must be retained by employers for a minimum of one year after use and be made available for inspection by authorised examiners. Police and authorised examiners may enter premises at any reasonable time to examine tachograph charts.

The instrument

A tachograph is a speedometer with mechanical or electronic drive incorporating an integral electric clock and a chart recording mechanism. It is fitted on the vehicle dashboard. The instrument indicates and records time, speed and distance. In particular the recordings on charts show the following information:

1. The speed at which the vehicle was driven.
2. The total distance travelled, the distance between stops and other intermediate distances.
3. The number of hours of driving time and the time taken to drive between intermediate points.

4. The number of hours of standing time in total and during the working day.
5. Whether driving was steady and economical or fast and erratic and consequently wasteful in fuel and in wear and tear on the vehicle
6. Whether a continuous record was made or if there are unexplained gaps in the recording.

Recordings

Recordings are made inside the instrument by three styli on special circular charts, each chart covering a period of 24 hours. One stylus records distance, another records speed and the third records driver activity in the time mode. The styli press through a wax recording layer on the chart, revealing the carbonated layer between the surface and the backing paper.

Charts are pre-marked with time, distance (in kilometres) and speed (in kph) reference radials and when the styli have marked the chart these factors can be easily identified and interpreted.

Movement of the vehicle creates an easily identifiable broad running line on the chart, recording accurately (normally readable to within about one minute) when the vehicle started running and when it stopped. After the vehicle has stopped, the clock stylus continues to mark the chart but with an easily distinguishable thinner black line. The speed trace gives an accurate recording of the speeds attained at all times throughout the journey. The distance recording is made between five radials on the chart, each upward and each downward stroke representing five kilometres travelled. After every five kilometres, the stylus reverses direction to form a 'V' for every ten kilometres travelled. To calculate the total distance covered, the 'V's are counted and multiplied by ten and odd tail-ends of the trace are added in.

NB: Examination candidates should take the opportunity to examine a number of tachograph charts to ensure they are fully familiar with the recording areas printed on them and the actual recordings made by the instrument.

Second-man recording

When a second chart is located in the rear position of a two-man tachograph, only a time recording of the second man's activities (ie other work, break or rest) is shown. Traces showing driving, vehicle speed or distance cannot be recorded on this chart.

Interference with recordings

Precautions against interference with the readings are incorporated in the instrument. It is opened with a key and a security mark is made on the chart every time the instrument is opened. When checking the chart it can be easily established at what time the instrument was opened and thus whether this was by an authorised person or not. Interference with the recording mechanism to give false readings, particularly of speed, can be determined quite simply by an experienced chart analyst.

Faults

Tachographs are generally robust instruments, but listed below are some of the faults which may occur:

1.   Failure of the cable drive at the vehicle gearbox
2.   Failure of the cable drive at the tachograph head
3.   Failure of the adaptor/corrector/triplex gearbox
4.   Cable breaking or seizure
5.   Electrical fault affecting lights in the instrument or the clock
6.   Incorrect time showing on the 24-hour clock (eg day-shift work becomes shown against night hours on the charts)
7.   Failure of the internal workings of the tachograph head
8.   Damage to the recording styli
9.   Failure of the distance recorder
10.   Damage to charts because of incorrect insertion.

Fiddles

A key feature of tachograph recordings is that careful observation will show results of the majority of faults in recordings as well as fiddles and attempts at falsification of recordings by drivers. The main faults likely to be encountered will show as follows:

1.   Clock stops – recordings continue in a single vertical line until the styli penetrate the chart
2.   Styli jam/seize up – recordings continue around the chart with no vertical movement
3.   Cable or electronic drive failure – chart continues to rotate and speed and distance styli continue to record on base line and where last positioned respectively. Time group recordings can still be made but no driving trace will appear.

Attempts at falsification will appear as follows:

1.   Opening the instrument face will result in a gap in recordings.
2.   Winding the clock backwards or forwards will leave either a gap in the recording or an overlap. In either case the distance recording will not match up if the vehicle is moved.
3.   Stopping the clock will stop the rotation of the chart so all speed and distance recordings will be on one vertical line (see item 1 above about how faults in instruments show on charts).

4. Restricting the speed stylus to give indications of lower than actual speed will result in flat-topped speed recordings while bending the stylus down to achieve the same effect will result in recordings below the speed base line when the vehicle is stationary.
5. Written or marked-in recordings with pens or sharp pointed objects are readily identifiable by even a relatively unskilled chart analyst.

Chart reading and checking

Employers have a responsibility under EU regulations (EU 3820/85) for 'periodically' checking tachograph charts to ensure that drivers have observed the regulations, have complied with statutory limits on driving time and such like and have been notified when the law has been breached. The regulations require employers to 'take appropriate action to prevent any repetition of such breaches' in these circumstances.

The principal items to be checked are:

1. that the chart has been properly produced
2. the driving time, indicated by a broad band
3. break and rest periods between driving periods
4. periods of other work
5. distances travelled, measured by reference to a series of radials set to indicate five kilometres for each full stroke.

To enable drivers to keep track of their times employers must give them, on request, a copy of their daily tachograph charts.

Chart analysis

Detailed analysis of the information on the tachograph charts provides valuable data for increasing the efficiency of the vehicle operation and for establishing productivity payment schemes for drivers. Tachograph manufacturers can supply accessories to enable detailed chart analysis to be carried out. For example, a simple chart analyser magnifies the used chart to the extent that detailed analysis, beyond the scope of a normal visual examination, can be made of the vehicle's minute-by-minute and kilometre-by-kilometre progress.

Analysis of charts by means of electron microscope allows for highly detailed evaluation of vehicle progress in accident situations. This is a specialised facility which cannot normally be undertaken by operators themselves or even on their premises.

2. Driving licences

Unified driver licensing

Radical changes to the long-established UK driving licence scheme have been introduced since 1990 to bring Britain into line with European Union requirements for harmonised driving licence categories plus common standards of competence and fitness to drive. EU-style licences have been issued for car and motorcycle drivers since 1 June 1990 and since 1 April 1991 vocational entitlements (ie LGV and PCV) have been added to the 'unified' licence

For these purposes:

1. vehicles are categorised in accordance with the EU standards (ie with main ategories identified as A, B, C, D and E plus sub-categories and combination categories as necessary);
2. the issuing authority for unified licences is now the Secretary of State for transport (via the DVLA at Swansea) replacing the previous functions of the licensing Authorities/Traffic Commissioners in respect of LGV/PCV driver licensing issues and administration;
3. goods vehicle driving entitlements apply to vehicles above 3.5 tonnes permissible maximum weight;
4. initial 'large goods vehicle' (ie LGV) driving medical status applies up to age 45 years after which a further medical examination is required at 5-yearly intervals;
5. new LGV driver testing arrangements have been introduced with minimum weights specified for goods vehicles used for tests;
6. HGV 'L' plates will eventually be replaced by ordinary 'L' plates.

Under the regulations, goods vehicles have been reclassified and the requirement for vocational licences for driving heavy goods vehicles (HGVs) exceeding 7.5 tonnes permissible maximum weight has been replaced by a need to hold a vocational entitlement to drive large goods vehicles (LGVs) exceeding 7.5 tonnes permissible maximum weight (subject to certain exemptions). Later, under a *second* EU Directive (from 1 July 1996), the vocational qualification will apply to vehicles exceeding 3.5 tonnes permissible maximum weight.

The specific definitions of goods vehicles for the purposes of the new scheme are as follows:

Large goods vehicles (LGVs) are:

1. Articulated goods vehicles
2. Motor vehicles (not being articulated vehicles) constructed or adapted to carry or haul goods and the permissible maximum weight of which exceeds 7.5 tonnes.

Age limits   No person may drive a heavy goods vehicle (large goods vehicle) of any class on a road unless they are at least 21 years of age. The various age limits for driving goods vehicles are shown below:

Minimum age	Maximum weight of vehicle which may be driven
17 years	not exceeding 3.5 tonnes (ie small goods vehicle)
18 years	not exceeding 7.5 tonnes (ie medium goods vehicle)
21 years	exceeding 7.5 tonnes (ie large goods vehicle)

Unified driving licences cover all vehicles and for this purpose they are categorised as follows:

New EU vehicle categories (ie all vehicles)

Category	Vehicle type	Other categories covered
A	Motorcycle (with or without sidecar) – excluding vehicles in categories K, P.	B1, P
B	Motor vehicle not exceeding 3.5 tonnes mass and not more than eight seats (excluding driver's), not included in any other category (including drawing trailer not exceeding 750kg mass).	B+E, B1, C1, C1+E, D1, D1+E, F, K, L, N, P
B1	Motor-tricycle not exceeding 500kg ulw and maximum speed exceeding 50mph.	K, L, P
C	Goods vehicle exceeding 3.5 tonnes mass (including drawing a single-axle trailer not exceeding 5,000kg mass, or any other trailer not over 750kg mass, but excluding a vehicle in category C).	—
C1	Goods vehicles exceeding 3.5 tonnes but not exceeding 7.5 tonnes mass (including drawing trailer not exceeding 750kg mass).	B, B+E, B1, C1+E, D1, D1+E, F, K, L, N, P
D	Passenger vehicles with more than eight seats (excluding driver's seat) including drawing a single-axle trailer not exceeding 5,000kg mass or any other trailer not over 750kg mass.	—
D1	Passenger vehicle (not used for hire or reward) with between 8-16 seats (excluding driver's) including drawing a trailer not exceeding 750kg mass.	B, B+E, B1, C1, C1+E, D1+E, F, K, L, N, P
B+E	Motor vehicle in category B drawing a trailer exceeding 750kg mass.	—

Cont...

Cont...

C+E	Goods vehicle in category C drawing a single-axle trailer exceeding 5,000kg mass or any other trailer exceeding 750kg mass.	—
C1+E	Goods vehicle in category C1 drawing a trailer exceeding 750kg mass but with a combination weight not exceeding 8.25 tonnes mass.	—
D+E	Passenger vehicle in category D drawing a single-axle trailer exceeding, or any other trailer exceeding, 750kg mass.	—
D1+E	Motor vehicle in category D1 drawing a trailer exceeding 750kg mass.	—
F	Agricultural tractor – excluding any vehicle in category H.	K
G	Road roller.	—
H	Track laying vehicle steered by its tracks.	—
K	Mowing machine or pedestrian-controlled vehicle.	—
L	Electrically-propelled vehicle.	K
N	Vehicle exempted from duty under the Vehicles Excise Act 1977 (s7).	—
P	Moped.	—

NB: In the above table the term 'mass' means the permissible maximum weight (pmw) for the vehicle/trailer.

The new regulations make a number of further significant changes to the UK driver licensing scheme as follows:

1. All driver licence applications are made to the Driver and Vehicle Licensing Agency (DVLA) at Swansea.
2. Traffic Commissioners/Licensing Authorities in the Traffic Areas no longer issue vocational licences but continue to exercise a disciplinary role in regard to licence holders and deal direct with cases of misconduct.
3. Applications for LGV/PCV licences may be submitted to the DVLA up to three months in advance.
4. Driving licence vocational entitlements remain valid until age 45 years from the initial medical examination and then a new medical examination is required at each five-yearly renewal up to age 65 years after which annual medical assessment is necessary.
5. Medical certificates which have to be submitted with

LGV applications may be signed up to four months before applications are made.

6. Drivers whose eyesight is below prescribed standards and those who are insulin dependent diabetics are precluded from obtaining licences with vocational (ie LGV) entitlement. However, an exception will be made for drivers who already held a full vocational (ie HGV) entitlement at the time the new system commenced and where the LA who issued the licence had knowledge of the condition prior to 1 October 1990.

7. The new system allows for Provisional entitlements* for prospective LGV drivers (ie in category C and C + E) who need to apply for a provisional entitlement before they can start learning to drive such vehicles – they must have already passed a test to drive vehicles in category B (ie cars and light vans).

8. Holders of full licences for rigid goods vehicles (ie licence category C) may use those licences as provisional licences for learning to drive large articulated vehicles (ie licence category C + E).

NB: Provisional driving entitlements are shown on a separate licence 'counterpart'. Endorsement of penalty points will also be made on this counterpart.

Driving test arrangements

New arrangements introduced for LGV testing take account of the wide range of vehicles represented by the various new driving licence categories. Currently, for rigid goods vehicle tests (ie licence category C) vehicles are required with a permissible maximum weight of at least 7.5 tonnes. For articulated or drawbar combination vehicle tests (ie licence category C + E), vehicles will be required which comprise a trailer with two axles and a permissible maximum combination weight of at least 15 tonnes.

Minimum Test Vehicles from 1 July 1996

From 1 July 1996, changes will be implemented to the current LGV driving test in regard to the minimum weight and speed capability of vehicles which candidates must supply for the test (known as minimum test vehicles – MTVs). The following such vehicles will be required:

1. Vehicles for category B tests must have at least four wheels and be capable of a speed of at least 100kph.

2. For category B+E tests the vehicle itself must comply with category B requirements (see above) and must be drawing a trailer of at least one tonne gross weight (ie one tonne mam – see p 223 for definition).

3. For category C1 tests the vehicle must be of at least four tonnes mam and capable of a speed of at least 80kph.

4. For category C1+E tests the vehicle must comply with the requirements for category C tests (see above), and must be drawing a trailer of at least two tonnes mam – the combined length of the combination must be at least eight metres.

5. For category C tests (ie rigid goods vehicles exceeding 3.5 tonnes pmw) the vehicle must be of at least 10,000kg pmw (or maximum authorised mass (mam) – see note on p 221), at least seven metres long and capable of at least 80kph.

6. For a category C+E test (articulated vehicles) the vehicle must be articulated and have a permissible maximum weight (or mam – see above) of at least 18,000kg, be at least 12 metres long and capable of at least 80kph.

7. For a category C+E test (restricted to draw-bar vehicle combinations only) the rigid towing vehicle should meet the requirements for a category C test and the trailer should be at least four metres long. A minimum total weight for the combination of at least 18,000kg is required and the 80kph minimum speed capability also applies.

The Euro Theory Test

From 1 July 1996, under the terms of the EU 'second' Directive, driving test candidates (both for ordinary and vocational entitlements) will have to face a separate tough, written theory examination of 20 or more questions.

New-type 'L' plates

By 1 July 1996 the HGV 'L' plate is to be phased out and replaced by an ordinary red 'L' on white plate. Within this period 'L' plates of either type may be used, fitted front and rear on vehicles driven by learner LGV drivers.

Magistrates' powers to impose a driving test

If a person considers that a driving test in which he has taken part was not conducted in accordance with the regulations he may apply to a Magistrates' Court acting for the Petty Sessions area in which the person resides (in Scotland the Sheriff within whose jurisdiction he resides), and if the court considers that the test was not properly conducted the applicant may apply for another test before the expiry of the normal delay period and any fee due for the further test need not be paid.

Additionally, magistrates may order that a person who has been disqualified from driving should remain disqualified until he has passed another test. In practice such an order will only be made when the competence of the person is in question, and particularly in the case of elderly drivers who may never have taken a driving test.

Responsibility for driving licences

It is a driver's responsibility to ensure that he holds current driving licences valid for the type of vehicle to be driven at any time. The employer of a driver is also held legally responsible if the driver does not hold a current valid licence for the class of vehicle being driven. Besides being an offence for which prosecution can result, the insurance cover for a vehicle being driven by an unlicensed or incorrectly licensed driver may be invalidated.

Production of driving licences
To a police constable

A police constable can ask to see a driving licence in the following cases:

1. When a person is driving a motor vehicle on a road.
2. If a person is believed to have been the driver of a vehicle involved in an accident or when a traffic offence was committed.
3. If a person is supervising a provisional licence holder who is driving a vehicle and who has been involved in an accident or has committed a traffic offence.

The constable can also ask to see a licence which has been revoked or which is believed to have been obtained by giving a false statement.

In any of the above cases, if a driving licence cannot be produced at the time of the police constable's request, the person is allowed *seven* days in which to produce the licence at a police station nominated by him.

To a certifying officer

A certifying officer or an authorised goods vehicle examiner may request the production of a driving licence showing ordinary and any vocational entitlements of the driver of a goods vehicle in the circumstances detailed above.

If the driver cannot produce the licence when requested he may produce them at a Traffic Area Office within *ten* days.

To a Licensing Authority

The holder of an LGV driving entitlement can be requested by a Licensing Authority to produce his driving licence within *ten* days at the Traffic Area Office.

To a Magistrates' Court

When prosecuted for offences which involve the endorsement of penalty points on conviction or disqualification the person must send their driving licence to the Court to arrive on the day before the hearing.

To a traffic warden

A traffic warden can ask to see the driving licence of a person who may have committed an offence such as obstruction or offences related to parking, loading or unloading vehicles on a road or stopping on a pedestrian crossing.

3. Speed limits

Speed limits in Great Britain are applied to various types of goods vehicle on various types of road. The national limits applicable to roads have already been described under Module A (ie part 3/1 – Traffic Legislation); here the limits applicable to goods vehicles only are shown.

Speed limits for goods vehicles

	Motorways	Dual carriageways	Other roads
Car-derived vans			
Solo	70	70	60
Towing caravan or trailer	60	60	50
Goods vehicles not exceeding 7.5t mlw			
Solo	70	60	50
Articulated	60	60*	50
Drawbar	60	60*	50
Goods vehicles exceeding 7.5t mlw			
Solo	60	50	40
Articulated	60	50	40
Drawbar	60	50	40

mlw means maximum laden weight (ie maximum permissible weight for a vehicle as specified in Construction and Use regulations).

* In Northern Ireland these two limits are 50mph only. Also in NI, learner drivers and those who have only recently passed their driving test (ie when displaying 'L' and 'R' plates respectively) are restricted to a maximum speed of 45mph on all roads where higher limits are otherwise permitted.

Exemptions from speed limits

Fire, police or ambulance service vehicles when necessary in the performance of their duty may exceed speed limits if they can do so in safety.

Lower limit

Where speed limits for different classes of vehicle and road vary, *the lower limit always applies.*

4. Procedures in the case of traffic accidents

Duty to stop
and give
information

In the event of being involved in a road traffic accident, where injury to people (other than the driver himself) or to specified animals (other than those carried in the vehicle) or damage occurs to another vehicle or to roadside property, the driver must stop.

He should remain at the scene at least long enough to provide the requisite information, namely his name and address, the name and address of the vehicle owner, and the registration number of the vehicle, to anybody who has reasonable grounds to request such information.

If he does not give this information to a person requesting it at the scene of the accident, he must report the details to the police *as soon as is reasonably practicable* afterwards but in any case not later than 24 hours after the event.

A police constable can ask the driver to give his name and address and his age and the name and address of the vehicle owner. The driver may be required to produce his driving licence at the scene of the accident by a police constable, or at the police station when reporting the event or within seven days at a police station of his own choice. The police may ask to see proof of insurance for the vehicle (ie a certificate of insurance or a temporary cover note) and the vehicle test certificate (if appropriate).

In the case of injury to third persons, an insurance certificate must be shown to a police constable or any other person at the scene of the accident who has reasonable grounds to ask to see it. If the driver is not able to produce the insurance certificate at the time of the accident or within 24 hours at a police station, he will be requested to produce it within seven days at a police station of his own choice. The accident must also be reported to the vehicle owner and the insurers.

For the purposes of these requirements 'roadside property' means '(items) constructed on, fixed to, growing on, or otherwise forming part of the land in which the road is situated or land adjacent thereto'. This includes damage to trees, hedges, gardens, gate-posts, street furniture, etc. and other vehicles.

Animals for these purposes are specifically any horse, cattle, ass, mule (in Northern Ireland also a hinnie), sheep, pig, goat or dog.

Injuries to 'people' (which require reporting as stated above) does not include those to the driver. Other people injured in an accident are the 'third party' who may ultimately make a claim direct to the vehicle driver or the insurers for compensation for their injuries.

The Highway Code gives additional advice for situations where an accident involves a vehicle carrying dangerous goods. It states that the police and fire brigade should be given as much additional information as possible about the labels and other markings on the vehicle; other people should be kept away from the vehicle and if it is necessary to act to save life it should be done with the utmost caution because of the possible presence of dangerous liquids leaking on to the road and dangerous dust or vapours blowing in the wind.

Accident report to the insurers

Drivers are required to report accidents to the vehicle insurers (or via their employer) and the main points to be included in a driver's accident report are the date, time and place of the accident; a description of the weather and road conditions at the time; the speed of the vehicle; the direction of its travel and its position on the road in relationship to other vehicles; the position on the road and direction of travel of any other vehicles involved; the description of the damage caused to the insured vehicle and any other vehicle; a description of the damage or injury caused to any other property (including any other vehicle) or person; the names, addresses and the name of the insurers of any other person involved; the names and addresses of any witnesses to the accident; a note of any comments made by people at the scene of the accident; the name or number of any police constable in attendance at the accident; and details of any instructions given regarding the removal of the vehicle from the scene of the accident. It is also advisable to provide a sketch of the accident situation showing the relative position of the vehicles involved prior to and immediately after the accident.

Accident claims procedure
In the event of an accident where damage or injury is sustained, the driver should report the event to the vehicle owner (if the driver is not the owner) and to his insurer or the vehicle owner's insurer, usually within seven days. An accident report/claim form should be completed.

At the scene of an accident it is unwise to admit liability, to apologise to the other party for what has occurred or to enter into an argument about responsibility for the accident with the third party or with any other person. Such remarks could prejudice the outcome of any claims arising by compromising

227

the insurer's negotiations. It should be left for the insurers to establish blame and liability when the claim is made.

Where damage or injury is confined to the vehicle and driver and comprehensive insurance cover is operative, a claim can be made for loss or damage, apart from any excess. A vehicle owner can volunteer to pay the first part of an amount of a claim, usually £25 to £250 or even more depending on circumstances, so that for minor damage repairs any 'no claims' bonus on the policy is not jeopardised. Volunteering to pay an excess can result in premium discounts. In special cases the insurers will impose a compulsory excess, often in the case of young or inexperienced drivers. The insurers will assess the claims and will require estimates for repair work to vehicles, property or loss through injury. If claims are met, the 'no claims' bonus will be affected and this will result in a higher premium on renewal of the policy.

Where the damage or injury is confined to the insured vehicle and driver and no comprehensive insurance cover is operative, no claim can be made against the insurers for loss, damage or injury.

If no damage or injury is caused to the driver or the vehicle but is caused to roadside property, other vehicles, animals or other people, the insurers will deal with any claims from third parties for loss, damage or injury. Claims which are received from third parties who have suffered loss or damage should be passed immediately to the insurers for them to deal with. The driver should not enter into correspondence directly with third parties. The insurers will assess the claims and will require estimates for repair work to vehicles, property or loss through injury. If claims are met, the 'no claims' bonus (if applicable) may be affected and this could result in a higher premium on renewal of the policy.

International Syllabus

Module D

Part 1: Law

EU drivers' hours regulations
Goods vehicle drivers undertaking international journeys within the territories of the EU member states (ie the UK, Austria, Belgium, Denmark, Eire, Finland, France, Germany, Greece, Italy, Luxembourg, the Netherlands, Portugal, Spain and Sweden) must observe fully the requirements of the EU drivers' hours rules as specified in EU Regulation 3820/85 and described in detail on pages 202–07 of this manual.

AETR agreement
When drivers are engaged on international journeys which extend beyond the territories of EU member states and involve travel into or transit across the territories of national states which are signatories to the AETR agreement, the AETR drivers' hours rules must be observed *for the whole of the journey*. In fact, the AETR rules are now fully aligned with those of the EU as contained in EU Regulations 3820/85, referred to above.

The European Agreement Concerning the work of Crews of Vehicles Engaged in International Road Transport 1971 (AETR) was established by the Economic Commission for Europe to control the hours of work and rest for drivers engaged in international road transport operations to or from third countries which are contracting parties to the Agreement (see below), or in transit through such countries for the whole of the journey where such operations are carried out by vehicles registered in an EU member state or in one of the contracting countries.

This Agreement arose from a need to increase the safety of road traffic and the requirement to make regulations governing certain conditions of employment (notably in respect of driving time, breaks and rest periods, etc) in international road transport in accordance with the principles of the International Labour Organisation.

Parties to the agreement
The AETR Agreement has been signed (ie ratified by) the EU member states plus the following non-EU countries: CIS (formerly the USSR), the Czech and Slovak Republics (formerly Czechoslovakia), Norway and the former Yugoslavia.

Tachographs
The rules applying to the fitment and use of tachographs for international journeys (within the EU and on AETR journeys) are exactly the same as those already described fully on page 209.

Part 2: Control of Road Haulage Operations

Border controls

The single European market has brought with it significant change in the hitherto bureaucratic, time consuming and costly administrative procedures which were a necessity when transporting goods across national boundaries. Fundamental to the whole concept of the single European market is that EU citizens, goods, money and services should be able to pass (or be transacted) freely across internal borders between member states. However, it is still a legal requirement that EU citizens carry their national passports when travelling abroad (even within the Union). This applies equally to transport drivers whose passports also provide suitable identification for other purposes (eg to substantiate travellers' or Euro-cheque encashments and other payments). However, within the Union most travellers find that frontier crossing authorities take only a cursory glance at the cover of the document.

Community Road Haulage Authorisations

One of the most important legislative steps, taken to allow freedom of movement for goods between member states, directly affects road transport. The complex and restrictive system of Union and bi-lateral permits and quota allocations necessary for international road haulage journeys within the EU, which also applied to transit traffic travelling to and from non-EU member countries, have been abolished. From 1 January 1993 a new system of 'Community Authorisations' was implemented to enable EU hauliers to operate freely (ie to undertake as many journeys as they wish) *between* member states – not to be confused with the quite separate Cabotage Authorisations which are necessary to operate *within* member states other than their own (see below). However, it is important to note the continuing requirement for certain permit authorisations when operating road haulage journeys *outside* the EU (see page 235).

EU Regulation 881/92 – Community Authorisation

EU Regulation 881/92 is the regulation providing for the new system of Community Authorisations for intra-Union international road haulage. It amends earlier legislation (ie EU Regulations 1841/88 and 3164/76 on access to the market in the international carriage of goods by road) by effectively introducing qualitative criteria in place of the previous system of quantitative restriction. The qualitative criteria are as specified in EU Regulation 561/74 as amended by 438/89, namely requirement for the operator to be of good repute, of adequate financial standing and professionally competent in road haulage operations.

International carriage
For the purposes of this regulation, 'international carriage' means:

1. where a goods vehicle departs from one and arrives in another, different, member state (whether transiting other member states or non-member countries *en route*); or
2. where a vehicle departs from a non-member country and arrives in a member state or vice versa (with or without transit through one or more member states or non-member countries *en-route*); or
3. where a vehicle departs from and arrives in a non-member country but travels via a member state *en route*.

This definition also includes all unladen journeys undertaken in conjunction with the carriage of goods on the defined journeys.

UK issue of Community Authorisations

The UK issues these authorisations (under the provisions of EU Regulation 881/92) via Traffic Area offices on an automatic basis to all existing operators holding a standard international licence (ie there will be no need for existing operators to apply for these authorisations) and to new operators, as a matter of course, with the issue of their new licence documents.

The authorisation comprises an original document to be retained safely at the licence holder's main place of business, and a number of certified copies equalling the total number of vehicles authorised on the operator's licence. One of the certified copies of the authorisation must be carried in each vehicle undertaking international journeys within the EU.

Penalties for infringement of Authorisations

An international haulier who jeopardises his 'O' licence by reason of failing to meet the requirements of good repute, financial standing or professional competence will also jeopardise his Community Authorisation. In other words, where circumstances arise which require suspension or revocation of an 'O' licence, the Community Authorisation will also be automatically suspended or withdrawn (ie revoked). Where curtailment of an 'O' licence is deemed to be necessary, the certified true copies of the Community Authorisation will be temporarily or partially suspended, according to the seriousness of the infringement of relevant regulations.

In member states where no 'O' licence or its equivalent is issued, failure to meet (or maintain) standards of good repute, financial standing and professional competence will result in direct jeopardy of the Community Authorisation.

It is a specific requirement that where one member state becomes aware of an infringement of Community Authorisation legislation by a haulier from another member state, it shall inform the authorities in that member state and may ask that state to impose sanctions on the haulier in accordance with the regulations (ie for temporary or partial suspension of certified copies or withdrawal of the Community Authorisation).

Community Authorisations and the certified copies carried on vehicles must be produced for inspection on request. Failure to do so, and not to carry the certified copy on a vehicle while on an international journey within the EU, is an offence.

Validity and duration of Authorisations

Community Authorisations are to be made out in the original licence holder's name and are not transferable to any third party. They are valid for five years. Certified copies, as mentioned above, must be carried on the relevant vehicle when on an international journey and must be produced by the driver for examination whenever he is required to do so by an authorised inspecting officer.

On the expiry of a Community Authorisation, it is a requirement that the issuing authority (ie in the UK the Traffic Commissioners on behalf of the Department of Transport) must verify whether the operator still satisfies the legal conditions for its issue. Since these conditions are identical to those on which renewal of the haulier's 'O' licence depends, namely good repute, financial standing and professional competence, UK operators whose 'O' licences are renewed will have their Community Authorisation automatically renewed at the same time.

Authorisation document

Annex I to the EU Regulation (EU 881/92) illustrates a model for the Community Authorisation, the front page of which contains details of the haulier, date and authority for its issue and dates of its validity; on the rear are the general provisions for the use of such Authorisations, in particular that while within the territory of any member state the holder (ie operator and driver) must comply with the 'laws, regulations and administrative provisions in force in that state' especially in regard to transport and traffic.

Exemptions from requirement for Community Authorisation

Certain transport operations are specifically exempt from the requirement for Community Authorisations in accordance with Annex II to the regulations, as follows:

1. Carriage of mail as a public service.
2. Carriage of vehicles which have suffered damage or breakdown.
3. Carriage of goods in vehicles with a permissible laden weight (including that of any trailer drawn) which does not exceed 6 tonnes or the maximum permitted payload of which does not exceed 3.5 tonnes.
4. Carriage of goods in vehicles owned (including hired) by an own-account firm solely for its own purposes plus where the transport is no more than ancillary to its overall activities and where the vehicle is driven only by an employee of the firm.
5. Carriage of medicinal products, appliances, equipment and other articles required for medicinal care in emergency relief, in particular for natural disasters.

Bilateral road haulage permits for non-EU journeys

Certain road haulage operations from the UK and other EU member states to non-member states still require the issue of a bilateral road haulage permit (see table below). At the present time road haulage journeys to or through Russia (formerly the USSR), Turkey and the former Yugoslavia require such permits for specified transport operations (see table below). The issue of road haulage permits for entry to the former Yugoslavia is suspended due to the current conflict.

Bilateral road haulage permits are not required for transport operations within the EU or for journeys to or through Bulgaria, the Czech Republic and Slovakia (formerly Czechoslovakia), Hungary, Norway, Romania, Poland and Switzerland. However, hauliers on transit journeys across EU territory to such destinations must be in possession of a Community Authorisation.

Bilateral and ECMT permits

Bilateral road haulage permits are still required for operations to Estonia, Russia, Turkey and the Ukraine. These are available on a general quota basis on request, one permit being valid for one return journey. ECMT* permits for unlimited third-country operations are required for Bulgaria, Croatia, Estonia, Latvia, Lithuania, Romania, Slovenia, Switzerland, Turkey and the EU member states. These permits are in restricted supply.

European Conference of Ministers of Transport, an inter-governmental organisation established by Protocol (Brussels 17 October 1953) constituting a forum for the Ministers of Transport of 29 European countries (listed on page 236).

Associate members are Australia, Canada, Japan, New Zealand and the United States. Morocco is an observer country, as are the newly admitted states of Russia and Moldova.

Household removals and abnormal loads

Special ECMT permits are available for carrying out household removals between EU and ECMT member countries, namely the 15 EU member states plus the Czech Republic, Hungary, Norway, Poland, Switzerland, Turkey and the former Yugoslavia (plus newly admitted members from the beginning of 1993, namely Bulgaria, Croatia, Estonia, Latvia, Lithuania, Romania and Slovakia), or which involve journeys crossing such countries. These permits are available only to firms employing the specialised equipment and staff needed to undertake such operations.

The transport of abnormal loads requires additional authorisation, which usually has to be obtained by direct contact with the relevant transport authorities of the country concerned. Additionally, in France for example, advance permission is normally required from the police (ie gendarmerie) for each district through which the load is to pass.

Validity of permits

Where bilateral road haulage permits are required as described above (see also table below), such permits are available covering single journeys only, allowing just *one* return journey to be undertaken between the dates shown on the permit. Outside of these dates the permit is invalid and it would be illegal to commence or continue the journey.

In the case of Turkey, single journey permits as described above are available as well as multiple journey permits authorising four journeys.

For Austria, normal termination permits are available for journeys destined for that country, but for transit traffic a new Eco-points system has been established whereby the haulier has to obtain stamps to affix to an Eco card (see below). Single journey permits are valid only between the dates shown, as mentioned above.

Permits for Austria are valid for six months from the date of issue while those for Russia, Tunisia, Turkey and the former Yugoslavia are valid from the date of issue until 31 December.

Permit
requirements

Type of transport operation	Turkey	Russia	Former Yugoslavia
Own-account carriage	Q	N	Q
Unaccompanied trailer/semi-trailer	Q	N	Q
Unladen in transit	Q	N	Q
Unladen as relief for vehicle with original permit	–	N	–
Unladen entry to collect goods	Q*	N	Q
Airports – re-routed goods	–	N	Q
Airports – carriage of luggage	–	N	Q
Carriage of broken-down vehicles	–	–	–
Funeral transport	–	–	–
Carriage of works of art for fairs/exhibitions	Q	–	–
Carriage of works of art for commercial purposes	–	N	–
Carriage of antiques	Q	N	Q
Carriage of goods for publicity or information purposes	Q	N	–
Carriage in connection with sports/theatre/media	–	–	–
Carriage in connection with fairs and exhibitions	Q	–	–
Carriage of animal carcasses *not* for human consumption	–	N	Q
Carriage of animal carcasses *for* human consumption	Q	N	Q
Household removals	Q	N	–
Carriage of mails	–	–	–
Carriage in connection with refuse and sewage	–	N	Q
Carriage of bees and fish fry	–	N	Q
Carriage of valuable goods	–	N	Q
Carriage in connection with medical emergencies	–	N	Q
Vehicles with plw** not over 6 tonnes	Q	N	–
Vehicles with ulw† and goods not over 6 tonnes	–	N	Q
Vehicles with payload not exceeding 3.5 tonnes	Q	N	Q
Carriage of abnormal loads	Q	N	Q
Carriage of dangerous goods	Q	N	Q
Carriage of spare parts for ships (ie sea-going vessels)	Q	N	Q
Carriage of spare parts for aircraft	Q	N	Q
Carriage of ships provisions (ie for sea-going vessels)	Q	N	Q
Carriage of perishable foods under ATP††	–	N	Q
Carriage of perishable goods in special vehicles	–	N	Q

Carriage of live animals in special vehicles	Q	N	Q
Carriage within 25 kilometres of frontier zones	–	N	–
Carriage across frontier zones to EU countries	–	N	–
Transit traffic	Q	N	Q
Carriage on road/rail§ journeys	Q	N	Q
Carriage using direct ferry services	Q	N	Q

Q: Quota permit N: Non-quota permit
*   *Permit free for unaccompanied trailer/semi-trailers using ferry*
**   *Permissible laden weight*
†   *Unladen weight*
†† *The ATP Agreement on the carriage of perishable foodstuffs (see p 280)*
§   *Journeys involving the use of combined road/rail facilities (see p 279)*

Third country traffic

Third country traffic, which is the carriage of goods between two countries other than the country in which the vehicle is registered, is permissible in certain cases (ie between any EU country) but not in others, as shown in the following list:

1. **Journeys are permissible between any EU country and:** Austria, France, Eire, Hungary, Luxembourg, the Netherlands, Norway, Poland, Sweden, Russia and Denmark.
2. **Journeys are permissible between any EU country and:** Germany, Portugal, Spain and Switzerland, but only where the vehicle passes in transit through its home state (ie in which it is registered).
3. **Journeys are permissible between any EU country and:** Finland, Greece (except for UK vehicles carrying goods to that country from Eire), Romania and the former Yugoslavia, subject to special permission first being obtained from the competent authorities concerned.

Third-country traffic permits are available for journeys between the Czech Republic, Slovakia, Turkey and the former Yugoslavia. At the present time the issue of permits in respect of the former Yugoslavia is suspended due to the current conflict.

Issue of permits

Road haulage permits where necessary, as described above, are issued by the relevant authority in each member state. Normally, this involves completion of application forms, advance payment of the relevant fee and submission by the applicant of a copy of his authority to operate (eg in the UK his 'O' licence).

'O' licence).

Return of used permits
Used and expired permits must be returned to the issuing authority not later than 15 days after the relevant journey has been completed or the permit expiry date, whichever is earlier. Journey record sheets issued with period permits (eg the four-journey permit for Turkey) must be returned within the same time-scale.

Lost or stolen permits
Road haulage permits are valuable transit documents and as such should be treated with care and appropriate security. They are not transferable to another operator and such misuse is illegal throughout the EU, with harsh penalties imposed on offenders (see below). Replacement of lost or stolen permits is not normally automatic, and in any case a full written explanation of the circumstances surrounding the loss or theft is required, together with a copy of the police report.

Journeys to or through non-agreement countries
If vehicles are to travel to or through a country with which an EU member state has no agreement, permission to operate in that country has to be sought direct from its transport authority. Application should be made well before the journey is due and full details of the vehicle, the load and the route should be given.

Permit checks
As a result of the exposure of a number of cases of permit frauds, stringent regulations have been made to prevent vehicles on international journeys travelling without valid permits (see above) and checks are made on vehicles to ensure that these regulations are complied with. A vehicle will be prevented from continuing its journey if it does not carry a valid permit.

In the UK the International Road Haulage Permits Act 1975 makes it an offence to forge or alter permits, to make a false statement to obtain a permit or to allow one to be used by another person.

Eco-points system for transit journeys through Austria
Transit permits previously required for authorising journeys through Austria have been abolished but have been replaced by a new system involving the issue of Eco-point stamps. This scheme is intended to reduce the effects of air pollution created by exhaust emissions from heavy lorries in transit through the country, hence Eco (ie ecology) -points. It is intended to benefit operators who use 'less polluting' vehicles. The number of Eco-points available (both to the UK and other EU member states) will decrease annually, thereby reducing the total number of transit journeys permitted unless greater use is made of ecologically-friendly vehicles.

The broad principle of the system is that the greater the potential exhaust emission, the greater the number of

Eco-point stamps the haulier will have to submit to fulfil his journey. Conversely, the lower the potential exhaust emission, the fewer the number of stamps required.

Verification of vehicle exhaust emissions will be by means of a CoP (Conformity of Production) document issued to vehicle operators and required to be produced at the border on entry to Austria.

It is emphasised that for journeys terminating in Austria existing permit requirements continue to apply (see above), but Eco-point stamps are *not* required. They are not required either for operations carried out under an ECMT permit.

Eco-point exemptions
Certain transport operations are exempt from the Eco-points system as follows:

1. Occasional freight movements by road to and from airports in the event of diversion of air services.
2. Transport of baggage in the trailers of vehicles intended for the carriage of passengers and baggage transport using vehicles of any kind to and from airports.
3. Transport of post.
4. Transport of damaged vehicles or vehicles requiring repair.
5. Transport of refuse and faecal matter.
6. Transport of animal carcasses intended for disposal.
7. Transport of bees and fish fry.
8. Funeral transport.
9. Transport of objects d'art and works of art for exhibitions and for professional purposes.
10. Occasional freight transport for reasons exclusively relating to publicity and education.
11. Removals transport (ie household removals) carried out by companies employing qualified workers and having the necessary equipment.
12. Transport of instruments, accessories and animals to and from theatrical, musical, cinema, sport and circus performances, exhibitions or fairs and to or from radio recordings, filming sessions or television recordings.
13. Transport of spare parts intended for ships and aeroplanes.
14. An unladen journey by a freight transport vehicle intended to replace a vehicle which has broken down *en route* and the subsequent transport operation carried out by this replacement vehicle under cover of the authorisation allocated to the defective vehicle.
15. Transport of emergency medical aid (in particular during natural disasters).

16. Transport of securities (for example precious metals) in specialised vehicles, accompanied by the police or other security services.

The Eco-points system

The new Eco-points system comprises Eco-point stamps and Eco cards (plus the issue of the CoP document for relevant vehicles as described below). To undertake international road haulage journeys which involve a transit crossing of Austria, operators need a supply of Eco-point stamps and an Eco card on which to stick the stamps for each leg of the journey (ie one each for the outward and homeward bound transit of Austria).

Eco cards

These cards are readily available on application to national transport authorities (ie in the UK, the International Road Freight Office – IRFO), usually free with the issue of Eco-points stamps (see below), or they may be purchased from the Austrian authorities on reaching the border.

The Eco card comprises three pages which have to be completed by the haulage operator or the driver prior to entering Austria:

1. Page one has space for affixing the Eco-points stamps, which must be cancelled by the driver signing across their face before crossing into the country. This page will be detached and retained by the Austrian authorities.
2. Page two (with carbon copies) requires details to be completed of the vehicle, load and journey (including, where possible, the postcode of both loading and unloading locations – but an offence is not committed if this information is omitted). This page will be stamped by the authorities at the border, confirming the number of Eco-points stamps used, and a copy will be given to the driver to be carried for the rest of the journey as proof that Eco-points stamps have been paid*.
3. Page three lists the appropriate codes for the Austrian border controls and international distinguishing signs to be used when completing page two of the document.

* It is important to note that this copy (ie page two of the Eco card) must be returned to the issuing authority, complete with operator's name, address and reference number within seven days of use (ie of completing the journey) – future issues of Eco-points stamps will depend on it.

Eco-points stamps

Eco-points stamps (each worth one Eco-point) are issued solely by national transport authorities in connection with international road haulage journeys involving transit in Austria. For this purpose, the Austrian authorities 'charge' vehicles with Eco-points in accordance with the following rules:

1. Vehicles first registered prior to 1 October 1990 and those not carrying a CoP document (see below) – 16 Eco-points (ie 16 Eco-points stamps).
2. Vehicles carrying a CoP document – the number of Eco-points equal to the rounded (ie up or down) CoP value shown on the CoP document.

Conformity of Production (CoP) documents

CoP documents are issued by the relevant transport authority (eg in the UK, the International Road Freight Office – IRFO) on application by road hauliers for vehicles first registered from 1 October 1990 whose engines have a lower Nox emission than older vehicles.

Operators are required to supply the following information in respect of each vehicle (ie those to be used for journeys involving transit through Austria):

1. Vehicle registration number.
2. The date of first registration.
3. The type approval number.
4. The chassis number.

The CoP document (each vehicle will carry an individual one which is non-transferable) shows the Nox emission value and the CoP value (ie the Nox emission value plus 10 per cent) for the vehicle. It also indicates the corresponding number of Eco-points stamps that will be needed for each single-leg journey by that vehicle.

The document must be carried on the vehicle to verify its so-called 'greener' performance. When shown at the Austrian border, the authorities will charge fewer Eco-points stamps to permit the transit journey through the country (see above).

Own-account transport operations

Own-account transport operations within Community territory are now free from all road haulage permit requirements (under the provisions of EU Regulation 881/92 Annex II) provided that goods are carried solely in connection with the trade or business of the vehicle user and are not carried for hire or reward, and that the following conditions are also met:

1. The goods carried must be the property of the business (of the vehicle user) or must have been sold, bought, let out or hired, produced, extracted, processed or repaired by the business.

2. The purpose of the journey must be to carry the goods to or from the business or to move them, either within the business or outside, for its own needs.
3. Motor vehicles used for the carriage must be driven by employees of the business.
4. The vehicles carrying the goods must be owned by the business or having been bought by it on deferred terms or hire (this does not apply where a replacement vehicle is used during a short breakdown of the vehicle normally used).
5. Road haulage must not be the major activity of the business.

Own-account operations between the UK, Austria, Cyprus and Hungary are free from permit requirements, but in the case of such journeys, drivers should carry on the vehicle a document containing the following information to confirm that the operation is solely for own-account purposes:

1. The name and address of the vehicle operator (ie user).
2. The nature of the operator's trade or business.
3. The nature of the goods being carried.
4. The location of the loading and unloading points.
5. The registration number of the vehicle on which the goods are carried.
6. Details of the route to be followed.

In all cases, own-account vehicle operators (and their drivers) should be aware that they may be asked to provide satisfactory evidence to help the authorities to determine the ownership of the goods, and also prove that the goods are being carried solely for own-account purposes.

Cabotage operations

Cabotage operation is provided for under the Treaty of Rome. Formerly a prohibited activity in any freight mode, road freight cabotage operation within EU member states under EU Regulation 4059/89 is now permitted, subject to road hauliers holding a valid Cabotage Authorisation permit.

Prohibited operations

Cabotage by EU own-account operators remains prohibited, as is cabotage by hauliers and own-account operators in non-EU states. It is illegal for road hauliers to undertake any cabotage journey without obtaining in advance (and carrying on the vehicle) a valid authorisation permitting such operations.

It is an offence to make a false statement to obtain such permits, and to misuse or alter a permit. Severe penalties are imposed on offenders (in the UK under the provisions of the International Road Haulage Permits Act 1975).

Issue of Cabotage Authorisations

Cabotage Authorisation permits (issued in the UK by the International Road Freight Office – IRFO – or by the relevant transport authority in other member states) are issued in the name of the applying haulier for vehicles authorised in his name (ie in the UK on his 'O' licence). They are valid for one vehicle for one month only, but any number of cabotage movements may be undertaken by that vehicle within the one-month period. Authorisation permits must accompany the vehicle at all times (in the case of articulated vehicles it relates to the tractive unit).

Journey record books

Each Cabotage Authorisation permit is accompanied by the issue of a journey record book. This must be carried at all times when the vehicle is on a relevant journey and completed by the driver for each consignment of goods carried on a cabotage basis; ensuring that all cabotage operations are recorded.

Instructions are given on the use of the book by way of the 'General Provisions and Explanatory Notes' printed inside the front cover. Of particular note is the provision that in column three the date shown should apply to the vehicles' departure under a cabotage load, *not* departure from the UK.

Completed record sheets from the journey record book must be returned to the issuing authority (in the UK the IRFO) no later than eight days after the end of the month to which the sheet relates (as instructed in the book).

Lost or stolen cabotage permits

As with all forms of road haulage permit, care must be taken to ensure the safe keeping of cabotage permits. It is illegal to pass on, or otherwise allow, named cabotage permits to be used by another operator (ie to run vehicles).

Loss or theft of permits should be reported to the issuing authority (eg the IRFO) together with details of the report made to the appropriate police authority and with a full written explanation surrounding the circumstances of the loss. The issue of replacement permits is not automatic or guaranteed.

Correct use of cabotage permits

Holding a cabotage permit is not an automatic entitlement, and their use will be monitored. Breach of permit conditions, may lead to its withdrawal.

Legal compliance under cabotage operations

UK operators are warned by the IRFO (and the same applies to hauliers from other EU member states), that when undertaking cabotage operations they must comply with the internal law and road traffic requirements of the countries in which such movements take place. They should also beware of special conditions and restrictions relating to the carriage of particular traffics and of the application of special rates and tariffs. Normal EU standards apply to vehicle construction, use, weights and dimensions, and to drivers' hours rules and the use of tachographs.

VAT on cabotage operations

Internal transport operations under Cabotage Authorisation requires operators to comply with national VAT requirements. For this purpose, operators may need to register in the member states in which they are operating or appoint a suitable VAT agent or fiscal representative to handle these matters.

For UK operators, reclaiming of VAT charged abroad may be (as it is commonly described) an 'administrative nightmare', but the use of an agent can reduce the difficulties and result in worthwhile returns, especially when viewed against the high rates paid on vehicle fuel and such like.

Documentation to be carried on the vehicle

International haulage operations largely depend for their efficiency on having the correct documentation. Incorrectly completed or missing documents cause problems for drivers at points of entry to and exit from national states (within the EU and beyond) and can result in extensive delays for vehicles and, consequently, considerable extra cost.

The following documents should be carried on a vehicle making an international journey:

1. For the driver:
   (a) his national (ie new EU-type) driving licence
   (b) an international driving licence (where appropriate – see below)
   (c) a translation of driving licence (where appropriate – eg for Italy)
   (d) his passport (current and valid to cover period away from UK)
   (e) an entry visa (where appropriate – see list of countries below)
   (f) a letter of authority to have charge of the vehicle (ie on company letter-heading)
   (g) a bail bond (for Spain only – usually issued with the insurance green card)
   (h) tachograph charts (where applicable – ie for vehicles over 3.5 tonnes)
   (i) ADR training certificate (if applicable).
2. For the vehicle:
   (a) the registration document (original form V5 – log book for NI vehicles)

    (b) a current tax disc displayed in the windscreen (ie showing full duty paid)

    (c) the current 'O' licence disc displayed in the windscreen

    (d) the certificate of insurance

    (e) insurance green card (not compulsory but advisable)

    (f) copies of the vehicle annual test and plating certificate

    (g) road haulage/Cabotage Authorisation permit (as appropriate)

    (h) Carnet de passage en douane for certain countries (see also pages 258-9)
- (i) France (no longer required for trailers and semi-trailers fitted with DoT 'plates')
- (ii) Gibraltar
- (iii) Greece (if staying longer than 10 days)
- (iv) Italy (for vehicles remaining more than three months)
- (v) Portugal (triptype for spare parts)

    (i) nationality plate (ie GB plate)

    (j) Eco-points card and stamps (for Austria).

3. For the load:

    (a) road haulage/cabotage permit/Community Authorisation (where applicable)

    (b) CMR consignment note (for haulage operations or own-account certificate)

    (c) carnet (as appropriate)
- (i) TIR
- (ii) ATA (for temporary importation of goods)

    (d) copies of invoices for the goods

    (e) certificate of origin/health/consular certificates (where appropriate)

    (f) certificates issued under the following conventions (as appropriate)
- (i) ADR (for dangerous goods – see page 282)
- (ii) ATP (for perishable foodstuffs – see page 280).

Full details of the requirements for documents in respect of individual countries may be obtained from the International Road Freight Office. It should be noted that when on an international journey, certain documents may be required only in particular circumstances, whereas others are required at all times.

A *national identification plate* should always be fixed to the vehicle when it is travelling in a country other than that of its registration.

The driver should carry his *passport* (and visa which is usually stamped in the passport – see also below) with him at *all* times, when in the vehicle and when away from it (eg when out for a meal in the evening). The passport provides a means of identification and carrying it everywhere helps to prevent it being stolen, which could then result in difficulties when crossing borders.

The driver should have with him in the vehicle the original of the *vehicle registration document* and a *letter of authorisation* from the vehicle owners, confirming that he is authorised to be in possession of the vehicle.

In some countries a British/Euro driving licence is not sufficient to meet national requirements. In these circumstances the driver should have an *international driving permit* which is obtainable from the AA, RAC or RSAC and the National Breakdown Recovery Club. Spain and Italy are two examples of countries where the old British green-type licences are not generally acceptable. An applicant for an IDP must be a UK resident and aged 18 years or over.

A *visa* is required by the driver for visiting certain countries (not EU member states). Employers should obtain the visas from the relevant country's embassy in Britain or from the British embassy in countries to be visited. Among the countries for which visas are required are:

- Bulgaria
- Commonwealth of Independent States (CIS)
- Romania
- Turkey

Part 3: Practice and Formalities Connected with International Movements

Special note: Following the opening of the Single European Market many changes have taken place in the systems and documents used by Customs for controlling and monitoring imports and exports as part of the liberalisation of trade procedures. Many long established procedures are being progressively eliminated and document systems abolished. The pace of change in this area is rapid, consequently the material covered by this text is undergoing constant change so the reader is advised to keep up to date with progress on these measures through the trade press.

Customs procedures – export

Under the provisions of the Customs and Excise Act 1952 and the Customs and Excise Management Act 1979 exporters must ensure that all goods exported go through one of the following procedures for export declaration and clearance:

1. Pre-entry with Customs and Excise
2. Simplified Clearance Procedure (SCP)
3. Local Export Control (LEC)
4. Low Value Procedure.

Pre-entry
All goods which are exported in the following circumstances must be pre-entered (using the appropriate forms – see below) at the Customs House at the port of exportation:

1. Goods exported from a bonded warehouse and goods from licensed premises
2. Tobacco products from registered premises
3. Goods in transit through a UK port other than those under TIR carnet or those moving under full Community Transit Procedure
4. Goods exported for processing, repair or exhibition, which are to be re-imported into the UK
5. Goods which are under restriction for the purposes of exportation

6. Goods exported by exporters who have not been issued with an assigned number
7. Goods exported on drawback (of duty) or where repayment of duty is to be claimed
8. Goods exported under an export licence (apart from those on an open general export licence).

Omission of details from pre-entry
Certain details as follows may be omitted from pre-entry declarations if not available in advance:

1. Date of shipment
2. Ship name/flight number
3. Dock/station
4. Port or airport of export
5. Flag code
6. Port code.

Full details of export procedures can be found in various Customs' Notices available free of charge from local offices of HM Customs and Excise.

CRN entry/ SCP

The Simplified Clearance Procedure (SCP) is an alternative to pre-entry. It involves the use of an approved commercial document showing a Customs Registered Number (CRN) which the exporter must have for export consignments if the goods are to be pre-entered under the SCP.

This number must be shown on all relevant export documents (ie bills of lading and air waybills) when they are given to the carrier and the number should also be shown on all other related documents (delivery notes, etc).

Once the consignment has been despatched, Customs must be provided with completed SAD (see below), from which the shipping information may be omitted, within 14 days, at the Statistical Office.

Local Export Control (LEC)
Where an exporter has large or regular consignments for Customs pre-entry application can be made to HM Customs and Excise for clearance at the exporter's (or carrier's) premises – subject to certain conditions – under what is known as the Local Export Control (LEC) procedure.

Low value procedure
This procedure can be used for non-dutiable goods not destined for the Channel Islands and where their value does not exceed £600 FOB and the net weight does not exceed 1000kg.

Customs Procedure Codes

The Customs Procedure Codes identify the customs and/or excise regimes to which goods are being entered and from which they have been removed.

Single Administrative Document (SAD)

To simplify documentation, facilitate trade and computerise communication of customs data within and between commerce and Government in the EU, new Customs procedures were introduced under the 'Customs 88 Project'. This scheme, which started in January 1988, replaced pre-existing export, import and transit documents with a new Single Administrative Document (SAD) which is used in the UK and throughout the whole of the European Union as an export, import and transit declaration for any consignment moving within the EU.

Additionally, the SAD form is used for declarations for exports to and imports from non-Community countries.

Most of the previous export, import and Community Transit (ie CT) declarations are replaced by the SAD and forms previously used for Customs pre-entry such as the C 271 (pre-shipment advice for goods exported under the Simplified Clearance Procedure (SCP), also used as export declaration for low value exports) and the C 273, as well as many others, are no longer used.

New tariff scheme

Also part of the Customs '88 Project was the introduction of a new Customs tariff based on the world-wide Harmonised Commodity Description and Coding System (HS) which is currently being adopted by all the world's major trading nations. The new tariff is referred to as 'TARIC'.

Customs procedures – import

Goods imported under a Community movement certificate (form T2L) or the full T-form procedure must still comply with the usual UK entry procedures.

Where the office of destination is situated at the place of importation, the Community movement certificate or T-form must be attached to the Customs entry (SAD) form and the type and registered number of the certificate or form endorsed on it, eg 'Forms T2 no ... attached'. Where the T-form is a T1, the appropriate full rate of duty must be inserted in the rate of duty column. In other cases, the letter 'M' and the appropriate intra-Community rate of duty (or 'free' where applicable) should be entered. In all cases *all* the copies of the T-forms must be attached to the entry. The usual supporting documents such as invoices will still be required in addition to any Community movement certificates or T-forms.

Procedure when documents are unavailable or unsatisfactory

Under the full Community transit procedure, the T-forms must accompany the goods and are therefore not available if entry is made prior to the arrival of the goods. In such instances the importer or his agent should give the following undertaking on the entry: 'Transit documents will be produced to the import office'.

If the movement certificate or T-form to establish entitlement to an intra-Union rate of duty is not produced or is unsatisfactory in some way, the importer or agent may obtain delivery of the goods on payment of duty on deposit at the full rate. Alternatively, if there is no reason to doubt the entitlement of the goods to an intra-Union rate of duty, a deposit equivalent to the duty calculated at that rate may be accepted, provided the importer or agent gives a guarantee endorsed by a bank approved by the Commissioners of Customs and Excise for such purposes (or Guarantee Voucher – see page 254). The request for delivery on deposit in such circumstances should be made on the entry in the following terms: 'I request delivery on deposit under Section 255 of the Customs and Excise Act 1952 pending production of evidence of entitlement to Union treatment.'

Goods removed for clearance elsewhere than at the place of importation

Where goods, other than spirits and tobacco, are removed for clearance to an office of destination away from the place of importation, for instance an Inland Clearance Depot (ie a depot inland from the port of entry/exit where Customs have facilities to process and clear import/export consignments), the normal UK removal procedures must be followed except that a bond or other security to cover the duty on the goods during removal will not be required if a guarantee, other than a cash deposit, is in force under the Community transit system. If the guarantee is in the form of a cash deposit, a fresh cash deposit or bond will be required to cover the removal of the goods within the United Kingdom.

The place of importation must be an approved office of transit.

In the case of spirits and tobacco, the port or place of importation must be the office of destination. If removal for clearance elsewhere is desired the goods must be moved under the UK removal procedures.

'Fast Lane Procedure'

Goods arriving for import from other EU member states can be processed through what is known as the 'Fast Lane Procedure' (or Route 7 clearance) whereby details of the goods are entered with Customs before the vehicle/trailer is off-loaded from the ferry ship. Then, unless Customs have a query on the shipment the Direct Trader Input (DTI) system (ie an electronic data input system used by import agents) will authorise an immediate clearance. In fact, once the documents accompanying the load have been presented to the import agent and DEPS (ie the Customs and Excise Departmental Entry Processing System – a computer located at Hemel Hempstead)* has been notified of the arrival of the load a special rapid clearance system starts to operate. Under this system, 24 minutes are allowed for the details to be entered into the computer and a further 30 minutes are allowed for Customs to consider whether they wish to intervene (ie to request further information or actually stop the vehicle and inspect the load). If they do not intervene after this 30 minute delay the load will automatically be cleared 54 minutes after notification of arrival – hence use of the term 'Fast Lane'.

NB: The DEPS system described above is now replaced by the full CHIEF (ie Customs Handling of Import and Export Freight), a computerised pre-entry import and export processing system.

Goods in transit through the UK

The normal UK transit documentation (SAD) and procedures apply to goods imported under the full Community transit procedure which are in transit through this country for a destination elsewhere, except that no security by bond or deposit is required to cover removal through the UK provided there is a Community transit guarantee in force. If the goods are moving in circumstances where the Community guarantee requirement is waived, security is required.

Unless the full procedure is terminated there, the place of importation must be an approved office of transit.

With consignments of spirits and tobacco, if the goods are being moved on a single transport document to an office of destination in another member state, the port or place of importation into the UK should be the office of destination and removal of the goods through the UK should be covered by security for the duty under normal procedures.

Community Transit

The Community Transit (CT) system was introduced on 1 January 1973 in connection with the reduction in Customs duties between EC member countries which came into effect from 1 April 1973. The full scheme came into effect with the publication in 1977 of EC Regulations 222/77 and 223/77. The aim was for duties to be reduced to nil and tariff barriers between the member states to be removed to allow 'free circulation' of goods within the Community (ie from 1992 when the Single European Market came into being).

The CT system is intended to ease the passage of loads between EU member countries to comply with the concept of a Customs-free Union with no tariff barriers. It replaces the need for TIR carnets and the involved procedures for the technical approval of TIR vehicles for all inter-Union journeys, (eg from Britain to Austria, Belgium, Denmark, Eire, Finland, France, Germany, Greece, Italy, Luxembourg, the Netherlands, Portugal, Spain and Sweden).

CT also applies to journeys to Switzerland (a non-Union state which has accepted the terms of the Community Transit agreement) although loads will still need to be 'satisfactorily sealed', a term which is not officially defined. Existing approved TIR vehicles will obviously comply but there may be difficulties with other vehicles not reaching this standard of load-area security.

Normal rates of duty and procedures still apply to trade with non-EU member countries.

In order to take advantage of duty concessions, special documents comprising the Community Transit system are required. These documents confirm that the goods being carried originated in, and are travelling to, EU countries and are therefore eligible for reduced/nil duty.

Under the full Community Transit procedure using the SAD the status of goods is determined as being either;

1. T1 for goods imported from non-Union countries which are not in free circulation in the EU.
2. T2 which applies to Union goods which are in free circulation.
3. T2ES and T2PT which applies to goods in free circulation in Spain and Portugal respectively.

The appropriate classification (ie T1, T2 or T2ES/T2PT) is indicated in box 3 on the SAD.

Where 'free circulation goods are exported from one EU state to another without crossing any other EU state (eg direct from Britain to France or from the Netherlands to Germany) the full CT procedure is not necessary. In this case the T2L (or T2LES/T2LPT as appropriate) procedure is followed and the SAD is used only for purposes of providing evidence of the Union status of the goods. The same procedure applies when goods have to cross non-Union territory to reach a destination elsewhere in the EU and the TIR procedure is therefore being used for transit purposes.

The operator must complete the SAD form showing appropriate status for the goods (ie T1, T2 or T2L/ES/PT) and have it certified when it has been completed by a Customs officer. The certified document must travel with the vehicle and be shown on request to Customs officials en route.

On arrival at the destination, one copy of the document must be given to local Customs officials and the other two copies must be brought back, one to be given to Customs at the point of origin of the journey to match a copy which was retained when it was certified, and the other to be retained for statistical purposes.

Guarantee/
deposit against
Customs'
claims

A deposit or guarantee against Customs claims for any duties which may be payable must be made when using the Community transit system, or with TIR operation. This guarantee can be arranged through banks or other approved sources, either on an individual journey basis or as a comprehensive guarantee. The acceptance of any guarantee is subject to the approval of the guarantor by the Customs. Alternatively, guarantee vouchers can be obtained from the FTA, RHA or the Prudential assurance Company (see also page 260).

To protect the interests of guarantors, operators must ensure that documentation relating to loads is properly completed and that the T-form is returned to the office of departure on completion of the journey to release the guarantor from his obligations provided, of course, that there was no irregularity while the goods were in transit.

TIR
Convention

Under the Customs Convention on the International Transport of Goods by Road (TIR Carnets) 1959, to which the UK is a party, goods in Customs-sealed vehicles or containers may travel through intermediate countries with the minimum of Customs formalities provided a TIR carnet has been issued in respect of the journey.

The carnet is a recognised international Customs document intended purely to simplify Customs procedures; it is not a substitute for other documents, nor is it mandatory for any operator to use it; it does not give any operator the right to run vehicles in any European country. Use of a carnet frees the operator from the need to place a deposit of duty in respect of the load he is carrying in each country through which the vehicle is to pass.

The issuing authorities for the carnets (in this country the FTA and the RHA) act as guarantors on behalf of the IRU (International Road Transport Union – the international guarantor), and for this reason carnets are only issued to bona fide members of these two associations.

Goods may only be carried under a TIR carnet provided the vehicle in which they are carried complies with special requirements and has been approved for this purpose by the DoT.

Approval for vehicles is only given if they are constructed so that the load-carrying space can be sealed by Customs, after which it must not be possible for any goods to be removed from or added to the load without the seals being broken, and there must be no concealed spaces where goods may be hidden.

Detailed requirements are laid down concerning the structure of the body, particularly regarding the manner in which it is assembled, so that there is no possibility of panels being removed by releasing nuts and bolts and so on. The manner in which doors and roller shutters are secured must also meet stringent specifications. Sheeted vehicles or containers may be used provided conditions relating to the construction of the sheet are observed and as long as, when the closing device has been secured, it becomes impossible to gain access to the load without leaving obvious traces.

The DoT examines vehicles to ensure that they meet the technical requirements for operation under the TIR Convention and issues a certificate of approval, which must be renewed every two years and *must* be carried on the vehicle when it is operating under a TIR carnet.

This latter point is particularly important as Customs authorities make random checks on vehicles leaving the UK to ensure that this certificate is being carried where necessary.

Application for TIR certification
Application for the examination of vehicles or containers must be made to the Clerk to the Licensing Authority for the traffic area in which they are available for inspection. These offices provide the application form GV 62, and a leaflet setting out the technical conditions which have to be met. If a TIR-approved vehicle is sold to another operator, the TIR certificate (form GV 60) is not transferable and the new owner must have the vehicle re-certified if he wishes to use it for TIR operations.

TIR plates
When a vehicle has been approved it must display at the front and the rear a plate showing the letters 'TIR' in white on a blue background. Such plates are obtainable from the FTA and RHA. They should be removed or covered when the vehicle is no longer operating under TIR.

TIR carnets
TIR carnets are internationally recognised Customs' documents. They are in four parts and contain 6, 14 or 20 pages (ie volets in French). A 6-page carnet is valid only for a journey between the UK and one other country. Journeys to

more than one other country require 14- or 20-page carnets which are valid for two months and three months respectively. A carnet covers only one load and if a return load is to be collected, a separate carnet is needed (each individual voucher covers one frontier crossing) and the driver should take this with him on the outward journey. Careful attention must be paid to the completion of the carnet if delays and difficulties are to be avoided.

Carnets are in pairs and have counterfoils in a bound cover. At each Customs point *en route* a voucher is detached and the counterfoil is stamped. Therefore a 14-page carnet may be used to cross six frontiers, the other pair of vouchers being required at the Custom's office of departure.

The four parts of the carnet comprise the following:

1. Details of the issuing authority, the carnet holder, the country of departure, the country of destination, the vehicle, the weight and the value of the goods as shown in the manifest (see part 3).
2. A declaration that the goods specified have been loaded for the country stated, that they will be carried to their destination with the Customs seals intact and that the Customs regulations of the countries through which the goods are to be carried will be observed.
3. A goods manifest giving precise details of the goods, the way in which they are packed (the number of parcels or cartons) and their value.
4. Vouchers which Customs officials at frontier posts will remove, stamping the counterfoil section which remains in the carnet.

Before obtaining a carnet the member must sign a form of contract with the issuing authority, agreeing to abide by all the necessary legal and administrative requirements. A financial guarantee is required to ensure that the member meets any claims which may be made against him.

Carnets are valid for limited periods only (see above), and if not used they must be returned to the issuing authority for cancellation. Those which are used and which bear all the official stampings acquired *en route* must also be returned within ten days of the vehicle's return.

Strict instructions regarding the use of carnets are supplied by the issuing authorities both for the operator and the driver. For example, the driver should never leave the carnet with any Customs authority without first obtaining a signed, stamped and dated declaration quoting the carnet number and certifying that the goods on the vehicle conform with the details contained in the carnet. Drivers should also ensure that the Customs officials at each departure office, transit office and arrival office take out a voucher from the carnet and stamp and sign the counterfoil accordingly.

If a Customs seal on a TIR vehicle is broken during transit for any reason, Customs officials or the police must be contacted immediately to endorse the carnet to this effect.

Combined transport documents

Many international transport operations use a combination of transport modes such as road, sea, air, rail, roll-on/roll-off (vehicles on ships), piggy-back (vehicles on rail).

With this complexity of operation and the liability and documentation requirements, there is an increasing movement towards the use of combined transport documents where the issuing carrier accepts responsibility for the whole operation. Normally in these circumstances a 'network' system of liability applies, subject to the conditions of the carrier who undertakes the leg of the journey where the possible loss occurs.

The Hague-Visby Rules, dealing with the law of carriage by sea (United Nations publication), normally apply to sea journeys and the conditions of carriage of the road or rail carrier to inland journeys.

TCM Convention

In 1969 a convention covering Combined Transport Operations (CTO) was agreed, under the title TCM Convention. Under the Convention, combined transport operators can issue a document headed 'Combined Transport Document Governed by the TCM Convention'. The Convention permits this to be either a negotiable document, giving title to the goods, or a simple receipt for the direct delivery of the goods to a named consignee.

When goods are carried in containers it is often impossible to ascertain at which point loss or damage has occurred. In such circumstances the Convention makes the combined transport operator (CTO) liable, by the issue of a CT document, for the loss or damage to the goods occurring while the goods are in his charge, subject to certain exceptions embodied in the TCM Convention. However, if it is known where the loss or damage occurred, liability is normally determined by the 'network' system of liability – under this system, liability is determined in accordance with the appropriate convention or national law, or in certain exceptional circumstances and with prior agreement, by the subcontract between the CTO and the actual carrier.

The principal contents of the Convention are as follows:

1. Voluntary application of the Convention by the issue of a clearly identified document likely to be accepted by all parties.
2. It is the responsibility of the CTO to undertake (or arrange for others toundertake) the carriage, and to accept liability throughout the whole combined transport. At any particular stage the CTO may be either a basic carrier or an operator, arranging for others to provide the actual carriage. Thus the document mentioned above may be the combined transport equivalent of either a shipping line's or forwarders' bill of lading.
3. The information which should be contained in the CT document, leaving it to commercial practice which party should complete the document. The Convention avoids the ambiguity arising from the use of the word 'containers' by such expressions as 'coverings in which goods are packed', ie traditional packings, and 'unit loads', ie palletised or containerised cargo.
4. The responsibility of consignors and the CTO respectively for information given in the CT document. They are now satisfactorily based on commercial and transport practices.
5. Provides for the alternatives of a negotiable or non-negotiable type document, ie a document of title enabling a holder to claim delivery of the goods or a simple receipt for the direct delivery of the goods to a named consignee. It also introduces a 'fail-safe' mechanism to govern a case where a document does not state which of these it is.
6. A 'dangerous goods' clause follows precisely the wording of certain existing conventions.
7. Stipulates the period in which notice of loss or damage to the goods should be given to the CTO, including loss or damage not immediately apparent with, for example, containerised cargo.
8. The CTO's overall liability, and certain exemptions plus the limit of financial liability of the CTO, leaving the amount to be fixed at a diplomatic conference.
9. Establishes the 'network' system of liability; it also deals with the problem of containerised cargo being carried on deck without specific reference being made to this fact in the document.

Carnets
Carnets de passage

Most European countries permit the temporary importation of foreign vehicles and containers (not to be confused with the loads they carry) free of duty or deposit and without guaranteed Customs documents. However, a *carnet de passage en douane pour l'admission temporaire* is required for the following:

1. Vehicles and trailers entering Gibraltar, Iran, Iraq, Jordan, Kuwait, Lebanon, Saudi Arabia, Syria, Turkey and other Middle East countries.
2. Vehicles remaining in Italy for more than three months, and those remaining in Portugal for more than one month.

A deposit of duty in lieu of a carnet de passage is required for unaccompanied trailers entering Norway and Denmark. Vehicles entering the Benelux countries (Netherlands, Belgium and Luxembourg) do not require carnets provided they show signs of use (ie they are not new imports).

Carnets de passage are issued by the Automobile Association, the Royal Automobile Club and the Royal Scottish Automobile Club.

ATA carnets

Goods which are only being imported temporarily can be moved under an ATA carnet (an international Customs clearance document – valid for 12 months). Normally these documents are used in connection with the movement of samples for demonstration, display material for exhibitions and trade fairs and equipment for use by service or maintenance personnel fulfilling overseas contracts. They are issued by Chambers of Commerce or by the RHA to members without the need for payments of, or deposits against, duty. Holding an ATA carnet, however, does not relieve the transport operator from observing Customs requirements in each individual country.

Other Customs/ transit documentation Bills of lading

A bill of lading is a legal document of title. It acts as a receipt for goods delivered to a carrier and as evidence of a contract of carriage for such goods. A bill comes in two forms, the traditional 'long' form and the new shortened form. The shortened bill was devised by the General Council for British Shipping and SITPRO (Simplification of International Trade Procedures) in order to reduce the costs of export documentation and to simplify completion procedures.

House bill

This is an alternative to a bill of lading in that it is used by shipping and forwarding agents and groupage operators when making up consolidated loads or arranging through transit of goods by land and sea. Therefore, whereas a bill of lading normally covers only a sea journey (between two ports), the house bill covers both the sea journey and the inland journeys at either end. This document is also referred to as a 'combined transport document', as a result of the TCM Convention for Combined Transport (see p 257).

Invoice	An invoice is a document giving details of a sale of goods showing the supplier, the purchaser and any other parties involved. It identifies the goods, the quantity, the price and any other charges to be paid to the supplier, the terms or arrangements for payment, and details of the origin of the goods. Some countries insist on details of invoices being certified by suitable authorities (eg Chambers of Commerce).
Consular invoice	This is an invoice document similar to that described above, but prepared on a special form and given legal status (ie legalised) by the Consul of the importing country. Consular invoices are required by some countries to confirm the specific details of the goods and the transaction, as well as the origin of the goods – this conforms to the Customs requirements of the country concerned. Forms can usually be obtained from the Consul of the appropriate country and when completed, they normally have to be lodged with the country for visa purposes.
Certificates of insurance	These certificates of insurance are issued as confirmation and evidence that a policy of insurance exists to cover risks involved in the movement of goods for export. The certificate indicates the type of risks covered, eg all risks, with average (WA) or free from particular average (FPA).
ECGD certificates	Insurance for British exporters against the risks of export movement is provided by the Export Credits Guarantee Department. Guarantees are given in respect of goods manufactured in this country for sale abroad and the risks covered include loss or damage in transit plus the risk of non-payment by the overseas customer. The ECGD certificate provides evidence of the cover against specified risks.
Guarantee vouchers	To avoid having to make individual guarantees or deposits of duty in respect of individual consignments when moving goods under the full Community Transit documentation system operators can obtain Guarantee Vouchers against possible Customs' claims for duty. Vouchers are obtainable from the FTA, RHA and the Prudential Assurance Company on payment of the appropriate fee. Guarantee vouchers are valid in all EU member states plus Switzerland.
Bail bonds	When vehicles travel to Spain, an additional insurance requirement is a Spanish bail bond which should be taken out to protect the driver in the event of his being involved in an accident or infringing local regulations. It is the practice of the Spanish police, in the event of an accident or incident, to hold all the parties involved until the blame has been clearly established. The purpose of the bond is to secure the release of the driver and the vehicle, pending the outcome of any investigation into the event. The bonds are supplied by

insurance companies (usually equivalent in value in pesetas to approximately £1,000/£1,500) usually in conjunction with the issue of a green card (see page 276).

SITPRO

These initials stand for the Simplification of International Trade Procedures. The United Kingdom Committee for the Simplification of International Trade Procedures was set up in 1968 by the National Economic Development Council, to 'study documentation in international trade and the commercial and governmental procedures associated with it and to make recommendations to assist the more efficient flow of trade'. Its purpose was to establish simplified procedures and forms of documentation to ease trade between countries, thereby reducing costs and improving efficiency in the administration of export and import trade. The documentation is referred to as *aligned documentation* (see below).

With the 'aligned' method, the size of essential documents is standardised and their layout is designed in such a way that they can be produced in a unified set from a single master document. By typing the details on the master the aligned forms can be prepared by the 'one-run' system. Various methods can be used – spirit duplicating, dyeline and electrostatic are examples. Items of information which are not required can be omitted by the use of plastic masks or other techniques. This system reduces the cost and time taken to prepare documents and, once the master is checked, ensures that the information on all forms is accurate. The most up-to-date example of aligned documentation is the Single Administrative Document (SAD) used for inter-Union movements since January 1988.

EDI – Electronic Data Interchange

Widescale computerisation in the road freight, shipping and export/import industries and by Customs and Excise departments has led to the introduction of modern systems for passing shipping and export/import data between traders, shippers and HM Customs via direct or indirect computer links without the need for paper documents to pass or confirm information. This whole concept is known as EDI – Electronic Data Interchange, sometimes also called paperless systems of trading and its use results in automatic handling and actioning of data. To ensure uniformity in this method of trading the United Nations has set a standard for EDI known as EDIFACT (an acronym for Electronic Data Interchange for Administration, Commerce and Transport) under which there are standard procedures and messages for passing such matter as shipping instructions.

CMR (Convention Merchandises Routiers)

Operators carrying goods for hire and reward on international journeys must comply with the Convention on the Contract for the International Carriage of Goods by Road 1956 (CMR) which relates to carriers' liability and documents to be carried on vehicles. The Convention was adopted in the UK under the Carriage of Goods by Road Act 1965.

The following countries in addition to the UK are party to the CMR Convention:

□ Austria	□ Italy
□ Belgium	□ Luxembourg
□ Bulgaria	□ Netherlands
□ Czech and Slovak Republics	□ Norway
	□ Poland
□ Denmark	□ Portugal
□ Finland	□ Romania
□ France	□ Spain
□ Germany	□ Sweden
□ Gibraltar	□ Switzerland
□ Greece	□ former Yugoslavia
□ Hungary	

The Convention applies to all contracts for the carriage of goods by road for hire or reward between one country and another, as long as one is a party to the Convention.

Exemptions apply in the case of:

1. carriage under an International Postal Convention
2. furniture removals
3. funeral consignments.

CMR is not applicable in respect of international haulage operations between the UK (including Northern Ireland) and Eire. Also, a recent High Court ruling stated that CMR conditions do not apply to contracts for the carriage of goods between the UK mainland and the Channel Islands (ie Guernsey, Jersey, Alderney, Sark and Herm. *NB: Vehicles are not normally allowed on the latter two islands in any case).* Such operations are not legally classed as being international journeys.

The principal conditions of the Convention are as follows:

1. The Convention terms apply to the complete carriage, whether this is wholly by road or partly by road and partly by rail, sea or inland waterway, as long as the goods remain in the original vehicle.
2. The carrier is responsible under the Convention for the actions and omissions of his agents and any other

persons whose services are used in carrying out the movement.

3. The contract of carriage is confirmed by making out a CMR consignment note in three original copies (see page 266) which should be signed by the carrier and the sender. Both keep one copy and the third copy travels with the goods.

4. If the goods are carried in different vehicles or are divided owing to their different nature, the carrier or the sender can specify that a separate consignment note should be made out for each vehicle or load of goods.

5. The consignment note must contain certain details (see page 266) but may also contain additional information of use to the parties to the contract.

6. The sender is responsible for all expenses, loss and damage sustained by the carrier as a result of inaccuracies in completion of the consignment note in relation to information supplied by the sender.

7. On receipt of the goods, the carrier must check the accuracy of details in the consignment note and the condition of the goods and their packaging.

8. The sender is liable to the carrier for damage and expenses due to defective packing of the goods unless the defects were known to the carrier when taking over the goods.

9. The sender must attach to the consignment note or make available to the carrier the necessary documents to complete Customs formalities.

10. The sender has the right of disposal of the goods and may stop transit of the goods or change the delivery address up to the time of delivery to the consignee unless he has stated on the consignment note that the consignee has this right. Once the goods are delivered to the address on the consignment note, the consignee has the right of disposal.

11. A carrier who fails to follow the instructions on the consignment note or who has followed them without requesting the first copy of the consignment note to be produced is liable for loss or damage caused by such failure.

12. The carrier must provide the consignee with a second copy of the consignment note at the time of delivering the goods.

13. If the carrier cannot follow the instructions on the consignment note for any reason, he must ask the sender or the consignee, depending on who has the right of disposal (see condition 10 above), for further

instructions.

14. The carrier is liable for the total or partial loss of the goods and for any damage to them occurring between the time when he takes over the goods and the time of their delivery unless the loss, damage or delay was caused by a wrongful act or neglect of the claimant. The burden of proof in this case rests with the carrier.

15. Failure to deliver goods within 30 days of a specified time limit, or within 60 days from the time when the first carrier took them over if there is no time limit for delivery, results in the goods being considered to be lost.

16. When goods of a dangerous nature are consigned, the carrier must be informed of the nature of the danger and the precautions to be taken.

17. Calculation of compensation in the event of loss or damage is related to the value of the goods at the place and time they were accepted for carriage but will not exceed a set value (ie related to SDR – see page 265 for explanation).

18. Carriage charges, Customs' duties and other charges in respect of the carriage are refunded in the case of total loss of the goods and proportionately in the case of partial loss.

19. Higher levels of compensation may be claimed where the value or a special interest in delivery has been declared or where a surcharge has been paid in respect of a declared value exceeding the limit mentioned in condition 17.

20. In the case of damage the carrier is liable for the amount by which the value of the goods has diminished.

21. The claimant may demand interest in respect of the amount of any claim at 5 per cent per annum from the date on which the claim was sent to the carrier.

22. A carrier cannot avail himself of exclusions or limiting clauses if damage to goods was caused by his wilful misconduct or default which constitutes wilful misconduct.

23. The consignee is considered to have accepted the goods in a satisfactory condition if he does not indicate his reservations at the time of delivery or within seven days (excluding Sundays and public holidays).

24. In legal proceedings, the plaintiff may bring an action in any Court or Tribunal of a contracting (ie CMR contracting) country or of a country in which the defendant is normally resident or has his principal place of business, or of a country where the goods were

       taken over by the carrier or where they were designated for delivery, and in no other Courts or Tribunals.

25. The period of limitation for an action under the Convention is one year, or three years in the case of wilful misconduct.

26. Where successive road carriers are involved in a contract under the Convention, each is responsible for the whole operation as a party to the contract. Each successive carrier must give the previous carrier a dated receipt and must enter his name and address on the second copy of the consignment note.

27. A carrier who has paid compensation arising from a claim may recover the compensation plus interest, costs and expenses from other carriers who were parties to the contract subject to:
    (a) the carrier responsible for the loss or damage paying the compensation
    (b) each carrier responsible for loss or damage jointly caused shall be liable to pay proportionate compensation or compensation proportionate to their share of the carriage charges if responsibility cannot be apportioned.

28. If a carrier who is due to pay compensation is insolvent, his share must be paid by other carriers who are parties to the contract.

CMR liability insurance

Transport operators in Britain normally carry goods either under their own conditions of carriage or under those of the Road Haulage Association, and consequently carry Goods in Transit (GIT) insurance cover in respect of their liability under those conditions. The cover usually varies between £800 per tonne minimum and £1200 per tonne.

In international road haulage operations (but *not* own-account operations), the carriage automatically comes within the terms of the International Convention on the Carriage of Goods 1965, known as CMR. Under this Convention the carrier's liability is determined by comparison with a measure known as 'special drawing rights' (SDR), whereby compensation must not exceed 8.33 units of account per kilogramme of gross weight short (gws). Special drawing rights are defined by the International Monetary Fund and are converted to the national currency of the country in which any claim is dealt with in Court and is assessed as to value on the date of the judgment or on a date agreed to by the parties. To gain a rough idea of what this value represents, on 12 April 1995 a conversion of SDR to sterling represented approximately £8484 per tonne. The daily rate for SDR can be found in the financial papers.

(ie 8.33 units × 1,000 kg × SDR rate £1.01860 = £8,484.94 per tonne as at 12 April 1995)

NB: the value or exchange rate of SDRs on the date of judgment or agreement referred to above must not be confused with the date of calculation of the value of the goods which are subject to the claim as referred to in item 17 on page 264).

With changing values it is essential that the current value should be established at any particular time, and adequate insurance cover to at least this level of liability should be carried.

Since all international road haulage movements are subject to CMR and a CMR consignment note accompanies the transit, operators should be aware that with any such movement their liability is for the CMR levels and that they need appropriate cover.

However, there are circumstances when a domestic haulier could unwittingly be involved in an international movement. These may arise when a haulier is asked, for example, to carry a loaded trailer or container from one place in the UK to another place in the UK. If the trailer or container has entered the country from abroad and has not been unloaded, any internal movement in the UK is still part of the international journey and is therefore still subject to CMR. The UK haulier who moves such a trailer or container may not be aware of this, particularly if the facts are not drawn to his attention or the relevant documentation is not pointed out, and he may only have standard GIT or RHA levels of insurance cover. Similarly, a haulier may be involved in an international haulage journey within the UK by taking a loaded trailer to a port for onward shipment or even to an inland clearance depot. If the trailer goes forward loaded the haulier should realise that he needs to be covered for CMR levels of liability despite the fact that his tractive unit and driver do not leave this country.

CMR consignment notes

The following details must be entered on CMR consignment notes:

1. The date of the consignment note and the place at which it is made out.
2. The name and address of the sender.
3. The name and address of the carrier and subsequent carriers.
4. The place and date of taking over the goods and the place designated for delivery.
5. The name and address of the consignee.

6. A description in common use of the nature of the goods and the method of packing (in the case of dangerous goods, their generally recognised description).
7. The number of packages and their special marks and numbers.
8. The gross weight of the goods or their quantity otherwise expressed.
9. Charges relating to the carriage (carriage charges), supplementary charges, Customs' duties and other charges incurred from the making of the contract to the time of delivery.
10. Appropriate instructions for Customs and other formalities.
11. A statement that the carriage is subject, notwithstanding any clause to the contrary, to the provisions of the CMR Convention.

Where applicable, the consignment note should also contain the following information:

1. A statement that transhipment is not allowed.
2. The charges that the sender undertakes to pay.
3. The amount of COD charges.
4. A declaration of the value of the goods and of the amount representing special interest in delivery.
5. The sender's instructions to the carrier regarding insurance of the goods.
6. The agreed time limit within which the carriage is to occur.
7. A list of those documents handed to the carrier.

Any other particulars which the parties to the contract feel will be useful may be added to the consignment note.

The CMR consignment note must be carried by the driver on all hire and reward journeys abroad.

Supplies of CMR consignment notes can be obtained from the Road Haulage Association and the Freight Transport Association.

International Convention on the Taxation of Road Vehicles

The International Convention on the Taxation of Road Vehicles Engaged on International Journeys 1957 (Command Paper 4206) makes provision for exemption from the taxes and charges levied on the possession or circulation of vehicles by contracting countries (ie those contracting to the Convention) for vehicles temporarily imported from another contracting country.

Details of the main provisions of the Convention are as follows:

267

Definitions:

'Vehicle' covers all self-propelled road vehicles and all trailers, whether imported with the vehicle or separately.

'International goods transport' is the industrial or commercial transport of goods, with or without remuneration, when the route taken crosses at least one frontier between two countries.

'Taxes or charges' cover three basic types of tax:

1. Turnover taxes and taxes of a similar kind, such as taxes on added value (VAT)
2. Fees for the issue of transport licences and other necessary documents
3. Taxes or supplementary taxes payable on account of the transport operation concerned, in addition to taxes charged solely for the right to possess a vehicle or put it on the road.

The main purpose of the Convention is as follows:

'Vehicles which are registered in the territory of one of the contracting parties and are temporarily imported in the course of international goods transport into the territory of another contracting party shall (under the conditions laid down below) be exempted from the taxes and charges levied on the circulation or possession of vehicles in the territory of that contracting party. This exemption shall not apply to tolls, taxes or charges on consumption, or taxes or charges on transport'.

Goods vehicle taxation

Goods vehicles are normally subject to the vehicle taxation system of any country through which they pass. However, as a result of Britain's acceptance of the terms of the International Convention on the Taxation of Road Vehicles mentioned above and as a result of bilateral agreements, goods vehicles are exempt from paying further taxation in the following countries *provided that they are correctly taxed in the country of registration* (see below for the list of countries where additional taxes are payable).

To ensure that vehicles are correctly taxed to meet this requirement, valid excise licence discs must be displayed on the vehicle windscreen on all journeys abroad.

Countries where further lorry tax (ie excise duty) *has* to be paid are:

- □ Austria (tax payable on transit of goods vehicles)
- □ Hungary (where single axle weight of 10 tonnes or 16 tonnes on two axles)

- □ Switzerland (road tax payable based on gross weights and time in country)
- □ Turkey (transit tax payable)
- □ former Yugoslavia (road tax payable for vehicles in transit).

Fuel duties
Generally, road fuel used to power vehicles carries tax/duty payable in the country of origin at the time of purchase and no further tax/duty is payable when it is carried into other countries in vehicle fuel tanks (the general allowance within the EU is 200 litres). However, since many vehicles used on international operations have high-capacity, long-range fuel tanks, some countries charge additional tax or duty above certain limits.

Motorway tax
Goods vehicles exceeding 12 tonnes gross weight are subject to a motorway tax when travelling to or through Germany, the Benelux countries (Belgium, Luxembourg and Holland), and Denmark. A vehicle certificate (vignette) is issued upon payment of the sliding-scale tax depending on the number of axles (ie up to three and four or more) and the period of time for which the certificate is required (ie from one week to one year).

Part 4: Operations, Technical Standards and Road Safety

Traffic regulations in EU member states
Vehicle weights and dimensions

The maximum articulated vehicle and road train weights and dimensions (lengths and widths) within individual EU member states are as follows:

Member State	Nationality Sign	Max Width (metres)	Max Length (metres) Rigid/Artic/RT	Axle*	Max Weight (tonnes) Rigid*	Artic/RT/CT* (tonnes)
Austria	(A)	2.5/6	12/16/18	10	16/22	38/38/42
Belgium	(B)	2.5/6	12/16.5/18.35	12/20/30	19/26/32	44/44
Denmark	(DK)	2.55/6	12/16.5/18.5	11.5/20	18/24/32	48/48
Eire	(IRL)	2.5/6	12/16.5/18	10.5	17/26/32	40/40
Finland	(SF)	2.6	12/16.5/18.35	11.5/19	Depends on axle distance	
France	(F)	2.5	12/16.5/18.35	13/21/24	19/26/32	38/40/44
Germany	(D)	2.5/6	12/16.5/18.35	11.5/20	18/25/32	40/40/44
Greece	(GR)	2.5/6	12/16.5/18.35	11.5/20	18/26/33	40/40/44
Italy	(I)	2.5/6	12/16.5/18.35	10/19/25	18/25/32	40/44/44
Luxembourg	(L)	2.5	12/16.5/18	13/20/26	19/26	38/40
Netherlands	(NL)	2.6	12/16.5/18.35	11/20/27	20/30/40	50/50
Portugal	(P)	2.5/6	12/16.5/18.35	12	19/26/30	40/40/44
Spain	(E)	2.5/6	12/16.5/18.35	11.5/19	20/26/32	40/40/44
Sweden	(S)	2.6	24	11.5/19/24	Depends on axle distance	
United Kingdom	(GB)	2.5/6	12/16.5/18.35	10.5	16/26/32	38/38/44

Source: *IRU Handbook of International Road Transport* – 1994 (13th edition)

Notes:
* Axle = drive axle/double axle. Rigid = 2/3/4 axles. Artic/RT = 5/6 axles. CT = vehicles used exclusively for combined transport operations or container carrying. Most member states permit a 2.6-metre width limit for refrigerated vehicles.

Height
There is a height limit of 4 metres on goods vehicles entering Austria, Belgium, Denmark, Germany, Greece, Italy, Luxembourg, Netherlands, Portugal, Spain and Switzerland. Where vehicles registered in EU member states enter other states this limit is not usually enforced.

Speed limits

Speed limits applicable to goods vehicles in EU member states (plus Switzerland) are as follows:

Country	Built-up areas	Motorways	Other roads
Austria	50kph	80kph 70kph (road trains)	70kph 60kph (road trains)
Belgium	50kph	90kph (over 7.5t) 70kph min speed	60kph (over 7.5t)
Denmark	–	70kph	70kph
Eire	48kph	–	64kph
France	50kph	90kph (0ver12t) 80kph (DG)	80kph 60kph (DG)
Germany	50kph	80kph	80kph (up to 7.5t) 60kph
Great Britain	30mph (48kph)	60mph (96kph)	40mph (64kph)
Greece	50kph 40kph (DG)	70kph (main roads) 50kph (DG)	60kph
Italy	50kph 30kph (DG)		60kph (over 8t) 40kph (DG)
Luxembourg	60kph 40kph (DG)	90kph	75kph (over 5t) 60kph (DG)
Netherlands	50kph	80kph	80kph (A roads) 60kph (B roads)
Portugal	50kph		70kph
Spain	60kph	100kph	70kph
Switzerland	50kph	80kph	80kph (rigids) 60kp (artics/RT)

DG = Vehicles carrying dangerous goods

NB: Where member states have no motorways or where common speed limits apply to motorways and other roads (usually classified as being outside built-up areas) these are shown above midway between the two headings.

Route planning

Planning routes for international journeys becomes a matter of experience as operators and drivers learn from previous trips which are the best roads, where the delays occur, the most efficient channel ferry crossings and so on. Much depends on the nature of the traffic, the size and weight of the vehicle, the stopping places for services (driver accommodation, technical assistance with vehicles, refuelling, etc).

AGR Convention 1975

Europe has an extensive motorway/autobahn/expressway road system – the principal routes are designated 'E' routes (under the AGR Convention 1975 which established a system for numbering road networks) and these provide the facility for rapid and efficient transcontinental travel.

Road traffic bans/other delays

The operator should bear in mind restrictions on goods vehicle movement, especially bans on vehicles at certain times (ie at the weekend and on public holidays – see below). He should also allow for border crossing delays, mountain pass

271

crossings and bad weather on these particular routes, channel ferry crossing delays and greater restrictions on speed than are in force in the United Kingdom.

Bans on goods vehicles

Some EU member states and other neighbouring countries do not allow goods vehicles to use the roads at weekends or on public holidays. Operators should make inquiries about this with the transport association before planning journeys since public holidays vary from country to country and do not always coincide with those of Great Britain.

France, for instance, restricts the movement of goods vehicles over 6 tonnes laden weight on public holidays (eg Bastille Day – 14 July) and at weekends; Germany prohibits the use of goods vehicles over 7.5 tonnes gross weight on Sundays up to 22.00 hours and on public holidays; and goods vehicles may not be driven in Switzerland on Sundays, public holidays and during certain night hours (see list below).

EU member states and neighbouring countries where such bans apply at various times:

Country	Goods vehicle ban

Austria	over 3.5 tonnes and when drawing trailer (except for carriage of milk):
	  – after 15.00 hours Saturday
	  – all day Sunday
	  – on public holidays until 22.00 hours

Eire	no traffic/vehicle bans in operation but it is not possible to pass through Customs' posts (ie from Northern Ireland) except between 09.00 and 17.00 hours daily (weekdays only) except by special request and fee payment

France	vehicles over 6 tonnes laden weight (except those carrying perishables, live animals, newspapers, hydrocarbons and vehicles returning to their home country):
	  – 22.00 hours Saturday (or the day before a public holiday) to 22.00 hours Sundays and public holidays
	vehicles carrying dangerous goods:
	  – 12.00 hours Saturday (or the day before a public holiday) to 24.00 hours Sunday and public holidays

Cont...

Cont...

Country	Goods vehicle ban
Germany	vehicles over 7.5 tonnes laden weight (except en route to Berlin and those carrying fresh milk, meat and produce): – Sundays and public holidays
Greece	goods vehicles (except those carrying perishables): – 17.00 hours Saturday to 24.00 hours Sundays and public holidays
Italy	goods vehicles with pmw over 5 tonnes, lorries with trailers (even if unladen) and those carrying dangerous goods: – 08.00 to 22.00 hours Sundays (Jan, Feb, Mar, Oct, Nov, Dec) – 07.00 to 24.00 hours Sundays (May, June, July, Aug, Sept)
Portugal	goods vehicles using certain main national routes: – 14.00 hours to 22.00 hours Saturdays – 06.00 hours to 24.00 hours Sundays and public holidays vehicles carrying dangerous goods: – 12.00 hours to 24.00 hours Saturdays – 06.00 to 24.00 hours Sundays and public holidays
Spain	goods vehicles except those carrying perishables: – Sundays and public holidays 17.00 to 24.00 hours goods vehicles carrying dangerous goods: – Saturday 13.00 hours to Sunday 24.00 hours
Switzerland	vehicles above 3.5 tonnes: – all day Sundays and public holidays – 22.00 to 05.00 hours daily
former Yugoslavia	vehicles over 5 tonnes during tourist season: – Sundays, public holidays and the eve of public holidays

Road signs   Britain's road sign system follows that of most European countries with the use of internationally recognised signs so those that are familiar on the roads in Britain will be recognisable abroad. See a current copy of the Highway Code. Certain road signs in Belgium and parts of northern Spain (Basque and Catalonian regions) are shown in dual language (eg French and Flemish in Belgium).

Driving on right/priority at junctions	The whole of Europe (except the UK and Eire) drive on the right and vehicles must overtake to the left. Priority at road junctions is mainly to traffic approaching from or turning right, viz 'Priorité à droite'.
Sources of information	It is essential for operators, when sending vehicles on international journeys, to be aware of the requirements in foreign countries for the following:

1. Driver licensing
2. Vehicle licensing
3. Traffic regulations
4. Restrictions on vehicle movement
5. Accident procedures
6. Movement of abnormal loads.

Information on these matters may be obtained from a number of sources:

1. The motor organisations: AA, RAC, RSAC.
2. *Your Lorry Abroad*, International Road Freight Office.
3. *International Services Manual*, Freight Transport Association.
4. Road Haulage Association.
5. Transport authorities for individual countries (eg the DoT in the UK).
6. Insurance companies, in the case of accident procedures.

Insurance and carriers' liability	Adequate insurance is necessary against civil liability claims in respect of the use of motor vehicles on international journeys. Details of the requirements are specified in EU Directive 166/72 'Council Directive on the approximation of the laws of the member states relating to insurance against civil liability in respect of the use of motor vehicles, and to the enforcement of the obligation to ensure against such liability' as follows:

Definitions:
- *Vehicle:* Any mechanically propelled motor vehicle intended for travel on land and any trailer, whether coupled or not.
- *Injured party:* Any person entitled to compensation in respect of any loss or injury caused by vehicles.
- *National Insurers' Bureau:* A professional organisation which groups together insurance undertakings authorised by member states to conduct the business of motor vehicle insurance against civil liability. Such bodies are constituted in accordance with a recommendation of the Road Transport Sub-Committee of the Inland Transport Committee of the United Nations Economic Commission for Europe.

- □ *Territory in which the vehicle is based:* The state in which the vehicle is registered.
- □ *Green card:* An international certificate of insurance issued on behalf of a national insurers' bureau (see above).

Other provisions of Directive

It provides that member states need not see evidence of insurance in respect of vehicles based in other member states. Similarly, it provides for a relaxation of checks on the evidence of insurance for vehicles based in third countries when entering member states from another member state.

It specifies that member states must take all appropriate steps to ensure that civil liability (in the UK commonly known as third-party liability or 'Road Traffic Act' cover) in respect of vehicles based in their territory is covered by insurance.

Member states must make sure that the insurance also provides cover for:

1. loss or injury caused in other member states according to the law in force in those states
2. loss or injury suffered by nationals of member states during a direct journey between two territories in which the Treaty establishing the EU is in force, if there is no national insurers' bureau responsible for the territory which is being crossed. In this case the loss or injury must be covered in accordance with the internal laws on compulsory insurance in force in the member state where the vehicle is normally based.

It allows for derogation (exemption) from the previous Article in certain respects. A list of exempted people must be drawn up by the member state and communicated to other member states and to the EU commission.

Member states must ensure that compensation is paid in respect of loss or injury caused in the territory of other member states by vehicles belonging to the exempt persons.

Further, derogation also applies to certain vehicles having a special plate, but member states may still request sight of valid green cards for vehicles entering their territory or they can request that suitable insurance cover is obtained at the point of entry to the territory.

It also deals with action in the event of accidents. Member states are required to ensure that where an accident is caused in its territory by a vehicle normally based in another member state, the national insurers' bureau must be given the following information:

1. Details of the vehicle registration mark and the territory in which the vehicle is normally based.
2. Details of the insurance of the vehicle from the green card or as they would appear on the green card.

This information must be given to the national insurers' bureau of the state in whose territory the vehicle is normally based.

The Directive requires EU member states to ensure that vehicles normally based in third countries (ie non-EU members) or in the non-European territory of any member state are not used in their territory unless any loss or injury caused by those vehicles is covered in accordance with the various laws on compulsory insurance against civil liability in respect of the use of vehicles.

It further requires that vehicles from third countries must have a green card or a certificate of frontier insurance before entering EU member states unless the national bureaux of all member states guarantee, in accordance with their own national laws, settlement of claims in respect of accidents caused by such vehicles.

Green cards An international motor insurance card (green card) issued by an insurance bureau (in the UK the MIB via insurance companies) will provide evidence of insurance against compulsory insurable liabilities in those countries in which the card is valid.

While green cards are no longer essential for travel within the EU and in certain other countries, drivers should continue to carry a green card (or at least their British insurance certificate) because although they will not be subjected to routine checks they may need to produce them in the event of an accident or other incident.

European Accident Statement It is usual for insurers to provide a copy of the European Accident Statement to operators who send their vehicles abroad. This document is a universally recognised form of words and layout for making a report (ie statement) of a motor vehicle accident. The document contains advice to drivers (eg 'don't get angry; be polite; keep calm') and instructions on completion of the form. It also instructs drivers to forward the form without delay to their own insurer (ie the vehicle insurer). It should not be sent to any other official body.

International transport operating systems A wide variety of transport modes and systems may be used by exporters, and frequently movements require the use of a combination of such modes. Although the principal forms of transportation require special study, brief outlines of some forms are given here with their relative advantages and some sources of information:

Freight forwarders

Exporters who do not wish to make their own arrangements with carriers and agents and deal directly with Customs can use the services of freight forwarders who will make all the necessary arrangements for them, negotiating the carriage, completing documentation, clearing Customs, etc. As an alternative, the services of freight forwarders may be used for only specific aspects of the whole export operation.

The principal advantages of using freight forwarders are relief from the need to co-ordinate all the activities of exporting and the availability of special expertise in this field. Information on freight forwarders and their services may be obtained from BIFA (the British International Freight Association).

Roll-on/roll-off

The development of roll-on/roll-off (ro/ro) short sea ferry ships has been one of the significant advances in modern transportation. On these ships, goods vehicles and trailers can make journeys abroad without their cargo having to be unloaded or the vehicle lifted aboard the ship. They offer speed and efficiency in loading and unloading and reduce the risks of loss or damage to goods through transhipment.

Progressively, the original channel crossing ro/ro services have developed to a point where an enormous variety of services and cross-channel routes are available to international transport operators. Information on these services may be obtained from the following bodies:

- □ Freight Transport Association
- □ Road Haulage Association
- □ Department of Trade and Industry
- □ Cross Channel shipping companies.

The Channel Tunnel

The Channel Tunnel (which opened in 1994) provides yet another alternative mode for international transport. Freight may travel through the Tunnel on a driver-accompanied basis, with complete road vehicles using Eurotunnel's Le Shuttle rolling motorway system whereby the vehicles are driven on at Folkestone and off at Calais (or vice versa), with only an 80-minute transit time from motorway to motorway. Other freight is carried on an intermodal basis by container or swap body on through train services from inland terminals in the UK to destinations in Europe. Conventional rail freight is also carried through the Tunnel.

Containerisation and swap bodies

This is another aspect of transportation which has changed the face of the industry in recent years. With the benefits of providing exporters with a means of transport, conforming to very rigid dimensions, being easily handled with the right equipment, being sufficiently strong to protect the goods inside in all the circumstances which may be met on overland

277

journeys and sea crossings and being capable of being sealed to provide security for the goods, the container has a special place among transport modes.

Swap bodies fulfil many of the roles of containers with the principal exception that they cannot be stacked. Extensive use of this form of transportation exists in Europe and with the opening of the Channel Tunnel (see above) the potential exists for a significant increase in this form of loading for UK–international intermodal freight traffic. It is worth pointing out that the term 'combined' or 'road–rail' transport has come to the fore as this concept develops, and as we have seen earlier in this manual legislative provision has been made in the UK and Europe for vehicles used in this traffic to be permitted to run at 44 tonnes gross weight.

Information on the use of containers and swap bodies may be obtained from many sources, including the Inter-Governmental Maritime Consultative Organisation

Other methods of unitisation

Besides containers/swap bodies which provide shippers with a means of packing their export consignments in a safe and secure way, there are other methods of unitisation used in international transport, as follows:

1. Sealed TIR vehicles and trailers.
2. On pallets with goods secured by:
   (a) netting
   (b) banding
   (c) shrink wrapping.
3. In air-freight-type igloos (small, specially-shaped containers).
4. For liquids, in tanks.

Unitisation of loads ensures more efficient handling, reduced risk of consignments becoming dispersed and lost and reduced risk of damage.

Groupage

For shippers and exporters who do not have consignments sufficiently large to fully occupy TIR vehicles or trailers or containers, the services of groupage companies are useful.

These firms combine the shipper's consignments with those of other similar small-scale shippers to fill vehicles and containers, thereby providing an economical means of sending 'less-than-container-load' (LCL) shipments.

Train ferry

For goods which are suited to rail shipment or where transit charges are more competitive than road movement, British Rail provides, in conjunction with European railway networks, a system of train ferry services by which means goods can make through transit by rail.

Road/rail

In some European countries*, the national rail network provides a system whereby road vehicles can be carried by rail. For example the French Kangourou system is available for use for the transit of unaccompanied trailers and semi-trailers and German railways operate the 'Piggy-back' service. The advantage of such systems is that the rail rate may be less than the vehicle operating cost over the route, but more significantly the systems provide a means of overcoming shortages in permit allocations. In the case of Germany, for example, operators wishing to travel through the country to reach more distant countries can put their vehicles on the railway at the western frontier and take them off at the eastern frontier and can thus eliminate the need for a permit. Full details of the services may be obtained from British Rail or from representatives of the German (DB) and French (SNCF) railway networks in London.

* NB: With the opening of the Channel Tunnel in 1994 the potential for such services is now being explored for UK–Europe freighting.

Financial considerations
Exchange rates

In international transport and the exportation of goods, the financial aspects of operation take on particular significance because of the increased direct costs and the vagaries of exchange rates between the currencies of one country and another.

The values of the currencies of various countries in relation to each other change frequently and often without prior warning. In some instances the effect is of considerable consequence, especially where foreign currencies rise in value to the pound sterling, and can seriously affect the British haulier's pricing of contracts (eg he should beware of quoting prices too far in advance because sudden currency fluctuations could have a significant effect on his prices).

A 'strong' pound sterling reduces the operator's costs (because he gets more value in foreign currencies in exchange for his one pound sterling) whereas a 'weak' pound will result in higher direct costs of operation outside Britain especially for such items as fuel and driver expenses for example (because he gets less value in foreign currencies in exchange for his one pound sterling). In order to understand the effects of exchange rates, it is useful to make a series of comparisons of the rates as published in the financial press.

European Currency Units (ECUs)
With the implementation of financial measures in connection with the Single European Market, a new universal currency,

the ECU (European Currency Unit), has been introduced. This will be useful in inter-Union trade because of the way in which it will help smooth out wide variations in individual national currencies. Haulage rates can be quoted in ECUs and the current daily value of these units is quoted in the financial press

Costs involved in international haulage

The international haulier is confronted with many additional costs compared to his domestic counterpart. These include the following:

1. The need for vehicles which meet the TIR specification or Community Transit requirements.
2. The costs of employing staff experienced in international operations.
3. The cost of documentation preparation such as; carnets, consignment notes and other documents.
4. Additional insurance costs for vehicles.
5. The cost of obtaining permits.
6. Other fiscal charges.
7. Cross-channel ferry fares.
8. Taxes, tolls and dues in foreign countries (see pages 267-9).
9. The extra costs of communication.
10. Driver expenses for food, accommodation, general expenses and cash for on-the-spot fines and 'gratuities'.
11. The higher costs incurred in the event of vehicle breakdown.
12. Insurance costs for CMR liability, green card, drivers' medical/accident cover and bail bonds.
13. Drivers' extra costs for passport, international driving licence (where necessary) and visas.

The carriage of perishable foodstuffs
The ATP Agreement

This is an International Agreement on the Transport of Perishable Foodstuffs and on the Special Equipment to be used for such Carriage (in its full French title – 'L'Accord relatif aux Transports internationaux de denrées Périssables et aux engins spéciaux a utiliser pour ces transports' – ATP) to which Britain acceded from 1 October 1979 by implementation of the International Carriage of Perishable Foodstuffs Act 1976 and The International Carriage of Perishable Foodstuffs Regulations 1985.

Its purpose is to improve the conditions of preservation of perishable foodstuffs during their carriage, particularly in international trade. It applies on journeys by road or rail (or a combination of both), and where sea crossings (eg by ferry ship) are involved, provided these do not exceed 150 kilometres (see item 3 in list below). It does not apply to national transport of such goods within the UK.

The principal terms of the Agreement are as follows:

1. The use of the following terms is prohibited unless the equipment (ie vehicles and containers) in question complies with the standards set out in the Agreement:
   (a) insulated
   (b) refrigerated
   (c) mechanically refrigerated
   (d) heated.

2. The equipment (ie vehicles and containers) referred to in point 1 must be inspected and tested for compliance at six-yearly intervals. Certificates of compliance, which must be carried on the vehicle and produced for inspection on request by an authorised inspecting officer, will be recognised by contracting parties to the Agreement. When a certificate has been issued, vehicles/containers must be fitted with a 'designated mark' showing the month and year of the inspection expiry (blue figures on white background).

3. The Agreement applies to carriage, if the carriage is between two different states, on own-account or for hire and reward by rail or road of:
   (a) quick (deep) frozen and frozen foodstuffs
   (b) other foodstuffs (including meats, offal, game, milk, fish, poultry and rabbits and dairy products) which are not quick frozen or frozen.
   This condition applies if the original vehicle containing the goods having travelled by road or rail is subsequently carried on a sea crossing of less than 150km between one or more land journeys.

4. The equipment referred to in point 1 must be used in movements covered by the Agreement unless the temperatures to be anticipated during the carriage make this unnecessary; otherwise the equipment must be used to maintain temperatures laid down in the Agreement.

5. The Agreement does not apply to carriage in containers by land where this is preceded by or followed by a sea crossing other than as described in point 3 above (ie if it is more than 150km).

6. Parties to the Agreement must ensure observance of its conditions.

Countries which are party to the ATP Agreement include all EU member states plus:

- Bulgaria
- Commonwealth of Independent States (CIS)
- Morocco
- Norway
- Switzerland
- former Yugoslavia

Vehicles (including trailers and containers) used on ATP operations must be examined at a DoT approved establishment of which there are currently five in Great Britain. On satisfactory completion of the test a certificate (or a metal certification plate for affixing to the vehicle/trailer/container) is issued which is valid for six years. This certificate is transferable to a new owner on request.

Transport of perishables to Italy

Vehicles used for the transport of frozen and deep frozen foodstuffs to Italy during the period from 1 April to 31 October each year must be tested to ensure that they comply with specific regulations relating to carriage in vehicles with thin side walls – The International Carriage of Perishable Foodstuffs (Vehicles with Thin Side Walls) Regulations 1987.

Carriage of dangerous goods
The ADR Agreement

The International Agreement on the Carriage of Dangerous Goods by Road 1969 (ADR – Accord Européen relative au transport international des marchandises Dangereuses par Route) deals with the safe carriage and safe packing of dangerous goods conveyed by road on international journeys – it does not apply to domestic haulage of such goods within Great Britain.

The purpose of the Agreement is to enable dangerous goods, which are packed and labelled and carried in vehicles which comply with the provisions in Annexes A and B to the Agreement, to travel unhindered to and through countries which are parties to the Agreement, namely, all EU member states with the exception of Eire (which although not a signatory to the Agreement nevertheless applies its provisions) plus Czechoslovakia (now the Czech and Slovak Republics), Hungary, Norway and the former Yugoslavia.

Vehicles for ADR operations

In order to convey dangerous goods by road to or through the countries listed above, vehicles must have been examined by the relevant national authority (the DoT in the UK) to ensure they conform to the strict technical requirements set out in the Agreement (full details of the requirements are specified in Annex B to the Agreement). This requirement applies to tanker vehicles (ie rigid, articulated tractive units, trailers and semi-trailers) used to carry dangerous goods in bulk and vehicles used for carrying explosives. Following inspection (which can be carried out at the same time as the annual vehicle test) a certificate will be issued to confirm that it complies with the ADR specification and with national safety regulations. A valid certificate must be carried on vehicles and will be accepted as evidence of conformity with ADR requirements. Certificates are valid for one year. In addition to technical requirements of the vehicle itself, the Agreement specifies that a vehicle must:

1. carry two portable fire extinguishers (one to deal with vehicle/engine fires and one suitable for a fire in the load) plus one further extinguisher which must be left with any detached trailer
2. carry a tool kit for emergency repairs and at least one wheel chock (suited to the weight of the vehicle and the diameter of its wheels)
3. be equipped with two amber lights (of the steady or flashing type and capable of operating independently of the vehicle electrics) when travelling in Europe. If the vehicle lights are not working when it is stopped on the road at night or in conditions of bad visibility these amber lights must be placed on the road approximately 10 metres ahead of and 10 metres behind the vehicle
4. display marker plates (of orange reflex reflecting material with black border and lettering) at the front and rear showing:
   (a) the identification number of the substance carried
   (b) the identification number indicating the degree of risk
   NB: Such markers must be displayed on each side of the tank if it contains more than one such dangerous substance and the front and rear vehicle markers in this case must be plain orange.
   All such markers must be covered or removed when the tank is empty and has been cleaned and purged.
5. display danger labels (sometimes referred to as hazard diamonds) on both sides and at the rear of tanker vehicles.

Additional points to note are that:

1. vehicles must not be left unsupervised when carrying goods under the ADR Agreement
2. passengers (other than crew members) must not be carried
3. if a vehicle has to stop and is likely to cause danger which the crew cannot deal with, the nearest competent authority must be notified whose name, address and telephone number the driver should have been provided with.

Driver training/ certification

Drivers and other crew members must be instructed in the safety aspects of international dangerous goods movement under the ADR Agreement and the action to be taken and the treatment to be given in the case of emergency or risk of danger. The driver must also carry with him a certificate of competence issued by a competent authority (in the UK such certificates are issued following Hazfreight training under The

283

National (Dangerous Substances) Driver Training Scheme – NDSDTS).

IMO/IMDG Code

These initial letters stand for the Inter-Governmental Maritime Organisation which has established an International Maritime Dangerous Goods (IMDG) Code. This is a standard code, recognised internationally, for the identification and marking of dangerous goods in transit (by sea). In the shipping trade, a Department of Trade and Industry publication *The Carriage of Dangerous Goods in Ships*, commonly known as the 'Blue Book', is referred to for information about the classification and methods of packing and freighting such goods. Its contents are relevant to international freighting of dangerous goods by road where sea crossings by ferry ship are involved.

Appendix 1
Typical Examination Questions

Readers who wish to prepare themselves for the examination are recommended to test their knowledge with the following typical questions, the answers for which are to be found on pages 298–9. For a more comprehensive test, and for examination practice, a further book called *1001 Typical Questions and Answers* by the author of this manual is available from Kogan Page.

National syllabus module A – sample examination questions

Select *one* answer only from (a), (b), (c), etc for each question.

1. Unless a lower speed limit is in force, the maximum permitted speed for any motor vehicle on a UK dual carriageway is
   (a) 40mph
   (b) 50mph
   (c) 60mph
   (d) 70mph

2. A traffic warden may enforce the law for an offence in connection with
   (a) stealing a motor vehicle
   (b) leaving a vehicle parked at night without lights
   (c) failing to stop after an accident
   (d) driving a vehicle with defective tyres

3. Endorsements for speeding offences remain on the driving licence for
   (a) 1 year
   (b) 3 years
   (c) 4 years
   (d) 5 years

4. A transport firm which is a private limited company wishes to employ additional labour for a short-term contract. This entails additional outlay of approximately £20,000. How might it reasonably try to raise the extra money?
   (a) by bank overdraft
   (b) a rights share issue
   (c) an additional share issue
   (d) on debenture

5. An increase in the annual rates that a transport company has to pay for its premises will show as
   (a) decreased revenue in the trading account
   (b) decreased revenue in the profit and loss account
   (c) increased expenditure in the profit and loss account
   (d) increased expenditure in the balance sheet

6. Which of the following information must an operator have before 'Return on Capital Employed' can be calculated?
   (a) working capital
   (b) net profit
   (c) debtors
   (d) gross profit

7. A 'Cash Budget' is a
   (a) plan for future cash expenditure
   (b) plan for future marketing techniques
   (c) record of cash receipts
   (d) record of cash expenditure

8. Effective stock control in a transport company can
   (a) reduce the amount of finance tied up in stocks of spares
   (b) lead to a worsening of the company's cash flow position
   (c) reduce the amount of finance available for other purposes
   (d) lead to the accumulation of excessive stocks of spares

9. A quotation is a notification
   (a) from a supplier to a purchaser detailing the amount owed for work done
   (b) from a customer instructing a supplier to supply specified goods or services
   (c) from a supplier to a purchaser reminding him how the account stands at a particular date
   (d) to a customer specifying a price for carrying out a particular job

10. A transport firm decides that in future instead of paying its suppliers by cheque it will pay them any monies owed direct into their bank accounts. This arrangement is known as
    (a) direct debit
    (b) credit transfer
    (c) deferred payment
    (d) standing order

11. Compulsory Employers' Liability Insurance is designed to meet claims
    (a) by customers injured by defective products
    (b) by employees alleging they have been unfairly dismissed
    (c) by employees injured at work
    (d) for loss of production due to strikes

12. An agent who makes secret profit from activities of the Principal
    (a) can be sued by the Principal for the equivalent sum
    (b) can retain the sum involved regardless of whether or not the Principal has suffered any loss
    (c) must return the sum involved to the person from whom it was obtained
    (d) can keep the sum involved as long as the Principal has not suffered any loss

13. A claim for damages for negligence against a transport operator can *only* be successful if the
    (a) operator has broken some statutory obligation
    (b) operator has committed a criminal offence
    (c) operator has entered into a valid legal contract with the plaintiff
    (d) plaintiff has suffered loss

14. A Plc must have an authorised share capital of at least
    (a) £1
    (b) £50,000
    (c) £500,000
    (d) £1,000,000

15. An employee who is dismissed after at least 4 weeks' service
    (a) is not entitled to a written statement at all
    (b) is not entitled to a written statement if he is dismissed for misconduct
    (c) must be given a written statement of the reasons if he asks for one
    (d) must be given a written statement of the reasons in all cases

16. Under employment legislation which of the following is entitled to time off work *with pay* to carry out the duties stated?
    (a) A person called for jury service
    (b) A shop steward for union business
    (c) A JP to carry out his public duties
    (d) A member of an independent trade union to attend a union meeting

17. Which one of the following benefits is dependent upon an employee having paid a certain number of National Insurance contributions?
    (a) Unemployment benefit
    (b) Disablement allowance
    (c) Income support
    (d) Retirement pension

18. An employee with a grievance under United Kingdom Equal Pay Legislation may seek redress by application to an Industrial Tribunal during employment or within a maximum period of
    (a) 6 months of termination of employment
    (b) 9 months of termination of employment
    (c) 12 months of termination of employment at any time
    (d) at any time

19. For what minimum period must a person who is appointed as a safety representative have normally been employed either by the present employer, or in similar employment elsewhere?
    (a) 5 years
    (b) 3 years
    (c) 2 years
    (d) 1 year

20. An application for a trade licence must be submitted to the
    (a) Driver and Vehicle Licensing Centre, Swansea
    (b) Local Vehicle Registration Office
    (c) Goods Vehicle Centre, Swansea
    (d) Department of Trade

The reader will find the correct answers to all these questions within the foregoing text but for ease of reference they are repeated on page 298.

National syllabus module B – sample examination questions

Select *one* answer only from (a), (b), (c), etc for each question.

1. Under EU Regulation 3820/85, a person driving vehicles coming within the scope of the regulation is limited to a maximum period of fortnightly driving of
   - (a) 88 hours
   - (b) 90 hours
   - (c) 92 hours
   - (d) 96 hours

2. Under EU Regulation 3820/85 the minimum break required after the maximum permitted driving period is
   - (a) 20 minutes
   - (b) 30 minutes
   - (c) 45 minutes
   - (d) 60 minutes

3. On a two-man tachograph, the chart for the non-driving crew member will record
   - (a) distance and activity mode only
   - (b) speed and distance only
   - (c) speed, activity mode, distance and time
   - (d) activity mode and time only

4. A new plaque must be fitted to the tachograph after re-calibration every
   - (a) 6 years
   - (b) 3 years
   - (c) 2 years
   - (d) 1 year

5. The police have the power to enter premises to inspect drivers' hours records
   - (a) only between 9.00 am and 5.00 pm
   - (b) at any reasonable time
   - (c) at any time
   - (d) they have no such power

6. A driver who is unavoidably delayed on a National road haulage journey which causes him to depart from EU Drivers' Hours Regulations must
   - (a) contact the Traffic Area Office as soon as possible to advise them of the occurrence
   - (b) report the circumstances to the police as soon as possible
   - (c) enter the details on the relevant tachograph chart
   - (d) report the circumstances within 24 hours to a motor vehicle examiner

7. The holder of a Category C LGV entitlement is also authorised to drive a vehicle of Category
   (a) D + E
   (b) B
   (c) C + E
   (d) A

8. A Licensing Authority revokes an LGV entitlement. The driver can appeal to the
   (a) Magistrates'/Sheriff's Court
   (b) Minister for Transport
   (c) Transport Tribunal
   (d) High Court

9. A 38 tonne articulated vehicle may travel at a maximum speed on a motorway of
   (a) 40mph
   (b) 50mph
   (c) 60mph
   (d) 70mph

10. At the scene of an accident on the public highway where no injury is involved, a driver is by law bound to provide, if required
    (a) his driving licence
    (b) his insurance policy
    (c) his certificate of insurance
    (d) his name and address

11. Any legal obligation by a haulage operator to pay for emergency hospital treatment to persons (other than employees) injured in a traffic accident involving one of his haulage vehicles would be covered by
    (a) Fidelity Insurance
    (b) Consequential Loss Insurance
    (c) Third Party Motor Insurance
    (d) Employer's Liability Insurance

12. A road haulage operator can carry his own third party motor insurance risks provided he deposits a sum of money with the Accountant General of the Supreme Court as a security. This sum is
    (a) £100,000
    (b) £150,000
    (c) £250,000
    (d) £500,000

13. The Code of Practice on the safe loading of vehicles states that to prevent movement of the payload in a forward direction, a load restraint device should be capable of withstanding a force equal to
    (a) 50% of the total weight of the load
    (b) 75% of the total weight of the load
    (c) the total weight of the load
    (d) twice the total weight of the load

14. An attendant must accompany a vehicle travelling under the Special Types Order when the
    (a) overall length of the vehicle and load is 18 metres
    (b) vehicle and load are 4 metres wide

    (c)   load projects to the front by 1 metre
    (d)   load projects to the rear by 2 metres

15. The colours which appear on a sign denoting a vehicle is carrying flammable liquids are
    (a)   black symbol on a red background
    (b)   red symbol on a black background
    (c)   black symbol on a white background
    (d)   white symbol on a black background

16. Under Construction and Use Regulations, the maximum permissible weight for a rigid vehicle having four or more axles is
    (a)   22,360 kilograms
    (b)   26,420 kilograms
    (c)   28,450 kilograms
    (d)   32,000 kilograms

17. The normal permitted maximum overall length of a road train consisting of a vehicle and one trailer in the United Kingdom is
    (a)   25 metres
    (b)   18.35 metres
    (c)   18 metres
    (d)   16.5 metres

18. Advance notice must be given to the police when it is proposed to move on to the public highway a vehicle and load having a rearward projection exceeding
    (a)   1.07 metres
    (b)   1.83 metres
    (c)   2.9 metres
    (d)   3.05 metres

19. A goods vehicle is classed as a motor car if its unladen weight does not exceed
    (a)   3050 kgs
    (b)   3500 kgs
    (c)   5075 kgs
    (d)   7250 kgs

20. Under Plating and Testing Regulations which of the following alterations must be notified to the DoT before the vehicle is used on the road?
    (a)   a change in the structure of the vehicle which varies its carrying capacity
    (b)   a change in the colour of the vehicle
    (c)   a change in the use of the vehicle
    (d)   a change in the owner of the vehicle

21. Under Construction and Use Regulations every vehicle having a fixed windscreen must have
    (a)   at least one automatic wiper
    (b)   at least two automatic wipers
    (c)   a method of clearing the windscreen which may be manual if this is efficient
    (d)   an adequate method of clearing the windscreen with no specific requirement as to method or the number of wipers

22. Rear underrun protectors must be fitted to most new rigid goods vehicles if the GVW exceeds
    (a) 3500 kgs
    (b) 2040 kgs
    (c) 1525 kgs
    (d) 1020 kgs

23. The minimum legal tread depth of a vehicle over 3.5 tonnes is
    (a) 1mm
    (b) 1.5mm
    (c) 2mm
    (d) 3.5mm

24. In accordance with current lighting regulations, which of the following lamps must be fitted to *all* goods vehicles?
    (a) two front spot lamps
    (b) two rear fog lamps
    (c) rear number plate lamp
    (d) reversing lamps

25. Which of the following persons can issue prohibitions and defect notices?
    (a) an officer of HM Customs and Excise
    (b) a weights and measures officer
    (c) a driving/traffic examiner
    (d) a Department of Transport vehicle examiner

26. The weight of a vehicle inclusive of body and parts normally used in operation but exclusive of weight of water, fuel, loose tools and equipment, and batteries, where these are used for propelling the vehicle, is defined as the
    (a) kerbside weight
    (b) plated weight
    (c) tare weight
    (d) unladen weight

27. A prohibition notice (PG 9) issued for a vehicle can only be completely removed by the issue of form
    (a) PG 9A
    (b) PG 9B
    (c) PG 9C
    (d) PG 10

28. Smith wishes to enter the transport industry for the carriage of goods for hire or reward. He will require a Standard National 'O' licence to operate which of the following vehicles?
    (a) a rigid vehicle of 3 tonnes gross plated weight
    (b) a rigid vehicle of 5 tonnes unladen weight
    (c) a dual purpose vehicle and trailer
    (d) an articulated vehicle of 3.5 tonnes combined gross plated weight

29. A road haulage operator applying for an 'O' licence
    (a) must lodge one application irrespective of how many operating centres he has throughout Great Britain
    (b) must lodge separate applications for each traffic area in which he has an operating centre

(c) must make a single consolidated application to the Department of Transport Head Office

(d) must make a single consolidated application to the Transport Tribunal

30. A haulier who acquires additional vehicles within the limit authorised by his licence
    (a) need not do anything
    (b) should have informed the Licensing Authority before he acquired them
    (c) must inform the Licensing Authority within one month of acquiring them
    (d) must inform the Licensing Authority within three months of acquiring them

31. Which of the following bodies has a statutory right to object to the granting of an operator's licence?
    (a) Industrial Training Board
    (b) Health and Safety Executive
    (c) Freight Transport Association
    (d) Department of Environment

32. Records of defects found during preventive maintenance inspections must be retained by the operator for a minimum period of
    (a) 6 months
    (b) 9 months
    (c) 12 months
    (d) 15 months

33. An operator parks his vehicles at the premises of a major customer. They are maintained at a commercial garage. The business is run from his home address. The operating centre is
    (a) his drivers' homes
    (b) his home
    (c) the garage
    (d) his customer's premises

34. A company applies for a restricted operator's licence. Which one of the following criteria can be *ignored* by the licensing authority?
    (a) the applicant must have sufficient financial resources
    (b) the applicant must be a fit and proper person
    (c) the applicant must hold a CPC
    (d) the arrangements for observing drivers' hours and records must be acceptable

35. Eighteen months after the death of his designated Transport Manager an operator has not employed anybody to take his place and as a result has his Standard Operator's Licence taken away. This constitutes
    (a) refusal to grant the licence
    (b) suspension of the licence
    (c) curtailment of the licence
    (d) revocation of his licence

36. Which of the following is a fixed (standing) cost?
    (a) lubricating oils used
    (b) drivers guaranteed wages

    (c)   fuel consumed

    (d)   tyres supplied on contract

37. A new vehicle costing £49,200 has 6 wheels with tyres worth £200 *each*. If it is to be written down to £6,000 over 7 years, what is its annual depreciation using the straight-line method?

    (a)   £6,000

    (b)   £6,171

    (c)   £6,500

    (d)   £7,029

38. The term 'Carriage Forward' means payment for transport

    (a)   has already been made by the consignor

    (b)   has been made by the consignor's forwarding agent

    (c)   will be the responsibility of the consignee

    (d)   will be the responsibility of the consignor

39. An organisation which is set up specifically to organise the movement of loads by the use of sub-contracted hauliers is known as

    (a)   an own-account operator

    (b)   a warehouse

    (c)   a hire and reward operator

    (d)   a clearing house

40. A sub-contractor is

    (a)   a haulage operator who undertakes to perform work on behalf of the original contractor

    (b)   an agent who works on a commission basis for a principal

    (c)   a haulage operator who sub-contracts work to other haulage operators

    (d)   an agent who arranges transport for a customer and prepares the necessary customs and transport documentation

The reader will find the correct answers to all these questions within the foregoing text but for ease of reference they are repeated on page 298.

International syllabus module D – sample examination questions

Select one answer only from (a), (b), (c), etc for each question.

1. Joe Bloggs, an LGV driver (based in Dover), has during the current week taken the following daily rest periods

    (a)   Monday   12 hours in Dover

    (b)   Tuesday   12 hours in Paris

    (c)   Wednesday   9 hours in Dover

    (d)   Thursday   11 hours in London

    If he takes his daily rest period on Friday in Dover what is the minimum length of rest he must take in accordance with EU drivers' hours regulations?

   (a) 8 hours
   (b) 9 hours
   (c) 11 hours
   (d) 12 hours

2. EU Regulation 3820/85, limiting driving time to a maximum of 9 hours daily, allows the following alternatives
   (a) 9 hours twice in any 7 days
   (b) 10 hours twice in any 7 days
   (c) 10 hours twice in a week
   (d) no alternatives are allowed

3. The minimum weekly rest period required by an LGV driver when operating to an AETR country is
   (a) 24 hours
   (b) 24 hours immediately preceded or followed by a daily rest period
   (c) 45 hours
   (d) 45 hours immediately preceded or followed by a daily rest period

4. If a tachograph breaks down on an international journey the operator must have it repaired, at the latest, as soon as the vehicle returns to his premises. However, the tachograph must be repaired en route if, counting from the day of the breakdown, the vehicle is unable to return to base within
   (a) 2 days
   (b) 3 days
   (c) 5 days
   (d) 7 days

5. An EU-approved tachograph being used on a heavy goods vehicle on a journey from Tunbridge Wells to Bordeaux must
   (a) be switched off during periods when the driver is taking official breaks from driving
   (b) only be kept running while the vehicle is on the road in England and France (and not during the ferry journey)
   (c) be kept running continuously from the time the driver takes over the vehicle until he finishes the day's work with the vehicle
   (d) only be kept running while the driver is at the wheel of the vehicle

6. An own-account operator will require a journey permit if he is transporting his own goods from the United Kingdom to
   (a) Holland
   (b) Belgium
   (c) Turkey
   (d) Germany

7. Which of the following work performed by a British registered vehicle would be described as cabotage?
   (a) collect Paris and deliver Dublin via London
   (b) collect Paris and deliver Hamburg
   (c) collect Dover and deliver Calais
   (d) collect Paris and deliver Marseilles

8. EU multilateral permits covering hire or reward operations only are valid for a maximum of
   (a) 6 months
   (b) 12 months

(c) 18 months

(d) 2 years

9. Entry into Austria is controlled by a points system requiring stamps and a card. This is known as the
   (a) Nox system
   (b) Pre-entry system
   (c) Eco-points system
   (d) Road-rail carnet system

10. An international driving permit may be obtained from the RAC or AA provided the applicant has a current valid driving licence and he has satisfied one of the following conditions
    (a) he must be domiciled in the United Kingdom and be at least 18 years of age
    (b) he must be domiciled in the United Kingdom and be at least 21 years of age
    (c) he must prove a one-year accident-free record
    (d) he must have no motoring convictions

11. For a journey to which of the following countries would it be necessary for a UK road haulage driver to have a visa in addition to a passport?
    (a) Greece
    (b) Yugoslavia
    (c) Italy
    (d) Bulgaria

12. Most EU countries limit the amount of fuel that may be allowed to enter in vehicle fuel tanks to
    (a) 200 litres
    (b) 250 litres
    (c) 200 gallons
    (d) 250 gallons

13. There is a limitation on the amount of fuel that can be imported in the fuel tanks of a heavy goods vehicle when entering France before excise duty is payable.
    (a) True
    (b) False

14. Under Export Procedures, if pre-entry is chosen which of the following could be omitted from the Export Entry?
    (a) value
    (b) shipping information
    (c) weight
    (d) tariff number

15. A British vehicle moving goods from the UK via Italy and the ferry to Greece must use which one of the following customs transit systems?
    (a) National transit systems
    (b) Community Transit through to Greece
    (c) Community Transit to the Italian border only
    (d) TIR carnets

16. A 14-voucher TIR carnet could be used for the international transportation of goods by road from the United Kingdom across a maximum of
    (a) 6 frontiers
    (b) 7 frontiers
    (c) 10 frontiers
    (d) 14 frontiers

17. The purpose of a *carnet de passage en douane* is to
    (a) enable a goods vehicle to pass through international frontiers without customs examination
    (b) allow temporary importation of samples and personal effects
    (c) allow temporary importation of exhibition goods without payment of duty, deposit or bond
    (d) allow temporary importation of foreign goods vehicles free of duty or deposit

18. The SITPRO system provides the operator with
    (a) automatic customs pre-entry
    (b) automatic ECGD cover
    (c) aligned documentation
    (d) customs clearance at intermediate frontiers

19. A green card is carried when travelling abroad and is
    (a) evidence of insurance
    (b) an import licence
    (c) a customs document
    (d) an insurance policy

20. In the case of loss of a consignment of goods despatched under CMR terms the value is calculated by reference to the value at the place and time at which
    (a) they were due for delivery to the consignee
    (b) they were accepted for carriage
    (c) they are believed to have been lost
    (d) the consignee lodges his claim

21. Haulage drivers who are involved in road accidents in Spain are taken into custody irrespective of whether the accident is their fault or not. In order to arrange for the driver's release as quickly as possible the employer should have taken out a
    (a) Bail bond
    (b) Community Transit Guarantee
    (c) Fidelity guarantee
    (d) Fidelity bond

22. If the exchange rate fluctuates, and the French franc is raised in value in relation to the pound sterling, expenses for a UK haulage operator in France will be
    (a) lower
    (b) the same
    (c) higher

23. The AGR Convention establishes
    (a) a system for the carriage of dangerous goods
    (b) a set of conditions of carriage

(c) a system for the numbering of import quotas

(d) a system of numbering for road networks

24. The height of a vehicle and its load going through Holland and Germany should not exceed
    (a) 4.5m
    (b) 4m
    (c) 3.8m
    (d) 3.5m

25. French lighting regulations state that headlights on vehicles must be yellow. British operators have to comply when entering France.
    (a) True
    (b) False

26. If a road tanker carrying hydrochloric acid is travelling from Dover to Dusseldorf, which regulations must the vehicle comply with?
    (a) ATP Convention
    (b) The UK Corrosive Regulations
    (c) ADR Convention
    (d) ADR and IMDG/Blue Book

27. The ATP Convention applies to journeys made by road or rail, excluding domestic transport, air transport and sea crossings exceeding
    (a) 150 kilometres
    (b) 100 kilometres
    (c) 65 miles
    (d) 70 miles

28. It is a requirement that the original vehicle registration document be carried on the vehicle when it is engaged on international road haulage.
    (a) True
    (b) False

29. Which of the following countries imposes a Sunday driving ban on goods vehicles over 6 tonnes?
    (a) Luxembourg
    (b) Belgium
    (c) France
    (d) Finland

30. Which one of the following provides a groupage service?
    (a) The Freight Transport Association
    (b) International Road Freight Office
    (c) The Road Haulage Association
    (d) A freight forwarder

The reader will find the correct answers to all these questions within the foregoing text but for ease of reference they are repeated on page 299.

Acknowledgement is due to the Royal Society of Arts from whose example examination papers these questions have been taken.

Appendix 2:
Answers to Typical Examination Questions

National Examination – Module A

Question	Answer	Question	Answer
1	(d)	11	(c)
2	(b)	12	(a)
3	(c)	13	(d)
4	(a)	14	(b)
5	(c)	15	(a)
6	(b)	16	(b)
7	(a)	17	(a)
8	(a)	18	(d)
9	(d)	19	(c)
10	(b)	20	(b)

National Examination – Module B

Question	Answer	Question	Answer
1	(b)	21	(a)
2	(c)	22	(a)
3	(d)	23	(a)
4	(a)	24	(c)
5	(b)	25	(d)
6	(c)	26	(d)
7	(b)	27	(d)
8	(a)	28	(b)
9	(c)	29	(b)
10	(d)	30	(c)
11	(c)	31	(c)
12	(d)	32	(d)
13	(c)	33	(d)
14	(b)	34	(c)
15	(a)	35	(d)
16	(d)	36	(b)
17	(b)	37	(a)
18	(d)	38	(c)
19	(a)	39	(d)
20	(a)	40	(a)

International Examination – Module D

Question	Answer	Question	Answer
1	(b)	16	(a)
2	(c)	17	(d)
3	(a)	18	(c)
4	(d)	19	(a)
5	(c)	20	(b)
6	(c)	21	(a)
7	(d)	22	(c)
8	(b)	23	(d)
9	(c)	24	(b)
10	(a)	25	(b)
11	(d)	26	(d)
12	(a)	27	(a)
13	(a)	28	(a)
14	(b)	29	(c)
15	(b)	30	(d)

Index

Index